This is a true story by
Author & Publisher
Brian Dale Bailey

Written while being a student
at Palm Beach State College.

Table of Contents 2

Christ Fellowship Church

This is the story of, "Brian Dale Bailey"

As a youngman who saw the ocean as a living dream, & loved to surf in the sunshine. Sharing a story of true history from mid 2019 to late 2019, while being enrolled as a college state student & becoimg incarsersted after a charge of Trespass at the local church.

Christ Fellowship Church

2019mm005685AXMB

Statue Violations: 92.525(1)(A)(4)(A)(B)(C)
Verification of documents,
perjury by false written
declaration, penalty
90.604 *Lack of Personal Knowledge*

At this time, Mr. Bailey was **self-employed** with a valid license through the **Department of State** knownas **SUNBIZ**. Also, collecting income through a web-based company known as **Google ADsense**.

Department of State / Division of Corporations / Search Records / Search by Entity Name /

*Above is the title of **Division of Corporations** listed by the **Florida Department of State** known as **SUNBIZ**.*

Detail by Entity Name

Florida Profit Corporation
BLACKWATER DIVE EXPERTS, INC   Self-Employed

Filing Information

Document Number	P16000019034
FEI/EIN Number	81-1721771
Date Filed	02/26/2016
Effective Date	02/26/2016
State	FL
Status	ACTIVE Active

Principal Address

3200 SUMMIT BLVD
15532
WEST PALM BEACH, FL 33416

Mailing Address

3200 SUMMIT BLVD
15532
WEST PALM BEACH, FL 33416

Registered Agent Name & Address

BAILEY, BRIAN D
3200 SUMMIT BLVD
15532
WEST PALM BEACH, FL 33416

Officer/Director Detail

Name & Address

Title P

BAILEY, BRIAN D
3200 SUMMIT BLVD
WEST PALM BEACH, FL 33416

Annual Reports

Report Year	Filed Date
2017	01/10/2017
2018	04/25/2018
2019	02/08/2019

Document Images

02/08/2019 -- ANNUAL REPORT	View image in PDF format
04/25/2018 -- ANNUAL REPORT	View image in PDF format
01/10/2017 -- ANNUAL REPORT	View image in PDF format
02/26/2016 -- Domestic Profit	View image in PDF format

*On this document it shares the data necessary to comply with **Florida Department of State** in order to conduct business in the **State of Florida**. This is proof that Brian Dale Bailey was a President of a valid company while being injured & arrested.*

ADMIN

Agency ORI Number		Agency Name			Agency Report Number		
FLO 500000		PALM BEACH COUNTY SHERIFF'S OFFICE			06- 19- 070132	Special Notes	

Charge Type / Check as many as apply: ☐ 1. Felony ☐ 2. Traffic Felony ☒ 3. Misdemeanor ☐ 4. Traffic Misdemeanor ☐ 5. Ordinance ☐ 6. Other

CHARGES

Name (Last, First, Middle)		Alias			Race	Sex	Date of Birth
Bailey, Brian, Dale					W	M	2/24/1979

Charge Description				Charge Description		
TRESPASS AFTER WARNING	810.09 OR					

Charge Description

VICTIM

Victim's Name (Last, First, Middle)					Race	Sex	Date of Birth
CHRIST FELLOWSHIP, ,					N/A	N/A	
Local Address (Street, Apt. Number)	(City)	(State)	(Zip)	Phone		Address Source
9905 Southern Blvd @ Christ Fellowship, Royal Palm Beach, FL 33411				( )		IN PERSON
Business Address (Name, Street)	(City)	(State)	(Zip)	Phone		Occupation
9905 Southern Blvd @ Christ Fellowship, Royal Palm Beach, FL 33411				(561) 214-2463		N/A

The undersigned certifies and swears that he/she has just and reasonable grounds to believe, and does believe that the above named Defendant committed the following violation of law. The Person taken into custody:

☐ committed the below acts in my presence
☐ confessed to _____ admitting to the below facts.
☐ was observed by _____ who told _____ that he/she saw the arrested person commit the below acts.
☒ was found to have committed the below acts, resulting from my (described) investigation.

On the 12 day of MAY 2019 at 1205 ☐ A.M. ☒ P.M. (Specifically include facts constituting cause for arrest.)

PROBABLE CAUSE STATEMENT

On the above mentioned date and time, while working a PBSO extra duty detail at the above mentioned location; I was approached by head of security, later identified as, Gerald Charles. Charles stated there was a white male standing outside infront of the religious building who had been trespassed on 05/05/2019 reference PBSO case #19067360 by Deputy Peitz, Robert I #6432.

I then approached the white male; I observed the white male standing at the front of the Religious Building located 9905 Southern Blvd @ Christ Fellowship, Royal Palm Beach, FL 33411. White male was later identified via FL DL as, Brian Bailey (suspect). After running Brian through F/Ncic, PALMS, and through PBSO's FIR system, it was confirmed Brian was ████████████

After confirming the above mentioned, The defendant was placed under arrest for violation of FSS 810.09. I order the defendant to place his hands behind his back to be handcuffed which he complied. The defendant was placed into handcuffs, checked for proper fit, double locked, and placed into the rear of my patrol car. The defendant was then transported to the Palm Beach County Jail where custody was transferred to corrections deputies without further incident.

Case cleared by arrest.

STATE OF FLORIDA
COUNTY OF _____ 84859 _____ D/S J. Carmenate
(Signature of Advisor/Complaining Officer)

The foregoing instrument was sworn to or affirmed and subscribed before me this 12 day of May 20 19 by D/S J. Carmenate _____ Known

(Printed name of Arresting/Complaining Officer) who is personally known to me and/or produced identification. Type of identification produced _____

O/S C. Pugonts _____ 17615
(Notary Public, Clerk of Court, Officer of F.S.S. 117.10)

	PAGE
	1 of 1

*When receiving the arrest report there was a black square after the word, "**was**" & is still unknown as to what has been written on the report.*

Brian Bailey   Time sheet   7/3/2019

Case # -50-2019-MM-005685-AXXX-MB

Date	Time-in	Time-out	Hours	Total	
5/12/2019 – 7/1/2019	background	—	1	1 Hr	1
7-2-2019	Brain search	—	3	4 Hr	2
7-3-2019	12:20 PM	4:20 PM	4	8 Hr	3
7-3-2019	4:45 PM	9:45 PM	5	13 Hr	4
7-4-2019	1:00 PM	3:00 PM	2	15 Hr	5
7-4-2019	6:00 PM	7:15 PM	1:15	16.25 Hr	6
7-4-2019	8:00 PM	9:30 PM	1:30	17.75 Hr	7
7-5-2019	1:45 PM	4:15 PM	3:30	20.25 Hr	8
7-8-2019	2:30 PM	3:30 PM	1	21.25 Hr	9
7-8-2019	9:15 PM	12:15 AM	3	24.25 Hr	10
7-9-2019	4:20 AM	5:00 AM	:30	24.75 Hr	11
7-9-2019	5:00 AM	8:00 AM	3	27.75 Hr	12
7-15-2019	12:00 PM	2:30 PM	2:30	30.25 Hr	13
7-15-2019	6:00 PM	7:15 PM	1:15	31.50 Hr	14
7-17-2019	12:00 PM	3:30 PM	3:30	35. Hr	15
7-18-2019	11:45 PM	2:15 PM	2:30	37.50 HR	16
7-18-2019	7:15 PM	9:30 PM	2:15	39.75 Hr	17
7-19-2019	5:30 AM	7:00 AM	1:30	41.25 Hr	18
7-19-2019	12:30 PM	1:15 PM	:45	42 Hr	19
7-22-2019	3:00 PM	3:30 PM	:30	42.50 Hr	20
7-22-2019	6:00 PM	8:30 PM	2:30	45 Hr	21
7-24-2019	7:00 PM	9:15 PM	2:15	47.25 Hr	22
7-27-2019	6:30 PM	7:45 PM	1:15	48.50 Hr	23
7-29-2019	7:00 PM	7:15 PM	:15	48.75 HR	24
7-30-2019	4:45 PM	6:30 PM	1:45	50.50 HR	25
7-30-2019	7:30 PM	9:00 PM	2	52.50 HR	26
8-2-2019	2:15 PM	4:15 PM	2	54.50 Hr	27
8-3-2019	12:30 PM	3:30 PM	3	57.50 HR	28
8-7-2019	6:30 PM	10:30 PM	4	61.50 Hr	29
8-8-2019	12:00 PM	3:30 PM	3:30	65 Hr	30
8-9-2019	12:15 PM	4:00 PM	3:45	68.75 Hr	31
8-10-2019	No clock	—			32
8-11-2019	1:15 PM	5:00 PM	3:45	72.50 HR	33
8-11-2019	6:30 PM	8:00 PM	1:30	74 Hr	34
8-15-2019	7:30 PM	8:00 PM	:30	74.50 HR	35
8-16-2019	8:30 PM	9:00 PM	:30	75 HR	36
8-19-2019	1:45 PM	5:15 PM	4:30	79.50 HR	37
8-21-2019	2:00 PM	3:00 PM	1	80.50 Hr	38

Statute: 810.09 Trespass

Case# 50-2019-MM-005685-AXXX-MB

Dates Incarcerated: 5/12/2019 – 8/23/2019

On the date of **5/12/2019**, Mr. Brian Dale Bailey, was arrested at the **Christ Fellowship Church**, Royal Palm Beach, in the **State of Florida**. For a charge of: **Statute 810.09** - Trespass on property other than structure or conveyance. At the time, Mr. Bailey had been attending the Christ Fellowship Church regularly for close to one-year, & off & on around five-years. When first attending Mr. Bailey came with little knowledge of any religion, with open ears & eyes looking to learn what this church has to offer the people in our community.

The year 2013 was the beginning of this journey that would come with unknown roads & new faces. At the time, Mr. Bailey was a Florida business owner of company called, **"BB Tropical Services"**. Providing underwater maintenance throughout our community of Palm Beach County to golf courses & property management companies. After attending this church for a short period of time, Mr. Bailey was at a point in his life that he was looking for change. This came at a time, when Mr. Bailey was recovering from more than one surgery, causing financial, physical & mental stress.

Always having a love for surfing & using it as his outlet to escape the challenges and daily stressors. The State of Florida only comes with a quality wave a few times a year. Making it a difficult location to catch a wave if you're working the average 9 to 5 work schedule. Which in return created a decision to chase the wave of lifetime. Mr. Bailey put most of his belongs in a storage unit, & offered all of it to two local friend in the county. One was Mr. David Davis, who helped him in many ways through life's challenges, also supporting Mr. Bailey through business. The other was, Mr. Brian King a local surfer & family man who has traveled the world surfing & comes from a business background.

Once having the plane ticket to the island of Hawaii & packing a surfboard bag with a couple of surfboards & scuba gear to complete the equipment necessary for the adventure. Then two suitcases with clothes for summertime year-round, just thinking of waves & the sun. The friends & family around him were all at different stages in life, most of them starting their own families. While he just wanted adventure, excitement through adrenaline, wanting a career as a stuntman. But, as a single man, Mr. Bailey's lifestyle came with unique days & nights. Working various positions from the 9 to 5 & at times working in the South Florida night life.

Mr. Brian Bailey traded in a **2008 Toyota Tundra** that he had recently just paid off, creating a financial loss, due to being in a rush to leave. Having this truck was a dream of his, that dream truck that you see on the movie, "Back to the Future." Well, that's what this Toyota Tundra was to Mr. Bailey.

Mr. Bailey had tools that the average man did not group together, coming from a variety of business backgrounds. Always continuing to adapt with any working environment needed to make it happen. On this journey, Mr. Bailey was looking to offer his skills to build in another environment, without charging. After facing one to many disappointing endings in the construction industry, creating a financial loss.

So, Mr. Bailey packed a large plastic box & filled It with the most used tools for building residential & commercial building. He put a label on this box & called it, *"Hawaiianchristian"*.

Mr. Bailey was ready to leave for the islands, in the Pacific oceans. Not saying much to his friends or family & seeing what roads life was about to create. Leaving the box labeled, *"Hawaiianchristian"* at the storage & speaking with Mr. David Davis, in regard to shipping once having a safe place to store the tools in Hawaii.

After missing the first plane at the Miami International Airport heading for the island of Hawaii. Mr. Bailey rescheduled to catch another plane just a few weeks later, finally reaching he destination. When he got off the airplane, it was like that surfer movie, "**North Shore**" he had a surfboard bag in one hand & clothes in the other with no reservation on the island.

Then walking up to an officer & Mr. Bailey asked, "where is a safe place to stay on the island"? His answer was, "**Turtle Bay on the North Shore**". Then grabbing a taxi that could hold surfboards & cruising to the North Shore late at night. Not being able to see much out the window of the van, until arriving at the hotel. This place is a surfer's dream hotel, everything in the place revolves around a surfer's lifestyle.

That night Mr. Bailey hit the pillow & woke up to the most beautiful glassy waves he'd ever seen, 10 to 15-foot walls. Breaking off the backside of the hotel, right on a shallow reef. After eating breakfast on the back porch, just watching these perfect waves break one after another, Mr. Bailey knew that he was in surfer's paradise. Grabbing his surfboard & heading off to catch the wave of a lifetime. When paddling out off the back of the hotel, he didn't see any other surfers in the line-up. This was odd for him due to this being a vacation area with rental surfboards available. The current was pushing hard & created a drift that was moving a few miles an hour.

Mr. Bailey was finally in the right spot after a 20-minute paddle out. Having the entire ocean to himself & having a feeling of achievement, while preparing to surf in the sun. The first set rolled through & Mr. Bailey went for it, not wanting to mis the wave he started paddling hard. Just as Mr. Bailey was ready to drop in all he could see was dry reef & rocks, approximately about 6 to 8 feet under the board. Not a good feeling to have, when being pushed by this amount of power in the water. It was too late, & he was dropping in, he curled his fingers to the top of the surfboard. Trying to save himself from skin damaged when hitting the reef. Mr. Bailey hit the reef & was pounded by the next few waves. Now in a distressed situation, surfing where there is no lifeguard.

Needing to paddle hard heading for the shore, with some large surf continuing to come from the outside. He was caught in a rip tide, having currents pulling him back out into the ocean, while paddling towards a cove next to the hotel. This lasted for close to 20 to 30 minutes, that dream wave now become a life threating situation. Making it to the beach with a few minor scrapes & little skin damaged. Mr. Bailey now realized why no other local surfers were on those perfect looking waves. It was time to change it up, & he started where the beginners surf on the west side of Turtle Bay.

Well with his financial predication, it was time to leave Turtle Bay. Having a small budget to work with & no income at the time. Mr. Bailey found a family renting a newly renovated room for a few thousand dollars for close to a month. After that month he was completely broke, & during that month of exploring the island. He met Pastor Larry Garret, who was the lead Pastor at **Sunset Beach Christian Church**. This is where he remembers something that stuck with him, when asking Ms. Mary Ann Clay to walk him into the Christ Fellowship Church, Royal Palm Beach, Florida. The one word she used was, **"Transformer"** meaning changing your life for the, **"Lord your savior Jesus Christ"**. She used those words often & at the time he wouldn't of had a clue at the roads ahead of him after making a decision to challenge this goal & walk this road. Mr. Bailey still hadn't read the bible, nor did he know a verse off the top of his head, but was surrounding himself with those who did.

Most of which were polite & came with open arms. But, not all were kind & some were curious as to where Mr. Bailey came from, having questions without asking. Pastor Larry & him started communicating just after he started attending regularly on Sundays, offering to serve around the Sunset Beach Christian Church. Pastor Larry Garret was on of the shepherd of the North Shore of Hawaii, the North Shore is a universal location on this earth. Not all have the same beliefs & understanding of the Lord & who works closely with the Sheriff's Department. Looking out for the safety of the community & those traveling. Once starting to serve around the campus, Pastor Larry & Mr. Bailey became on a level of friendship.

As their relationship grew & over the next few months, Mr. Bailey shared his interested in regard to surfing the island, & how he landed on the island of Hawaii. Pastor Larry has a love for Christian surfers around the world. It was around **New Years of 2015**, & he was challenged by a financial decision. Mr. Bailey was living with little income & only able to find part-time work on the island. Mr. Bailey made a few poor decisions, according to those who oversee the property of the Sunset Beach Christian Church. This created an end for his stay at the church. At the time, he was at an extreme fitness level & unable to keep up with the finances necessary for daily living off the campus.

Mr. Bailey was working 7 days a week & only collecting for a part-time worker. This wasn't working out, causing him to leave the island & head back to Florida to open a new company. Come **February of 2016**, Mr. Bailey landed in West Palm Beach, Florida. Picked up by Mr. David Davis, who allowed him to stay at his house for a couple weeks while building the company called, "**Blackwater Dive Experts**." By April of 2016, this new small business was licensed & insured, with Mr. Brian Bailey listed as President owner. Working days nights building a back office & creating new administration tools necessary for organization & marketing purposes.

This is where he found himself being surround by many hours of working to create numbers for the business. Leaving the learning of religious beliefs that he had been surround by to, "new learners." Now by this time, he had moved out of Mrs. Davis home & was living with three other men. One was an FAU student, & the two others were from the military, one the Army & one the Navy. After a few months, the company made enough money, & Mr. Bailey was able to afford to rent his own room in another location. This created friction in the household due to the amount of income the company was bringing in. To his surprise before having all his personal property removed from the household.

The homeowner wiped out the company account, leaving him, "**no funds**" to continue with forward progress. While confronting the gentleman about the missing funds, things turned for the worse.
Mr. Bailey was beaten by both of the military men, leaving him with a fractured right orbital & lacerations on his face & body. Causing financial, physical & mental stress, losing time for the company & creating medical invoices, while healing.
Mr. Bailey was able to overcome some of the financial problems on the following day, by collecting a check from a company with an outstanding invoice. Then opening a new business bank account with Bank of America, while having bandages on his body, from head to toe.

It took around a month to heal his skin, making it where he was able to get back to work diving underwater. Now, the hurdles started coming at a higher rate, losing the company automobile to grand theft. Once again, needing to move, being in area that was unfit for my position. While still building a company in the field & on the web. After sharing this story with his father Mr. William Dale Bailey, he was kind enough to loan his son his personal automobile. There's only one challenge, he lives in the Carolina's & Mr. Brian Bailey was in Florida, with little funds in the account. Mr. Brian Bailey jumped on a plane & met with his father & then returned with a truck & trailer, ready to go at it again.

Then moving into a commercial building & living in unfit conditions of a warehouse in **The City of Lake Worth**. At the same time, pressing forward with marketing & the companies needs for growth. Putting his personal life completely to the side & only living for the reason of developing a new source of income. The company needed a more organized commercial area, with higher security. Moving again, to another commercial area in **The City of Riviera Beach**. Also, living in unfit conditions, showering out of a water hose & pressing forwards with the company needs. Mr. Bailey hadn't been to a church in quiet awhile & was receiving contracts that were out of the Palm Beach County area.

Only being tested by those overseeing new companies, checking him as new business owner. **February of 2017**, while showering at the Planet Fitness gym in Palm Beach Gardens. Mr. Bailey found himself on the floor of the shower, bleeding profusely from the head. He had hit his head on the shower tile floor & split the skin a few inches. Then being removed by Emergency Medical Services, known as Fire Rescue. Ending up in the hospital & staying for a few days while being evaluated by doctors & nurses.

Again, prolonging him from being able to dive for the company, "**Blackwater Dive Experts**". Pushing the timeline of predicted income back yet again. The steps of developing this company were continuing to be challenged. A few months passed & he was able to create enough income to rent his own commercial warehouse space, with an upstairs office. Separating the working warehouse space & office administrating area. This only lasted one month, after paying first, last & security, of over 4000.00 dollars. During that month he felt a very unnatural power in that office. That feeling of the unknown challenging the human power, while having health & money at the same time.

Mr. Bailey lost to the power of the unknown, only to find out the power of money rises again. This move ends up leaving Mr. Bailey with a truck full of tools & no home. Losing everything to new business ownership in the **State of Florida**. Unable to move forward with landing new projects, while having many lose ends of administration to be closed off, before being able to choose a new road. Also, being glued to the personal property in the automobile, due to the high criminal activity in the **Palm Beach County** Area. Not able to work for any other individual or business unless they were law abiding companies.

Completing many applications in various areas through the county & not being offered any position available. That's the power of the Lord creating down fall in our community. He spoke with his father about the situation & asked if he would come down & pick up the truck with a trailer. He's a busy guy with his own challenges in life & this wasn't how Mr. Brian Bailey wanted this situation to end. A few days went by & he showed up with a trailer, scooping up the truck & Mr. Brian Bailey. Heading back to North Carolina, with many things on his plate & loss ends that need closer in the **State of Florida.**

With the Power of churches comes the eyes of eagles, shepherds & wolves ready to devour anyone individual on their own path for their Lord. In layman's terms each one of us is grouped with certain individuals, whether you know it or not. In Mr. Bailey case, he was about to find out the hard way, with a very small percentages of people in his position on this planet. Once arriving in North Carolina, Mr. Brian Bailey was offered a home on the Mountain to stay for a few nights. His father stayed kind & packed him some food & drove Brian up to a house on the mountain side. Little did Brian know he was being picked up by the police.

The following evening of 10/22/2017, there was a knock at the door, while Mr. Bailey was making dinner. Once again, doing what he was asked of law enforcement, then being carried off to a hospital for a psychological evaluation, for close to a week. While totally sober, but alone with no transportation on the side of a North Carolina mountain.

This event takes place after Mr. Bailey created stock footage in 2016 in a **North Carolina airport**, while waiting for his plane to arrive.

https://www.youtube.com/watch?v=XBezmBmCh1I

24

10/22/17
to
10/25/17

Patient Name: BRIAN DALE BAILEY
Statement Date: 03/11/18
Guarantor Number: 5021125

Page 2 of 3

Charges				
Date	Description	Charges	Credits	Patient Balance
Visit on 10/22/2017 with STRAUSS, HEATHER LINDSEY at Pardee Emergency Department				
10/22/17	EMERGENCY DEPT VISIT	532.00		319.20
12/05/17	DISCOUNT (SELF-PAY, UNINSURED)		212.80	
Visit on 10/24/2017 with BIERRENBACH DECASTRO, RICARDO C at PATHS PRDH				
10/24/17	PSYCHIATRIC DIAGNOSTIC EVAL W/MEDICAL SERVICE	165.00		99.00
12/12/17	DISCOUNT (SELF-PAY, UNINSURED)		66.00	
Visit on 10/25/2017 with BIERRENBACH DECASTRO, RICARDO C at PATHS PRDH				
10/25/17	HOSPITAL DISCHARGE DAY	105.00		63.00
12/05/17	DISCOUNT (SELF-PAY, UNINSURED)		42.00	
	Total Outstanding Balance:			$481.20
	Current Amount Due:			$481.20

THIS BILL IS FOR PHYSICIAN CHARGES ONLY AND DOES NOT INCLUDE HOSPITAL CHARGES WHICH ARE BILLED SEPARATELY BY THE HOSPITAL

Contact Information

For questions, call Patient Services at (984)974-2222 or (800)594-8624, Mon-Fri. 8:00am to 5:00pm.
For written communication, our address is UNC Health Care, PO Box 168, Chapel Hill, NC 27514.

UNC Physicians
PO Box 602948
Charlotte, NC 28260-2948

Account Summary		Charge Summary	
Patient Name:	BRIAN DALE BAILEY	Total Charges:	$802.00
Statement Date:	03/11/18	Insurance Pending:	$0.00
Guarantor Number:	5021125	Insurance Payments:	$0.00
Due Date:	04/08/18	Patient Payments:	$0.00
		Adjustments:	$-320.80
		Amount You Owe:	$481.20
		Prepayments/Deposits:	$0.00

Insurance Information	Contact Us
Ins 1:	For questions, call our Customer Service Call Center at (984) 974-2222 or (800) 594-8624, Monday through Friday, 8:00am to 5:00pm.
Ins 2:	
Ins 3:	

Pay Your Bill Online!
https://myuncchart.org

Please detach the bottom portion and return with your payment. Keep the top portion for your records. There will be a $35.00 service fee for all returned checks. ***See reverse side for important information***

UNC Health Care
700 Eastowne Dr
Chapel Hill, NC 27514-2293

☐ PLEASE CHECK HERE FOR ADDRESS CORRECTIONS AND FILL OUT THE BACK OF THIS FORM.

*****************AUTO**MIXED AADC 275
11936 1 MB 0.424
BRIAN DALE BAILEY
3200 SUMMIT BLVD UNIT 15532
WEST PALM BEACH FL 33416-4021

To pay by credit card, complete the section below:

Card Number				Exp. Date
Signature				C V V Code
☐ VISA ☐ 🔴 ☐ ☐ DISCOVER				Amount Paid

Due Date	Guarantor #	Amount Due
04/08/18	5021125	$481.20

PLEASE MAKE CHECKS PAYABLE AND REMIT TO

UNC Health Care
P O Box 602948
Charlotte, NC 28260-2948

0103112018000502112500048120□

26

UNC Health Care
700 Eastowne Dr
Chapel Hill, NC 27514-2293

☐ PLEASE CHECK HERE FOR ADDRESS CORRECTIONS
AND FILL OUT THE BACK OF THIS FORM

To pay by credit card, complete the section below:	
Card Number	Exp. Date
Signature	

☐ VISA ☐ ☐ ☐ DISC VER

	Amount Paid

Due Date	Guarantor #	Amount Due
10/24/18	5021125	$2,384.13

PLEASE MAKE CHECKS PAYABLE AND REMIT TO

UNC Health Care
P O Box 603158
Charlotte, NC 28260-3158

02102420180005021125002384138

**10/22/17
t0
10/25/17**

Statement Date: 09/27/2018

Thank you for choosing UNC Health Care for your healthcare needs. Your account reflects a total balance due of $2,384.13. A minimum payment of $2,384.13 is due by 10/24/18. The minimum payment consists of the current amount due on any established payment plan, along with balance(s) remaining on account(s) not on an established payment plan. Please return the payment coupon above in the provided envelope with your payment or credit card details. For your convenience, you may also make payments or establish a payment plan using our automated online patient portal MyUNCChart at https://myuncchart.org.

If you are unable to make payment, please contact our office toll free at (800) 594-8624 or local at (984) 974-2222 for more information on our financial assistance program.

Questions?   ***See reverse side for important information***   Coverage(s) on file
   · How to contact us
   · Hours of operation
   · Payment options
   · Financial assistance information

Date of Service	Description	Charges	Insurance Pmts/Adjs	Patient Pmts/Adjs	Patient Balance
	Brian Dale Bailey's visit to Pardee Hospital		Acct #2353337302		

Our records indicate that you do not have medical insurance for this date of service. If you have active coverage for this date of service, please contact our Customer Service Call Center at (800) 594-8624. In order for this account to remain in a current status, the account balance must be paid in full or an approved payment plan must be established. If you are unable to make payment, please contact our office for more information on our financial assistance program.

Page 1 of 2

27

PLEASE INDICATE IF ANY OF THE FOLLOWING HAS CHANGED SINCE YOUR LAST STATEMENT:

CHANGE OF ADDRESS:
Street: _____ City: _____ State: _____ Zip: _____

CHANGE OF PHONE:
Residence Telephone #: _____ Employment Telephone #: _____

CHANGE OF INSURANCE:

PATIENT NAME	INSURANCE CO. NAME		
INSURANCE CO. PHONE	STREET OR P.O. Box	CITY	STATE / ZIP CODE
INSURED'S NAME (not patient)	EFFECTIVE DATE / INSURANCE ID #		GROUP #
RELATIONSHIP OF PATIENT TO INSURED ○ SELF ○ SPOUSE ○ DEP. CHILD ○ OTHER	IF OTHER IS CHECKED, NEED DESCRIPTION OF RELATIONSHIP		INSURED'S PHONE
INSURED'S EMPLOYER NAME	EMPLOYER'S PHONE		INSURED'S SOCIAL SECURITY
OTHER INFORMATION			

Need More Information? Need an Itemized Statement? Here s How to Contact Us

UNC Health Care provides automated access to Patient Account information available 24 hours a day, 7 days a week by calling our toll free number (800) 594-8624 or local at (984) 974-2222. You will need your account number and other patient identifying information to access your account.

The automated system allows you to:
- Verify your account balance
- Make a payment
- Request an itemization of charges
- Speak with a Customer Service Representative (available M-F 8:00AM – 5:00 PM)

All written correspondence, including checks indicating Payment in Full, must be mailed to UNC Patient Financial Services, 700 Eastowne Drive, Chapel Hill, NC 27514.

A $35.00 fee will be charged for each returned check.

You may also access your account at our online portal, My UNC Chart at https://myuncchart.org.

The patient portal allows you to:
- Pay your bill online for Hospital and Provider bills
- Access, view, and print your itemization of charges
- View outstanding patient balances
- Request account itemization free of charge
- Sign up for paperless billing
- Establish payment arrangements
- Post payments to a specific account

Payments received via mail will first be applied to payment plans and then oldest account balance.

If you want to apply a payment to a specific account you can access MyUNCChart or call our Customer Service line and speak to a representative.

NOTICE OF AVAILABILITY OF CHARITY CARE & FINANCIAL ASSISTANCE:

To inquire about potential financial assistance for your account(s), please contact UNC Patient Financial Services at (800) 594-8624 or (984) 974-2222.

https://www.uncmedicalcenter.org/uncmc/patients-visitors/billing/financial-assistance-programs/

¿Necesita mas informacion? ¿Necesita un estado de cuenta detallado? Asi es como puede comunicarse con nosotros.

Nuestros dedicados representantes de servicio al cliente estan disponibles para atender sus preguntas Lunes – Viernes, 8:00 Am – 5:00 PM al numero gratuito (800) 594-8624 o local al (984) 974-2222.

Usted puede checar el estado de cuenta, solicitor factura detallada de los cargos, y hacer pagos por este systema.

Toda correspondencia por escrito, incluyendo cheques para saldos vigentes, deben de ser mandados por correo a UNC Patient Financial Services, 200 Eastowne Drive, Chapel Hill 27514

Habra un cargo de $35.00 por cada cheque devuelto.
**Los servicios de los medicos facturan por seperado.

Tambien puedeacceder su cuenta por medio de internet portal. https://myuncchart.org

A traves de internet usted puede:
- Pagar su factura de Hospital o Medicos
- Pedir facturas detallada sin algun cobro
- Checar el estado de cuenta
- Ver saldos pendientes de pacientes
- Establecer planes de pago

Bill Pay/E-checks recibidos a traves de internet. Para poder aplicar los pagos a un saldo espesifico por favor de mandar el cheque con el talon. Pagos mandados sin talons seeran acreditados a los planes de pago o saldos vigentes del hospital y medic

AVISO DE DISPONIBILIDAD DE ASISTENCIA FINACIERA Y PROGRAMA DE BENEFICENCIA

Para indagar sobre la posibilidad de asistencia financierapara sus cuentas, favor de comunicarse con UNC Patient Financial Services al (800) 594-8624 o (984) 974-2222.

https://www.uncmedicalcenter.org/uncmc/patients-visitors/billing/financial-assistance-programs/

Your Responsibility	Due Date	Guarantor #
$2,384.13	10/24/18	5021125

Date of Service	Description	Charges	Insurance Pmts/Adjs	Patient Pmts/Adjs	Patient Balance
10/22/17 to 10/25/17	PSYCHIATRIC	2,100.00			
	PHARMACY	23.55			
	CHEMISTRY	248.00			
	EMERGENCY ROOM	1,489.00			
	OTHER BEHAVIOR HEALTH TREATMENTS/SERVICES	113.00			
	Patient Adjustments			-1,589.42	
	Totals	3,973.55	0.00	-1,589.42	2,384.13
	Patient Balance				**2,384.13**
			Balance Due		**2,384.13**

Our records indicate that you have not activated your MyChart access or that access will expire within 30 days. Please feel free to access MyChart using the Code V3DVN-QDZBH-BZN4N at https://myuncchart.org.

29

At the end of this week, his father was who they allowed to pick Mr. Bailey up from the hospital, only wasting his time of organizing his paperwork for the business, & charging obscene amounts to a disabled individual, while being a business owner. Providing no improvement for any psychological issue. Only using a hospital as a high price hotel, providing food & shelter, in attempt to get Mr. Bailey to draw. Not assisting in any mental illness, which is the claim of psychological evaluation. Requesting him to attend an AA class while being completely sober for some time.

Blocking Mr. Bailey from the time needed for clearing up his administration needs with, **"Blackwater Dive Experts"** one thing he was unable to do while having an automobile packed with personal property. Constantly needing to move the wheels. Once leaving the hospital we returned to the home he was staying in North Carolina. That move only created, another untrusting baring in Brian & his father's relationship. Mr. Bailey walked off the mountain, with what he could carry & a rolling suitcase & was on his way back to South Florida.

Landing back in Florida in a few days, still staying in contact with his father by telephone. Once arriving Mr. Bailey started tying up any lose ends that the company left behind. Now, he was challenged by this new world operating through computers. He needed to learn more about the program office 365 & the tools it had to offer. Over the next year he stayed outside while using many different locations for internet services, then learning the end & outs of office 365. Then returning to Christ Fellowship Church, only to offer what he had learned to share with others.

At the same time needing community service hours, while being on EBT food stamps. Back involved with serving at the church on the Production Team, Traffic Team & Greeting. While at the Christ Fellowship Church, Royal Palm Beach campus & holding a two-way radio. Mr. Bailey would see the EMS team walking around the church. Then making a request to be a part of the EMS team. The team leader, "Mr. Don Frey" explained Mr. Bailey would need to complete a course at Palm Beach State College called, **"Emergency Medical Technician." Late 2018**, Mr. Bailey enrolled in college at **Palm Beach State**, looking to complete with an AS & a degree in EMS.

January of 2019, starting his freshman year of college, with injuries to my left shoulder, causing sharp pain daily. After his first semester ended, he had A & B's with a high GPA of over a 3.0. Excited & wanting to share the good news with those he served with around the church. Not realizing, that sharing this news would lead to unpresedented disappointment. Over the break between semesters, Mr. Bailey was working on producing a short film, using various geological locations throughout the Palm Beach County Area. Of course, his style is not loved by all the elders, working to create things that don't exist on the worldwide web.

Mr. Bailey comes from a very pushy background to get things done, being a business owner most of his life. Always going out on a limb for success, this means taking on challenges that many people will never face, especially financial ones that come with extreme droughts. The surroundings of most are to follow & do what they are told, staying close to the trunk of the tree for financial success. That never worked for Mr. Bailey, constantly seeing the mistakes of our older generation & how they treat the younger generation. He was created to be a divergent, with only a small percent of people that fall under this category in each family.

After uploading my short film to a YouTube Channel called, *"BB's Life"* later in the month of *April* 2019. On the date of 5/5/2019, Mr. Bailey was on his way into the Christ Fellowship Church, when he was hit by an SUV at a high rate of speed, while on his bicycle. Fracturing Mr. Bailey's right wrist & continuing pain to the left shoulder. Then contacting Mr. Gary Borge, who serves with Christ Fellowship Church, Royal Palm Beach campus. Explaining that he had been struck by an automobile at a high rate of speed. He arrived at the accident scene & once the Sheriff's Department was finished with their report.

Mr. Bailey, & another individual riding with Mr. Gary Borge. They made their way back to the Christ Fellowship Church of Royal Palm Beach. When arriving & making his way inside, he was met by security & led into an office, to wait for the arrival of Pastor Oscar & a few other men including the Sheriff's Department. Where Mr. Bailey was confronted by Pastor Oscar Soto, who **violated statutes 836.05 Threats; extortion**. By sharing information that was meant to be **kept secret** on his **prayer card, embarrassing him** by violating his rights as a member of the Christ Fellowship Church.

Exposing personal information to others in the room, **disgracing Mr. Bailey, & exposing secrets** affecting his belonging in the community of Wellington, Florida. Choosing to impute & create a **deformity** or **lack of chastity**, between him & Mr. Bailey, with him being one of the leaders at the church. Leaving Mr. Bailey now **threated by our community** & asking him not to return to the church, sharing information in front of these men that was not true by any means. Making claims that Mr. Bailey harassed women of the church, & making claims that he was hugging women, when asked not to. In some cases, these women were walking up to him and shooting in for a hug, before he was able to explain that Pastor Oscar didn't want me hugging people in the church.

Making it not feel like family at all, with the words on the wall saying love, family & friends. Then escorted outside, to stand in front of a Sheriff's automobile, while the officer waited for Mr. Bailey to explain how he was leaving the property, while his bicycle was in an unrideable condition, in the back of a pickup truck of one of the other members, having a fracture right wrist. All this taking place just after being struck by an SUV at a high rate of speed. Not one person at this church asked if Mr. Bailey was ok, after being in auto accident.

Making it clear that this is a very large church meant for mass volumes of people with higher incomes, to flow in & out. Mr. Bailey had been serving here for just under one-year consistently on various teams & was known by many of the other members & now being shifted away from the church, for no wrongdoing taking place on this property, while tithing & giving his time. The following weekend, Mr. Bailey came back to worship wearing a dress on Mother's Day. Pastor Oscar Soto then had Mr. Bailey arrested for charges that match burglary, when all he's ever done at this church was offer a helping hand free of charge, never once taking anything that didn't belong to him!

Only to have his personal property gone through while serving outside for traffic, being separated from his bag, while someone in this church went through the backpack he was carrying regularly. Removing hardware from a Dell computer & cutting the spokes on the bicycle that is left is the warehouse area, while visiting this church. On the date of 5/12/2019, Pastor Oscar Soto was having Mr. Bailey hauled off to jail, with his bicycle & personal property left on the property of the Christ Fellowship Church.

Having other members of the church, tell Mr. Bailey that he should make better decisions, then being separated from the Iso-Pure powder protein in the duffle bag he was carrying. Which was needed for survival in the current situation. After becoming a member of Christ Fellowship Church & serving with individuals for close to One-year. Serving just about every Sunday & now sitting in the back of a Sheriff's Department patrol unit, with new charges being pressed against him. Mr. Bailey was now on his way to the West Detention Center - Belle Glade to be booked & incarcerated.

For the next hundred days plus this is what took place, while going through The Palm Beach County Court System & Sheriff's Department. Mr. Bailey was stripped of his freedom while gaining a higher education through the Palm Beach State College & being helped financially by the government through loans that he would be responsible for, having to pay back after being incarcerated.

Showing that the government is creating these financial problems for individuals, while making an attempt for those looking to achieving higher education, with criminal backgrounds. If, we were all on the same team, the government wouldn't be arresting nonviolent criminals who were serving in their community through community activities. Creating an invisible wall of those who they allow in & those who they're pushing out.

On the date of **5/5/2019**, after being struck by an SUV at a high rate of speed. Having the bicycle swiped out from under him & landing on both wrists. The right wrist sustained a fracture to the scaphoid bone, causing the wrist to swell with immediate pain. Then one week later, after having an appointment setup for X-Rays. Mr. Bailey was placed in handcuffs at Christ Fellowship Church, Royal Palm Beach, Florida. While being a religious member of the church with identification.

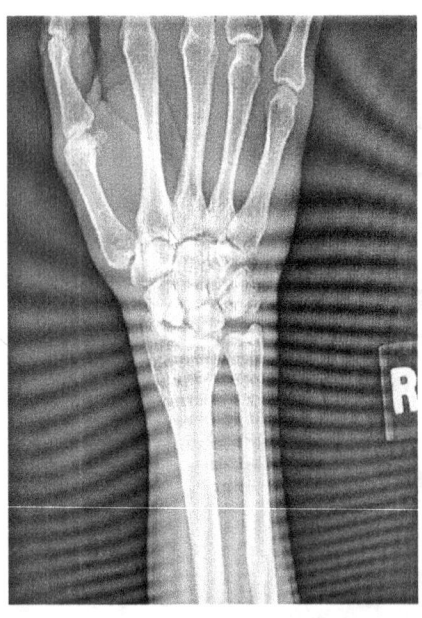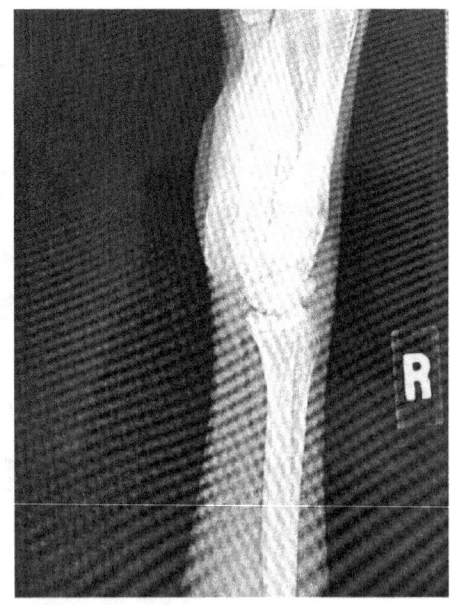

5/12/2019
LPN Elizabeth Lisanti

Dictation : INTAKE HEALTH SCREENING - ARMOR CORRECTIONAL HEALTH SERVICES, INC:

Name:	BRIAN DALE BAILEY
No:	0403731
DOB:	02-24-1979

155 lbs

Sex:	Male
Location:	WDC INTAKE

Pulse 53

VITALS:
VITAL SIGNS: (7) Weight: 155 lbs , Height: 6 ft., BMI: 21, BSA (Mosteller): 1.89, BSA (DuBois): 1.91, Blood Pressure: 100/68, Temperature: 98.4, Pulse: 53, Respiration: 18, Pulse Oxygen: 100

CURRENT PROBLEMS:

1. Do you have any medical, dental or mental health problems, including recent hospitalizations
    we should know about?
        YES - "I was in a car accident last week. I was riding my bike and I got hit by a car. I damaged my right wrist and when I lift things it hurts and I cant move my wrist backwards because it hurts. My left shoulder was hurt to and I can feel it going in and out of the socket. I was told I needed a reconstructive surgery and my insurance doesn't cover it."

Pain

2. Have you ever had or are you currently being treated for any illness or health condition?   No

3. Do you have any special health requirements?   No

4. Do you have health insurance?   YES - "health care district" **District Cares**

5. Have you ever had or are you currently being treated for HIV, AIDS, Tuberculosis,
        Hepatitis, STD's, skin infections or any other serious communicable disease?
            No

SKIN:
    ABNORMAL - "I was in a car accident last week. I was riding my bike and I got hit by a car. I damaged my right wrist and when I lift things it hurts and I cant move my wrist backwards because it hurts. My left shoulder was hurt to and I can feel it going in and out of the socket. "

Pain

SKIN ASSESSMENT QUESTIONNAIRE - ARMOR CORRECTIONAL HEALTH SERVICES, INC: **Right Wrist**
1. Do you currently have any wounds, bites, sores, redness, swelling?
YES - "swelling and redness to right wrist"

2. Do you have a history of recurrent skin infections?   No

3. Have you tested positive for MRSA in the past?   No

4. Do you have a history of IV drug use?   No

5. Have you shared personal items with another person?   No

INTAKE MENTAL HEALTH SCREENING AND ASSESSMENT - ARMOR CORRECTIONAL HEALTH SERVICES, INC:

Inmate Name: BRIAN DALE BAILEY
ID#: 0403731   Race: W
Gender: Male   DOB: 02-24-1979

1) Does officer believe individual may be a suicide risk?   NO   **Not Suicidal**

DIRECT QUESTIONS:

2) Have you ever received mental health treatment for depression, emotional problems, psychiatric illness or anything similar?   NO
3) Have you ever been in a mental health hospital?   YES
" I was baker acted last year in North Carolina, but I don't remember the name of the facility they took me to."
4) Have you experienced a major loss within the last six months?   No
5) Has anyone in your family or a close friend attempted or committed suicide?   NO
6) Have you had problems with drugs or alcohol?   NO
7) Are you a public official or professional, charged with a shocking crime, or especially embarrassed about being arrested?   NO
8) Are you currently thinking of killing or hurting yourself?   NO
9) Have you ever tried or seriously considered killing or hurting yourself?   NO
6. Have you ever had Chicken Pox?   YES- "as a child"

7. Do you now have or have you recently had any of the following:
         Cough > 2 weeks, bloody cough, lethargy, weakness, unexplained weight loss,
         loss of appetite, fever or night sweats?
         No

8. Have you ever been treated, hospitalized or taken psychotropic meds for a mental health illness?
         No

9. Have you ever been incarcerated (jail or prison) before?   YES

10. Have you ever intentionally hurt yourself or attempted suicide?   YES
         Within the last month: No
         When: "in 2008"
         How many times: 1
         Method: "I had no plan on how I was going to do it"

11. Are you currently thinking about harming yourself or committing suicide?   No

12. Has anyone in your family ever attempted or committed suicide?   No

13. Do you feel that there is nothing to look forward to in the future?   No

14. Have you experienced a major loss within the last 6 months?   No

15. Do you drink alcohol?   YES
         How much and how often? - "rarely and on social occasions"
Alcohol last use: 2018-11-21

When Mr. Bailey was arrested, he was polite while complying with officer & members of Christ Fellowship Church. Not harming anyone within the Church or himself, considered non-violent.

----

16.   Do you use any illegal drugs / medications?   No

17.   Have you ever had any problems with drug/medication withdrawal?   No

18.   Have you ever been in a drug or alcohol treatment program?   YES -
2018

19.   Are you currently taking any prescription or other medications?   No

20.   Allergies:
            NKDA

LEVEL OF CONSCIOUSNESS:
      Alert.   Oriented to x 4.
GENERAL APPEARANCE:
      Normal
BEHAVIOR/CONDUCT: Mr. Bailey Kind and Cooperative
      Cooperative.
AFFECT/MOOD:
      Normal.

GENERAL:
      WNL.
NEURO:
      WNL
EENT:
      WNL
10)   Do you feel that there is nothing to look forward to in the future?
NO
11)   Is this your first time in jail?   NO
11a) Do you identify as transgender, gender non-conforming, or intersex?
NO - Inmate does NOT identify as transgender, gender non-conforming, or
intersex.
            Inmate is neither < 25 years of age or > 70 years of age.

ASSESSMENT OF BEHAVIOR AND GENERAL APPEARANCE:
12)   Shows active symptoms of depression?   NO
13)   Presents afraid, overly anxious or angry about current situation?
NO
14.) Refuses to make eye contact, withdrawn, low verbal tones?   NO
15)   Psychosis?   NO   Not Psychosis
16)   Shows signs of mental retardation or developmental disability: No
17)   Does the patient identify as transgender, gender non-conforming, or
intersex and indicated it is ALSO their first time in jail?: NO

      TOTALS:
         YES: 1
         SHADED: 0

18)   Do you take any mental health medications?   NO
19)   Do you have other mental health concerns?   NO
20)   Have you been a victim of sexual assault or physical abuse?   NO
         Would you like to speak to a Mental Health Professional about past
sexual abuse?   NO
21)   Have you ever perpetrated sexual assault or physical abuse?   NO
22)   Have you ever suffered from a serious head injury, cerebral trauma or
seizure? YES - "February of 2017 I had a head injury at Planet Fitness"
23)   Did you receive special education placement while in school?   NO

RECOMMENDATIONS (based on answers):

```
# Yes:
--------------------------------------------------------------------
# Shaded:
--------------------------------------------------------------------
Position of Respect/Shocking Crime:
--------------------------------------------------------------------
Presentation and 1st Time in Jail:
--------------------------------------------------------------------
Offender's Age and 1st Time in Jail:
Presentation as Repeat Offender:
--------------------------------------------------------------------
Assault/Abuse:
S/W MHP regarding past abuse:
--------------------------------------------------------------------
Perpetrator of assault/abuse:
--------------------------------------------------------------------

DISPOSITION:
     No mental health symptoms; general population; follow-up as needed.

INFLUENZA SYMPTOM SCREENING - ARMOR CORRECTIONAL HEALTH SERVICES, INC::

1.  Have you been visited by or stayed with someone in the past 7 days
with a severe flu illness?      No
Are you presently experiencing any of the following symptoms:
     High fever over 101.5:       No
     Severe headache:             No
     Shortness of breath:         No
     Fever/Chills:                No
     Sore Throat:                 No
     New Frequent Cough:          No
     Nausea/Vomiting/Diarrhea:    No
     No influenza.

PLACEMENT:
     General Population

REFERRED for additional intake assessment/evaluation:      YES
Routine Medical referral initiated.

TREATMENTS:
ROI obtained.
Adult Health Assessment order electronically created.

IMAC ALERTS:41 LOW BUNK/LOW LEVEL
```
Sheriff's Department has been advised by Medical Staff to comply with a
Low Bunk / Low Level

```
FORMS CREATED FOR IM SIGNATURE:
     Release of Information
     Intake Medical/Mental Health Screening
Automated Entries:
The following items were created by ELIZABETH LISANTI, LPN on 05-12-2019
03:29:12 PM:
     ORDER: Provider - Sick Call - Routine (+7)
     Electronically Approved by ELIZABETH LISANTI, LPN on 05-12-2019 03:28:42
PM.

Weight: 155 lbs      Height: 6 ft 0 in   Blood Pressure: 100 / 68    Temp: 98.4
 Pulse: 53   Respiration: 18
Patient's Condition is Related to
Current Illness Date   :
1st Date Of Illness    :
```
155 lbs

When Mr. Bailey first arrived at the West
Detention Center – Belle Glade. He was placed on a
mattress on the floor in Block E-1, due to over
population. Arriving at a healthy weight with fit
body composer & injured.

4/19/2021 3:57:22 PM

Unable to Work Dates :
Hospitilization Dates :
DIAGNOSES:

PROCEDURES:

Attending Provider: LISANTI, LPN ELIZABETH, ARMOR   ID:

End Of Encounter.

Just day before the arrest at Christ Fellowship Church, Mr. Bailey transferred the business administrative data from "**Blackwater Dive Experts**" to an external hard drive. This data was complete with a database of existing clients & contract information, in order to continue business. Also, including details of logos of each company that Mr. Bailey was working with at the time of service. The drive was intended for Mr. Daniel Coston of **Coston Marine Services** & **Marine Construction**. After Mr. Bailey & Mr. Coston shared a short conversation in regard to expanding with Mr. Bailey's current information. While being injured & unable to continue commercial diving on his own.

IN THE CIRCUIT/COUNTY COURT OF THE FIFTEENTH JUDICIAL CIRCUIT
IN AND FOR PALM BEACH COUNTY, FLORIDA

CASE NO. 2019MM005685ARX MO

STATE OF FLORIDA vs.
Brian Bailey
Defendant/Minor Child

APPLICATION FOR CRIMINAL INDIGENT STATUS

✓ I AM SEEKING THE APPOINTMENT OF THE PUBLIC DEFENDER OR

___ I HAVE A PRIVATE ATTORNEY OR AM SELF-REPRESENTED AND SEEK DETERMINATION OF INDIGENCE STATUS FOR COSTS

Notice to Applicant: The provision of a public defender/court appointed lawyer and costs/due process services are not free. A judgment and lien may be imposed against all real or personal property you own to pay for legal and other services provided on your behalf or on behalf of the person for whom you are making this application. There is a $50.00 fee for each application filed. If the application fee is not paid to the Clerk of the Court within 7 days, it will be added to any costs that may be assessed against you at the conclusion of this case. If you are a parent/guardian making this affidavit on behalf of a minor or tax-dependent adult, the information contained in this application must include your income and assets.

1. I have __0__ dependents. (Do not include children not living at home and do not include a working spouse or yourself.)

2. I have a take home income of $____0____ paid (_) weekly (_) bi-weekly (_) semi-monthly (✓) monthly (_) yearly (Take home income equals salary, wages, bonuses, commissions, allowances, overtime, tips and similar payments, minus deductions required by law and other court ordered support payments)

3. I have other income paid (_) weekly (_) bi-weekly (_) semi-monthly (_) monthly (_) yearly. (Circle "Yes" and fill in the amount if you have this kind of income, otherwise circle "No")

Social Security benefits	Yes	$____	Veterans' benefit	Yes	$____ (No)
Unemployment compensation	Yes	$____	Child support or other regular support from family members/spouse	Yes	$____ (No)
Union Funds	Yes	$____	Rental income	Yes	$____ (No)
Workers compensation	Yes	$____	Dividends or interest	Yes	$____ (No)
Retirement/pensions	Yes	$____	Other kinds of income not on the list	Yes	$____ (No)
Trust or gifts	Yes	$____			

4. I have other assets: (Circle "yes" and fill in the value of the property, otherwise circle "No")

Cash	Yes		Savings	Yes	$____ (No)
Bank account(s)	(Yes) $ 246.2 No		Stocks/bonds	Yes	$____ (No)
Certificate of deposit or money market accounts	Yes	$____	*Equity in homestead real estate	Yes	$____ (No)
*Equity in motor vehicles	Yes	$____	*Equity in non-homestead real estate	Yes	$____ (No)
*Equity in boats/other tangible property	Yes	$____	*Include expectancy of an interest in such property		

5. I have a total amount of liabilities and debts in the amount of $ 33,000-

6. I receive: (Circle "Yes" or "No")
   Temporary Assistance for Needy Families – Cash Assistance Yes (No)   Supplemental Security Income (SSI) .... Yes (No)
   Poverty-related veterans' benefits .... Yes (No)

7. I have been released on bail in the amount of $____ Cash ____ Surety ____ Posted by: Self ____ Family ____ Other ____

A person who knowingly provides false information to the clerk or the court in seeking a determination of indigent status under s. 27.52, F.S., commits a misdemeanor of the first degree, punishable as provided in s. 775.082, F.S., or s. 775.083, F.S. I attest that the information I have provided on this Application is true and accurate.

Signed on May 13, 2019

X _____
Signature of applicant for indigent status

Print full legal name: Brian Bailey

Date of Birth 2/24/79

Address: P.O. Box 15532
City, State, Zip: West Palm Beach, FL 33406
Phone Number: 561-130-0181
E-mail Address:

Last four digits of Driver's License or ID Number

CLERK'S DETERMINATION

✓ Based on the information in this Application, I have determined the applicant to be (✓) Indigent ( ) Not Indigent

✓ The Public Defender is hereby appointed to the case listed above until relieved by the Court.

Dated this 13 day of May , 20 19

Clerk of the Circuit Court, by Deputy Clerk

Shamed HRhode
Clerk/Deputy Clerk/Other authorized person

APPLICANTS FOUND NOT INDIGENT MAY SEEK REVIEW BY ASKING FOR A HEARING TIME. Sign here if you want the judge to review the clerk's decision of not indigent. _____

This form was completed with the assistance of:

Florida Supreme Court Form 3.984, Updated 11/23/15

*Statue Violations: 92.525(1)(A)(4)(A)(B)(C)
Verification of documents,
perjury by false written
declaration, penalty*

90.604 Lack of Personal Knowledge

*(The document above has the **incorrect income amount & address**.)*

Google

Payments profile ID
6132

Name
Brian Bailey

Payments account nickname
Google AdSense

Summary created
Feb 7, 2020

Jan 1 – 31, 2019

Ending balance: $47.29

Date	Description	Amount (USD)
Jan 1 – 31, 2019	Earnings - YouTube	$7.49

Starting balance: $39.80

(2019)

Annual Income — 919.68

45

Google

Payments profile ID
6132

Name
Brian Bailey

Payments account nickname
Google AdSense

Summary created
Feb 7, 2020

Feb 1 – 28, 2019

Ending balance: $59.53

Date	Description	Amount (USD)
Feb 1 – 28, 2019	Earnings - YouTube	$12.24

Starting balance: $47.29

46

Payments profile ID
6132

Name
Brian Bailey

Payments account nickname
Google AdSense

Summary created
Feb 7, 2020

Mar 1 – 31, 2019

Ending balance: $78.78

Date	Description	Amount (USD)
Mar 1 – 31, 2019	Earnings - YouTube	$19.25

Starting balance: $59.53

Google

Payments profile ID
···· ··· 6132

Name
Brian Bailey

Payments account nickname
Google AdSense

Summary created
Feb 7, 2020

Apr 1 − 30, 2019

Ending balance: $629.50

Date	Description	Amount (USD)
Apr 1 − 30, 2019	Earnings - YouTube	$550.72

Starting balance: $78.78

48

Google

Payments profile ID
6132

Name
Brian Bailey

Payments account nickname
Google AdSense

Summary created
Feb 7, 2020

May 1 – 31, 2019

Ending balance: $175.32

Date	Description	Amount (USD)
May 1 – 31, 2019	Earnings - YouTube	$175.32
May 21, 2019	Automatic payment: Checking ····380. 0910000131091	–$629.50

Starting balance: $629.50

49

Google

Payments profile ID
6132

Name
Brian Bailey

Payments account nickname
Google AdSense

Summary created
Feb 7, 2020

Jun 1 – 30, 2019

Ending balance: $19.93

Date	Description	Amount (USD)
Jun 1 – 30, 2019	Earnings - YouTube	$19.93
Jun 21, 2019	Automatic payment: Checking ···· 380. 09100001729356	-$175.32

Starting balance: $175.32

50

Google

Payments profile ID
6132

Name
Brian Bailey

Payments account nickname
Google AdSense

Summary created
Feb 7, 2020

Jul 1 – 31, 2019

Ending balance: $42.07

Date	Description	Amount (USD)
Jul 1 – 31, 2019	Earnings - YouTube	$22.14

Starting balance: $19.93

Google

Payments profile ID
-6132

Name
Brian Bailey

Payments account nickname
Google AdSense

Summary created
Feb 7, 2020

Aug 1 – 31, 2019

Ending balance: $59.28

Date	Description	Amount (USD)
Aug 1 – 31, 2019	Earnings - YouTube	$17.21

Starting balance: $42.07

Google

Payments profile ID
6132

Name
Brian Bailey

Payments account nickname
Google AdSense

Summary created
Feb 7, 2020

Sep 1 – 30, 2019

Ending balance: $77.48

Date	Description	Amount (USD)
Sep 1 – 30, 2019	Earnings - YouTube	$18.20

Starting balance: $59.28

Google

Payments profile ID
6132

Name
Brian Bailey

Payments account nickname
Google AdSense

Summary created
Feb 7, 2020

Oct 1 – 31, 2019

Ending balance: $114.86

Date	Description	Amount (USD)
Oct 1 – 31, 2019	Earnings - YouTube	$37.38

Starting balance: $77.48

54

Google

Payments profile ID
6132

Name
Brian Bailey

Payments account nickname
Google AdSense

Summary created
Feb 7, 2020

Nov 1 – 30, 2019

Ending balance: $96.78

Date	Description	Amount (USD)
Nov 1 – 30, 2019	Earnings - YouTube	$96.78
Nov 21, 2019	Automatic payment: Checking ···· 613. 09100001397389	-$114.86

Starting balance: $114.86

55

Google

Payments profile ID
6132

Name
Brian Bailey

Payments account nickname
Google AdSense

Summary created
Feb 7, 2020

Dec 1 – 31, 2019

Ending balance: $181.20

Date	Description	Amount (USD)
Dec 1 – 31, 2019	Earnings - YouTube	$84.42

Starting balance: $96.78

56

Being released to find the P.O. Box held at USPS 3200 Summit Blvd. in West Palm Beach, Florida, filled with mail and coming due. The correct address and information are below:

Paid   8/23/2019
(Debt Card)

P.O. Box Service Fee Notice
WEST PALM BCH WINDOW UNIT
3200 SUMMIT BLVD, WEST PALM BEACH, FL 33416

WEBBATS BAT710B1

(561) 697-2122

BRIAN BAILEY
PO BOX 15532
WEST PALM BEACH, FL 33416

Date of Notice:	08/20/2019
Box#	15532
6 Months:	$53.00
12 Months:	$106.00
Due Date:	08/31/2019

Dear BRIAN BAILEY:

This is a friendly reminder that your Post Office Box or Caller Service renewal fee is due. If you have already paid this fee, please disregard this notice and thank you for your continued business with the United States Postal Service. If you have not yet submitted your payment, please do so now.

At your location, at least one of the following Additional Services is available: *Street Addressing* (allows private carrier package delivery) and *Signature on File* (easy pickup for some signature required items).

There is **no** extra charge for these Additional Services. Visit your Post Office to sign up for these services today! These services however, do not apply to Caller Service and Group E Box customers.

For your convenience, you can sign up at www.usps.com/poboxes and renew or manage your PO Box online. Use your credit card to make a one-time payment or sign up for automatic payments so you never miss a due date. You can also renew your PO Box at any of more than 2,900 self-service kiosks located at select Post Offices nationwide. Go to www.usps.com/locator/welcome.htm to look for a kiosk location near you.

As always, payments can be made at the Post Office or mailed to the attention of the Postmaster at the address indicated above. Please make checks or money orders payable to the US Postal Service and include your PO Box number and ZIP Code. If paying by mail, a receipt will be delivered to your PO Box.

Note: Caller Service may only be paid **in person** or **by mail** unless enrolled in Enterprise PO Box Online (EPOBOL). (Enroll at https://postalpro.usps.com/EPS under the "Quick Links" section). Please be sure to include this notice with your remittance. Caller Service receipts will be provided at the caller service pickup window.

If your payment is not received by the due date, access to your PO Box will be blocked and caller services will be limited. If we have not received your payment by the 10th day after the due date, your PO Box service will be terminated, incoming mail will be returned to the sender, and, in addition to any unpaid monthly PO Box fees, you will be charged a handling fee to reopen your box. To avoid this inconvenience, we encourage you to renew on time.

As a reminder, your account information must be current. If your physical address or other pertinent information has changed since you applied for your PO Box, please ask a Sales and Service Associate at your Post Office to update your *Application for Post Office Box Service* (PS Form-1093).

To update your information for Caller Service, you can ask a Sales and Service Associate to update the *Application for Caller Service* (PS Form-1093C).

You are a valued customer and we appreciate your business. Thank you!

POSTMASTER, WEST PALM BEACH

8/23/2019

WEST PALM BEACH
3200 SUMMIT BLVD
WEST PALM BEACH, FL 33416-3599
119446-0102
(800)275-8777
08/23/2019 07:59 PM

Product	Qty	Unit Price	Price
Box Renewal			$106.00

    (Zip Code:33416)
    (Box #:15532)
    (Box Size:Size 1 - 3 in x 5.5 in)
    (Rental Period:Annual)
    (Rental Start Date:09/01/2019)
    (Next Renewal Date:08/31/2020)
    (Customer Name:BRIAN BAILEY)

Total: $106.00

Debit Card Remit'd $106.00
    (Card Name:VISA)
    (Account #:XXXXXXXXXXXX2559)
    (Approval #)
    (Transaction #:133)
    (Receipt #:048581)
    (Debit Card Purchase:$106.00)
    (Cash Back:$0.00)
    (AID:A0000000980840   (chip)
    (AL:US DEBIT)
    (PTN:Verified)

In a hurry? Self-service kiosks offer
quick and easy check-out. Any Retail
Associate can show you how.

Preview your Mail
Track your Packages
Sign up for FREE @
www.informeddelivery.com

All sales final on stamps and postage.
Refunds for guaranteed services only.
Thank you for your business.

United States Postal Service
NOW HIRING numerous locations
$16.00 - $17.78 per hour
depending on position
Apply online at www.usps.com/careers
Search by state -
AL/AR/TX/GA/FL/LA/MS/OK
Must apply separately for each
position desired
Check daily for new opportunities

HELP US SERVE YOU BETTER

TELL US ABOUT YOUR RECENT
POSTAL EXPERIENCE

Go to:
https://postalexperience.com/Pos

840-5327-0103-008-00069-31180-02

or scan this code with
your mobile device:

or call 1-800-410-7420.

YOUR OPINION COUNTS

Receipt #: 840-53270103-8-6931180-2
Clerk: 20

Order of No Contact and Bond Amount

IN THE CIRCUIT COURT, 15TH JUDICIAL CIRCUIT, PALM BEACH COUNTY, FLORIDA

STATE OF FLORIDA

V.

BAILEY, BRIAN DALE

2019015844   05/12/2019

BOOKING NO/CASE NO. 50-2019-MM-005685-AXXX-MB

[ ] FELONY
[X] MISDEMEANOR
[ ] CRIMINAL TRAFFIC

ORDER

THE DEFENDANT is here for a non-adversary probable cause determination (a first court appearance). See Rule 3.131.

Fla.R.Cr.P. He/She is in custody charged with the offense(s) named in the Booking Slip and/or Charging Document of Record.

THE COURT FINDS AND ORDERS AS FOLLOWS:

PROBABLE CAUSE EXISTS for the pending charge(s) (unless otherwise checked below), AND while the defendant awaits trial.

[ ] RELEASE ON OWN RECOGNIZANCE is hereby ordered.
[ ] NO BOND is allowed because this is a capital or life felony and/or for good cause shown.
[ ] Defendant is ordered held NO BOND PENDING FORENSIC evaluation and return to Court.
[ ] Defendant is ordered held NO BOND PENDING SAAP (ie., substance abuse) evaluation and return to Court.
[ ] NO BOND PENDING FURTHER HEARING for _____
[✓] BOND is set in the amount of $ _2000_ (including the following ONE condition if checked).
    [✓] ALTERNATIVE S.O.R. (Supervised Release on Own Recognizance) is also authorized.
    [ ] PLUS S.R. (Supervised Release by SOR Program) if and only if the bond set above is posted.
    [ ] PLUS HOUSE ARREST per court order and only if bond as set above is posted. [_____
    [ ] The ALTERNATIVE of HOUSE ARREST is allowed only if Defendant qualifies for PBSO House Arrest.
[ ] COURT ORDERED HOUSE ARREST.
[ ] SOR Level _____
[ ] COURT ORDERED SUPERVISED RELEASE.
[ ] CUSTODY RELEASE to _____
[ ] NO PROBABLE CAUSE exists, THEREFORE Defendant is RELEASED ON OWN RECOGNIZANCE.
[ ] NO PROBABLE CAUSE but HEARING CONTINUED for supplement P.C. (not more than 72 hours) until ___/___/___.

CONDITIONS OF RELEASE

Defendant is required to: (1) appear at time set for arraignment and all other set times for court proceedings in this case, (2) keep the Clerk of Court notified to Defendant's current and correct mailing address, (3) understand that mailing of notice of court proceedings to Defendant's address as provided to Clerk constitutes legal notice of court proceedings if mailed at least 72 hours before time of hearing, and (4) comply with the following additional conditions:

[✓] NO CONTACT WITH VICTIM(S) direct or indirect (except through attorneys) _As per order_
[ ] NO CONTACT WITH ANY CO-DEFENDANT(S) direct or indirect (except through attorneys) _____
[ ] NO CONTACT WITH ANY WITNESSES _____
[ ] NO VIOLENT CONTACT WITH VICTIM(S) [per victim request only] _____
[ ] CHILD VISITS _____
[ ] CURFEW [ ] 24 hours a day, or [ ] from _____ to _____ . [ ] EXCEPTIONS _____
[ ] Sign up for and comply with BATTERERS INTERVENTION PROGRAM. (Select program now in Court records)
[ ] Immediately obtain a SAAP EVALUATION (substance abuse evaluation) within 48 hours, and comply with all recommendations
[ ] Be subject 24 hours a day to RANDOM TESTING at Defendant's expense for [ ] ALCOHOL and/or for [ ] DRUGS
[ ] Attend ANGER MANAGEMENT CLASSES, [ ] using a program WITH SUBSTANCE ABUSE COMPONENT.
[ ] NO ALCOHOL possession or consumption, no visits to bars or lounges or any place where alcohol is a primary business.
[ ] NO WEAPONS in Defendant's possession, constructive or otherwise, or in Defendant's residence or vehicle.
[ ] DO NOT LEAVE PALM BEACH COUNTY except with prior authorization of Court.
[ ] Prior to release from custody, submit to HIV/STD/HBS-Ag TEST with results returnable to victim(s) and Defendant only.
[ ] Submit to MENTAL HEALTH EVALUATION at Community Mental Health Center or by private psychiatrist (not psychologist) within 48 hours AND COMPLY with any and all recommended treatment and medication.

[ ] OTHER _____

DONE AND ORDERED this __13th__ day of __May, 2019__ at West Palm Beach, Florida.

Presiding Judge

FILED
MAY 13 2019
SHARON R. BOCK
Clerk & Comptroller

---

*The Bond amount had been set higher than Mr. Bailey's **annual income**.*

*Statue Violations: 787.02 **False imprisonment;***

4/19/2021 3:57:21 PM

BAILEY, BRIAN DALE
05-13-2019 Mon 11:19:15 AM
ENCOUNTER
    Dictation : PROVIDER CLINIC VISIT ROUTINE - ARMOR CORRECTIONAL HEALTH
SERVICES, INC:

    Resident Name: BRIAN DALE BAILEY
    ID#: 0403731
    DOB: 02-24-1979
    Location: B W E 01 1 02L B

    Allergies: NKDA
    Current Problems:
    41, LOW BUNK/LOW LEVEL   **Low Bunk / Low Level**

    Current Medications:

    DateTime: 05-13-2019 Mon / 15:21
                                              Right Wrist
    CHIEF COMPLAINT/HPI:
        BRIAN DALE BAILEY, 40 year old W Male complains of right wrist pain
    and swelling from bike accident he had few ago. Patient has also h/o left   **Pain**
    shoulder dislocation syndrome, has done repeated MRI of the shoulder and had
    received multiples intrarticular injections. He was scheduled for surgery
    prior he gets arrested.   **Left Shoulder**

    PAST MEDICAL HISTORY: none
    REVIEW OF SYSTEMS:
        Headache:
            Negative.
        Vision Changes:
            Negative.
        Chest Pain:
            Negative.
        Shortness of Breath:
            Negative.
        Leg Swelling:
            Negative.
        Abdominal Pain:
            Negative.
        Nausea/Vomiting:
            Negative.
        Diarrhea:
            Negative.
        Constipation:
            Negative.
        Hemoptysis:
            Negative.
        Hematuria:
            Negative.
        Hematochezia:
            Negative.

    PHYSICAL EXAM:
        Height: 6 ft.
        Weight: 155 lbs 4 oz   **155 lbs**
        Temp: 97.8

While Mr. Bailey was answering these questions for staff at **West Detention Center - Belle Glade**. Explaining that he's in pain due to bodily injury. Confused that after sharing this with the **Social Security Administration** & having an open case, writing his injuries on a **prayer card** at the local Church, he ends up in handcuffs.

B/P: 104/68
Pulse: 51   **Pulse 51**
Respiration: 16
Pulse Ox: %
EYES:
        Eyes clear bilaterally. PERRLA.
ENT:
        Ears clear bilaterally. Nares are patent. No congestion noted.
Pharynx clear.
NECK:
        Neck supple. No palpable lymph nodes of head/neck. No thyromegaly
noted. No JVD.
HEART:
        RRR. No murmur.
LUNGS:
        Respirations non-labored. Clear to auscultation.
ABDOMEN:
        Soft, non-tender. No CVA tenderness. Resident walks erect with
steady gait.

ASSESSMENT:RIGHT WRIST PAIN/ LEFT SHOULDER PAIN **Pain**

PLAN:
Radiology:
        X-Ray of Right Wrist ordered
Acetaminophen 325 mg, 325 mg #20, Sig: Take 2 tablets by mouth twice a day
for 5 days PRN
RTC in 2 weeks   **Pain Medication Denied**

Automated Entries:
The following items were created by Louidor Alliance, MD on 05-13-2019
03:34:47 PM:
        ORDER: X-Ray - Right Wrist
Electronically Approved by Louidor Alliance, MD on 05-13-2019 03:34:13 PM.

Weight: 155 lbs 4 oz   Height: 6 ft 0 in   Blood Pressure: 104 / 68   Temp:
97.8   Pulse: 51   Respiration: 16
Patient's Condition is Related to
Current Illness Date :
1st Date Of Illness   :
Unable to Work Dates :
Hospitilization Dates :
DIAGNOSES:

PROCEDURES:

Attending Provider: Alliance, MD Louidor, Armor - MJ   ID:

End Of Encounter.

During the last several years while owning his own company, "**Blackwater Dive Experts**" Mr. Bailey had to live outside & in warehouses. Now only being able to be released on an **S.O.R.** bases under supervision. Pushing him to use a residential address after losing everything to injury. Then blocking his release, while **Palm Beach County**, offers **John Prince Park** for temporary living. He's distant with his family, due to many years of being self-employed & their differences in working status. Most of them working in fields such as Authority, Military, Fire Department, & Medical.

Now being confined & needing to locate a residential address, after being advised by **APD Raymon A. Burns** that he needs a residential address. Then placing Mr. Bailey with an individual that he's never lived with, & who already has a conflict of interest. Nor do they see eye to eye, her name is, "**Brenda Taft**" twin sister to his mother, "**Linda Kay Hall**" & they didn't see eye to eye either. Ms. Taft's son also attends the Christ Fellowship Church & holds a leadership position with the Palm Beach County Fire Rescue, his name is, "**Adam Michael Taft**."

Which has fallen right into our next generation of family members. This creates cases for the **Sheriff's Department**, by displacing these individuals, instead of using county assistance & helping people find quality housing. Which was, "**not**" provided.

While going through his first semester at **Palm Beach State College** & starting school living outside. He found a home on the internet that had an open room, known as **Palm Beach Recovery Coalition GW House** Transitional housing program in Lake Worth, then understanding that this was a county assistance program providing housing. Address 311 N Federal Hwy, Lake Worth, FL 33460.

The house had many men, "none of which were going to college, physical fit or healthy" & continually smoked on the property.

https://sobernation.com/listing/palm-beach-recovery-coalition-gw-house-lake-worth-fl/

Mr. Bailey was sober & in college while volunteering.

*Mr. Bailey stayed in the room being offered & worked on studies, while volunteering at **Christ Fellowship Church** every **Sunday** through multiple worships. Not sharing anytime for relationships within the home of no common interest, while being injured. Mr. Bailey stayed in the room being offered & worked on studies, while volunteering at **Christ Fellowship Church** every **Sunday** through multiple worships. Not sharing anytime for relationships within the home of no common interest, while being injured.*

*After speaking with the social worker, & reviewing the contracts being offered. Explaining to the social worker that he would only be able to afford to stay on the property for **9 months**. With the amount of funds being received through school loans that Mr. Bailey had in transit. The county social worker was unable to process the request, even after speaking with upper management. This created another displacement just before the arrest by **Palm Beach County Sheriff's Department** at **Christ Fellowship Church**.*

5/13/2019

IN THE FIFTEENTH JUDICIAL CIRCUIT
CRIMINAL DIVISION IN AND
FOR PALM BEACH COUNTY, FLORIDA

☐ CIRCUIT COURT
☐ COUNTY COURT

STATE OF FLORIDA

CASE NO(S). _2019MM005685_

vs.

Brian Bailey

Defendant

AUTHORIZATION FOR COURT DATE REMINDER TEXT MESSAGES

I, Brian Bailey , hereby consent to receive text messages to my cell phone reminding me of court dates and times for my ongoing court case(s) in the Fifteenth Judicial Circuit. I understand that standard text messaging rates may apply. I further understand that I may revoke this consent via the text message system if I wish to do so. I authorize to receive these text messages at 561-720-0787.

(Spanish) Yo, _____, por la presente consiento en recibir mensajes de texto a mi teléfono celular recordándome las fechas y horas de la corte para mi caso (s) en curso en el Decimoquinto Circuito Judicial. Entiendo que las tarifas estándar de mensajería de texto pueden aplicarse. También entiendo que puedo revocar este consentimiento a través del sistema de mensajes de texto si lo deseo. El número de teléfono celular que autorizo a recibir estos mensajes de texto es _____.

(Creole) Mwen menm, _____, mwen dakò pou resevwa mesaj tèks nan telefòn selilè mwen an ki raple m dat ak lè tribinal pou pwosè kont mwen an (yo) nan Jidisye 15yem sik la. Mwen konprann ke konpayi telefon yo ka chaje mwen yon bil pou mesaj sa. Mwen plis konprann mwen ke mwen ka anile konsantman sa a atravè sistèm mesaj tèks la si mwen vle fè sa. Nimewo telefòn selilè mwen bay otorizasyon pou resevwa mesaj tèks sa yo se

_____   5- -19
Signature   Date
Firma   Fecha
Siyati   Dat

FILED
MAY 13 2019
SHARON R. BOCK
Clerk & Comptroller

65

Report :	CWRCDACT			CLERK OF THE CIRCUIT COURT		Date :	13-May-2019
Instance :	JISPROD			CROSS REFERENCE LIST		Time :	8:53 pm
				CRIMINAL DEFENDANT ACTIVITY REPORT		Page No :	1

— — — — — — CURRENT CASE — — — — — —   User ID : IRHO

Defendent Name		Arrest Date	Case ID		Booking	Assigned Div
BAILEY, BRIAN DALE		5/12/19	50-2019-MM-005685-AXXX-MB		2019015844	B

Charges : 1 - TRESPASS AFTER WARNING

Booking History

Case ID	Booking No	Div	Charge
50-2013-TR-163888-AXXX-NB		NI	TCATS FAIL TO DISPLAY REGISTRATION / TEMPORARY INTERNET RECEIPT. POSSESSION REQUIRED
50-2013-TR-163911-AXXX-NB		NI	TCATS SPEED/65 HIGHWAY/TURNPIKE (REQUIRES SPEEDS)
50-2013-TR-163918-AXXX-NB		NI	TCATS PROOF OF INSURANCE REQUIRED

Case ID	Booking No	Div	Charge
50-2019-MM-005685-AXXX-MB	2019015844	B	TRESPASS AFTER WARNING

Purged Booking History

Booking Number	Arrest Date	Booking Charge Narrative

Case ID	Initial Filing Date	Booking No	Charge
50-2019-MM-005685-AXXX-MB	05/13/2019	2019015844	TRESPASS AFTER WARNING

Disposition Date : Plea : Adjudication : Probation : Days-0.00, Months-0.00, Years-0.00

PENDING EVENT: 06/5/19 9:30   Type: AR - ARRAIGNMENT   Division : KK1
WARRANT TYPE: Type :

*Above in the left column, it shows **Booking History**. The first three cases are from 2013, where Mr. Bailey was stopped by Florida Highway Patrol while driving an automobile. It shows no dates & doesn't relate to the case of Trespass at Christ Fellowship Church, in 2019. Meanwhile using a religious location as an arresting destination. On more than occasion Mr. Bailey has had his identity stolen or lost.*

Creating an identity comprise after building on the worldwide web, looking for the American Dream of financial income & stability. Now being proven to show disfunctions in the System **We Trust in.**

5/13/2019

FIFTEENTH JUDICIAL CIRCUIT IN AND FOR PALM BEACH COUNTY, FLORIDA

STATE OF FLORIDA

v. Brian Dale Bailey

DEFENDANT

BOOKING NO.: 2019 015884

CASE NO.: 2019 MH 005685 MB

[ ] DOMESTIC
[ ] DATING
[X] NON-DOMESTIC

ORDER OF NO CONTACT

This "no contact order" is effective immediately and enforceable for the duration of the pretrial release or until modified by the Court.

1. The Defendant is specifically ordered to have NO CONTACT and to not attempt to contact the following person(s):

    [X] Alleged Victim(s)   Christ Fellowship in Royal Palm Beach
    [ ] Co-Defendant(s) _____
    [ ] Witness(es) _____

2. The Defendant shall NOT CONTACT or attempt to contact the above-listed person(s) until this case is closed or until further order of the Court, whichever occurs first.

3. For purposes of this Order, "no contact" means:

    • NO direct or indirect messages or communications by the Defendant.

    • NO direct or indirect contact by a third person on behalf of the Defendant. This does not prohibit an attorney for the Defendant, consistent with Rules regulating The Florida Bar from communicating with any person protected by the no contact order for lawful purposes.

    • NO communication of any kind including telephone calls, messages on answering machines and voice or electronic; all written forms of communication, including letters of apology; or any other means of communication, including the delivery of gifts at any time, either at a residence, school, or workplace.

    • The Defendant is prohibited from being within 500 feet of the victim's or other named person's residence, even if the Defendant and the victim or other named person share the residence.

    • The Defendant is prohibited from being within 500 feet of the victim's or other named person's vehicle, place of employment, or a specified place frequented regularly by such person.

    • The Defendant is prohibited from the following addresses (victim's home/job, if child involved school address/aftercare center/address for extracurricular activities): _____

5/13/19 emailed to PBSO

FILED

MAY 13 2019

SHARON R. BOCK
Clerk & Comptroller

October 2015   Page 1 of 2   Form 31

Brian Dale
Bailey

2019 015844

4. The Defendant has been expressly advised that if the above-listed person(s) attempts to contact the Defendant, he/she must avoid any such contact and the Defendant has been further advised that he/she would be in violation of this Order if the Defendant communicates with the above-listed person(s) even if contact is initiated by the above-listed person(s).

5. **Immediately surrender any firearms or ammunition to the custody of the sheriff.** (within 24 hours of release from custody) {possession of either may be a violation of Federal Statute 18 U.S.C. 922(g)(8)}

6. <u>Exceptions</u> (applies only if checked):

    [ ] The Defendant may return to the residence where the above-listed person(s) resides for the purpose of removing the Defendant's PERSONAL EFFECTS ONLY and then only in the presence of a uniformed law enforcement officer and on ONE occasion only.
    [ ] Contact may be in writing.
    [ ] Contact may be by telephone.
    [ ] Contact may occur but only through a third party and only to facilitate visitation with the Defendant's minor children.

7. The Defendant has been expressly advised that violation of this Order will subject the Defendant to arrest and commitment by the Court, plus, if applicable, bond forfeiture.

I have read and do understand this Order and agree to obey it. I fully understand that ONLY A CRIMINAL DIVISION JUDGE may modify this order. I understand therefore that the alleged victim in this case, the state attorney, and any other attorney or person DOES NOT HAVE THE AUTHORITY to modify <u>ANY PORTION</u> of this Order without APPROVAL BY THE JUDGE.

I completely understand and agree that if I disobey this Order, the Judge may possibly revoke and forfeit any bond, and/or order my immediate incarceration.

I understand that this Order supercedes any prior Order(s) relating to the above-listed person(s).

X _____
      DEFENDANT

DONE and **ORDERED** in West Palm Beach, Palm Beach County, Florida this _13th_ day of ___May___, 20 _19_.

_____
CIRCUIT/COUNTY COURT JUDGE

Copies Furnished To:
State Attorney
Public Defender/Defense Attorney
Defendant
Alleged Victim (provided by State Attorney)

October 2015   Page 2 of 2   Form 31

*Above is the **Order of No Contact**, provided by **Sheriff's Department**, at the request of **Christ Fellowship Church**. The **Sheriff's Department** are the same individuals that Mr. Bailey serves with, while assisting on the **Traffic Team**.*

*The URL below shows **Brian Dale Bailey** as Traffic Man:*
https://www.youtube.com/watch?v=EQRjG8QedAQ

PALM BEACH COUNTY SHERIFF'S OFFICE
Florida State Statute Exemption Sheet

Palm Beach County Sheriff's Office – Arrests Only

	x	Florida State Statute	Description	Page Number(s)
L/E Exemptions	☐	119.071(2)(d)	Surveillance techniques, procedures and personnel; inventory of law enforcement resources, policies or plans pertaining to mobilization deployment or tactical operations.	
	☒	943.053, 943.0525	NCIC/FCIC/FBI and in-state FDLE/DOC.	1
	☐	119.071(4)(c)	Undercover personnel.	
	☐	119.071(2)(f)	Confidential Informants (CIs).	
	☐	119.071(2)(e)	Confession.	
Public Info. Exemptions	☐	985.04(1)	Juvenile offender records.	
	☐	119.071(h)(1)	Assets of a crime victim.	
	☐	395.3025(7)(a), 456.057(7)(a)	Medical information.	
	☐	394.4615(7)	Mental health information.	
	☐	119.071(4)(d) (2)(e)	Home address, telephone, Social Security number, date of birth, or photos of active/former LE personnel, spouses, and children.	
Florida Rules of Judicial Administration 2.420 (Rule of 25)	☒	(ix) 119.0714(1)(i)-(j), (2)(a)-(e)	Social Security, bank account, charge, debit, and credit card numbers.	2
	☐	(viii) 394.4615(7)	Clinical records under the Baker Act.	
	☐	(xi) 741.30(3)(b)	The victim's address in a domestic violence action on petitioner's request.	
	☐	(xii) 119.071(2)(h), 119.0714(1)(h)	Protected information regarding victims of child abuse or sexual offenses.	
	☐			
	☐			
	☐			
	☐			
	☐			
Other	☐		Other:	
	☐		Other:	

REVIEW COMPLETED BY

Booking Number: 2019015844 WDC	Date: 05/13/2019
	Specialist Name/ID: AM/31562

Created 2/5/2016 | Updated 1/5/2018

*While being incarcerated & an enrolled student at a State college. **Never once** did & member of the **Sheriff's Department, Christ Fellowship Church** or the **College**. Present Mr. Bailey with the charges listed above as 943.053, 943.0525, 119.0714(1)(i)-(j),(2)(a)-(e).*

5/13/2019

IN THE COUNTY COURT OF THE FIFTEENTH JUDICIAL CIRCUIT
IN AND FOR PALM BEACH COUNTY, FLORIDA - CRIMINAL DIVISION
CIRCUIT/COUNTY COURT
Court Event Form

DEFENDANT: BRIAN DALE BAILEY
CASE NO: 50-2019-MM-005685-AXXX-MB

STATE OF FLORIDA

DATE: 5/13/2019

vs.
DEFENDANT: BRIAN DALE BAILEY
CASE NO: 50-2019-MM-005685-AXXX-MB
DIVISION: B: Cnty Crim - B (County)

JACKET #: 0403731
BOOKING #: 2019015844

PRESIDING JUDGE: COLLINS, JUDGESHERRI L
ASA: STATE, ATTORNEY
ATTORNEY:
PUBLIC DEFENDER: DEFENDER, PUBLIC
CO-COUNSEL:

START TIME: 9:27 AM
END TIME: 9:35 AM

DEPUTY CLERK: IR

COURT REPORTER CENTRAL
RECORDED
COURT TYPE: FAP - FIRST
APPEARANCE

COURT ROOM: #1 (West Branch)

Reset For
Court Date Scheduled - AR - ARRAIGNMENT - 6/5/2019 9:30 AM - #2 (Gun Club) GB, 3228 Gun Club Road
West Palm Beach FL 33406 - IN CUSTODY

Other: DEFENDANT PRESENT AND IN CUSTODY
Other: DEFENDANT FOUND INDIGENT
Other: PD APPOINTED PER COURT
Other: STAND IN ATTORNEY APD S. GRAVES PRESENT
Other: STAND IN ATTORNEY ASA T. BECKWITH PRESENT

New Bond - Count 1 - ALTSOR IV ($2,000.00)

Bond Condition - NO CONTACT WITH VICTIM ORDER FILED
Bond Condition - DEFT MUST PROVIDE VERIFIED HOME ADDRESS TO BE RELEASED ALT SOR IV
Total Criminal Court Costs and Fines: $50.00 - Due Date: 05/13/2019
Other Fees: $50.00
PD App Fee: $50.00

Count 1 - MF TRESPASS AFTER WARNING 810.09(2A)

FILED: PALM BEACH COUNTY, FL SHARON R BOCK, CLERK 05/13/2019 09:35:23 AM

IN THE CIRCUIT/COUNTY COURT OF THE FIFTEENTH JUDICIAL CIRCUIT
IN AND FOR PALM BEACH COUNTY, FLORIDA

STATE OF FLORIDA

-Vs-

BRIAN DALE BAILEY
GENERAL DELIVERY
WEST PALM BEACH, FL 32200

Date: 05/13/2019

Case No: 50-2019-MM-005685-AXXX-MB

Division: B: Cnty Crim - B (County)

NOTICE OF HEARING
THE DEFENDANT MUST BE PRESENT AT THIS HEARING

*For Criminal Charges: Failure to Appear will result in a Bond Forfeiture or
revocation of own recognizance (O.R.) and a Capias/Warrant being issued for your arrest.
For Civil Traffic Charges: Failure to appear may result in the suspension of your driver's license.*
IF YOUR CASE IS ON-CALL, CONTACT YOUR ATTORNEY FOR THE TIME TO APPEAR

YOU ARE HEREBY NOTIFIED that this case is scheduled

DATE:	TIME:	HEARING TYPE:	LOCATION:
6/5/2019	9:30 AM	AR - ARRAIGNMENT	#2 (Gun Club) GB, 3228 Gun Club Road West Palm Beach FL 33406

BE PREPARED TO PAY COURT COSTS AND FINES ASSESSED BY THE COURT AT THIS HEARING
*"IF YOU INTEND TO REQUEST THE SERVICES OF THE PUBLIC DEFENDER, YOU MUST FILE AN APPLICATION AT THE CLERK &
COMPTROLLER'S OFFICE AND BE APPOINTED THE PUBLIC DEFENDER BEFORE YOUR COURT DATE. THE APPLICATION FEE IS $50.00."*
Civil Traffic Charges are not eligible for a Public Defender.

SHARON R. BOCK,
CLERK & COMPTROLLER
BY: IR

Deft/Atty: DEFENDANT IN CUSTODY

Deputy Clerk

cc: ATTORNEY STATE
DEFENDER, PUBLIC

FILED: PALM BEACH COUNTY, FL SHARON R BOCK, CLERK 05/13/2019 09:35:21 AM

IN THE CIRCUIT/COUNTY COURT OF THE FIFTEENTH JUDICIAL CIRCUIT
IN AND FOR PALM BEACH COUNTY, FLORIDA

"If you are a person with a disability who needs any accommodation in order to participate in this proceeding, you are entitled, at no cost to you, to the provision of certain assistance. Please contact Tammy Anton, Americans with Disabilities Act Coordinator, Palm Beach County Courthouse, 205 North Dixie Hwy, West Palm Beach, FL 33401; telephone number (561) 355-4380 at least 7 days before your scheduled court appearance, or immediately upon receiving this notification if the time before the scheduled appearance is less than 7 days; if you are hearing or voice impaired, call 711."

"Si usted es una persona minusválida que necesita algún acomodamiento para poder participar en este procedimiento, usted tiene derecho, sin tener gastos propios, a que se le provea cierta ayuda. Tenga la amabilidad de ponerse en contacto con Tammy Anton, 205 N. Dixie Highway, West Palm Beach, Florida 33401; teléfono número (561) 355-4380, por lo menos 7 días antes de la cita fijada para su comparecencia en los tribunales, o inmediatamente después de recibir esta notificación si el tiempo antes de la comparecencia que se ha programado es menos de 7 días; si usted tiene discapacitación del oído o de la voz, llame al 711."

"Si ou se yon moun ki enfim ki bezwen akomodasyon pou w ka patisipe nan pwosedi sa, ou kalifye san ou pa gen okenn lajan pou w peye, gen pwovizyon pou jwen kèk èd. Tanpri kontakte Tammy Anton, kòòdonatè pwogram Lwa pou ameriken ki Enfim yo nan Tribinal Konte Palm Beach la ki nan 205 North Dixie Highway, West Palm Beach, Florida 33401; telefòn li se (561) 355-4380 nan 7 jou anvan dat ou gen randevou pou parèt nan tribinal la, oubyen imedyatman apre ou fin resevwa konvokasyon an si lè ou gen pou w parèt nan tribinal la mwens ke 7 jou; si ou gen pwoblèm pou w tande oubyen pale, rele 711."

On the date of **5/13/2019**, Mr. Bailey was in Custody at **Glades, West Detention Center**, also known as **Palm Beach Sheriff's Office - West County Jail**. Address 38840 FL-80, Belle Glade, FL 33430. Injured & hurt laying on a metal bunk in pain, not speaking out. After sharing on a prayer card that he needed medical assistance with **Christ Fellowship Church**, hurting in more than one place on his body. Mr. Bailey wasn't eating nor sharing any conversation after this experience. Below is a hand crafted & created calendar while being held in custody. Most inmates are having their timeline blown apart with little tools to mind stimulate or keep a recorded documentation on what's taken place. Mr. Bailey felt honored that the Sheriff's Department allowed him the right to keep his art & leave with these documents, as providing evidence.

Bike + SUV Fractured right wrist			MAL (
12 Arrested At Christ Fellowship (X)	13 ~~Covert Laid in~~ One position Left Shoulder going in + out socket (X)	14 Laid in One position ~~fractur~~ Fracture on wrist (X)	15 Laic One po Fractu Right w
19 Reading HB +	20 Reading HB +	21 Reading HB +	22 Rea H

5/14/2019   West County Detention Report 2019-05-14 - 2019-05-14

Physician Blandon

Portable Medical Diagnostics, Inc.
8080 Belvedere Rd. Ste. 6 West Palm Beach, FL 33411
Phone: 888.387.XRAY Fax: 888.493.1890
pmdxu.com

Radiology Interpretation

PATIENT NAME: BRIAN BAILEY
DATE OF BIRTH: 02/24/1979
ID/MRN: 0403731
PHYSICIAN: BLANDON
FACILITY: West County Detention
DATE OF EXAM: 05/14/2019
HISTORY: R/O FX

SIGNIFICANT FINDINGS

Portable RIGHT WRIST X-Ray Complete 3 view:

There is an acute fracture of the mid navicular. The radius is normal the metacarpals are normal.

IMPRESSION: Acute Fracture on the Navicular (Right Wrist)

1. Acute fracture of the navicular.

Electronically Signed By: Dr. Elliott Wagner M.D. 05/14/2019 13:51:15 EDT

Wagner notified Nelda NMXR of significant findings. Nelda NMXR notified VERIFIED W/ RHEN at Portable Medical
Diagnostics FL of significant findings at 2019-05-14 13:04.23.

Date: 05-14-19

Nom:
Ah:
N:
AL: ✓ scheduled for clinic
Pul:
Signature:

https://apps-lb.rapidrad.com/client/batch_report.php   1/4

74

5/17/2019
Dr. Louidor Alliance
ENCOUNTER
    Dictation : PROVIDER CLINIC VISIT FOLLOW UP - ARMOR CORRECTIONAL HEALTH
SERVICES, INC:

    Resident Name: BRIAN DALE BAILEY
    ID#:   0403731
    DOB: 02-24-1979
    Location: B W E 01 1 02L B

    Allergies: NKDA
    Current Problems:
    41, LOW BUNK/LOW LEVEL   Low Bunk / Low Level

    Current Medications:
    Acetaminophen 325 mg 325 mg

    DateTime: 05-17-2019 Fri / 12:26

    CHIEF COMPLAINT/HPI:
        BRIAN DALE BAILEY, 40 year old W Male complains of roght wrist pain. Pain
has XR done. He is here today for the resut..

    PAST MEDICAL HISTORY:none

    TESTING/OTHER EXAMS:

    PAST SURGICAL HISTORY:
    REVIEW OF SYSTEMS:
        Headache:
            Negative.
        Vision Changes:
            Negative.
        Chest Pain:
            Negative.
        Shortness of Breath:
            Negative.
        Leg Swelling:
            Negative.
        Abdominal Pain:
            Negative.
        Nausea/Vomiting:
            Negative.
        Diarrhea:
            Negative.

Constipation:
        Negative.
Hemoptysis:
        Negative.
Hematuria:
        Negative.
Hematochezia:
        Negative.

PHYSICAL EXAM:
    Height: 6 ft.
    Weight: 149 lbs 4 oz
    Temp: 97.6
    B/P: 106/61
    Pulse: 51
    Respiration: 18
    Pulse Ox: %
X-ray report:Fracture of the navicular bone   Fracture (Navicular Bone)
EYES:
    Eyes clear bilaterally. PERRLA.
ENT:
    Ears clear bilaterally. Nares are patent. No congestion noted.
Pharynx clear.
NECK:
    Neck supple. No palpable lymph nodes of head/neck. No thyromegaly
noted. No JVD.
HEART:
    RRR. No murmur.
LUNGS:
    Respirations non-labored. Clear to auscultation.
ABDOMEN:
    Soft, non-tender. No CVA tenderness. Resident walks erect with
steady gait.

ASSESSMENT: Fracture of left navicular bone   Fractured Bone

PLAN:Full restriction from lifting, carrying, pushing any weight over 5lbs
from the right hand x 8 weeks.
    RTC as needed   Restricted from caring over 5lbs

Electronically Approved by Louidor Alliance, MD on 05-17-2019 12:32:19 PM.

Weight: 149 lbs 4 oz   Height: 6 ft 0 in   Blood Pressure: 106 / 61   Temp:
 97.6   Pulse: 51   Respiration: 18
Patient's Condition is Related to
Current Illness Date   :
1st Date Of Illness   :
Unable to Work Dates   :
Hospitilization Dates :
DIAGNOSES:

PROCEDURES: 149 lbs

Attending Provider: Alliance, MD Louidor, Armor - MJ   ID:

End Of Encounter.

While Mr. Bailey was incarcerated & after Sheriff's' Department had been advised by Medical Staff for him not to carry more than 5 lbs. He was still required to carry a mattress, weighing more than 5 lbs & personal property.

BAILEY, BRIAN DALE
05-18-2019 Sat 05:03:48 PM
ENCOUNTER

5/18/2019
LPN Jannet Gomez

   Dictation : INITIAL HEALTH ASSESSMENT - ARMOR CORRECTIONAL HEALTH SERVICES, INC:

   Patient Name: BRIAN DALE BAILEY
   MNI #:   0403731
   DOB: 02-24-1979
   Sex: Male
   Location:
      B W E 01 1 02L B

   Date / Time: 05-18-2019 Sat / 17:04

   SIGNIFICANT PAST MEDICAL HISTORY: Hx of car accident in 05/2019- Right
wrist and left shoulder injury related to car accident per patient

5/5/2019 Auto Accident

   ALLERGIES:
      NKDA

   HOSPITALIZATION HISTORY: car accident in 05/2019
      Hemorrhoidectomy   May   2019
   Problems with current prescription medications? No

   SOCIAL HISTORY: **Self-Employed**
      Occupation: Unemployed   **Improper Documentation**
   Education Completed: Some college

   Family Health Conditions: Patient denies any family health
conditions.
         Alcohol Use: YES : Occasional drinker per patient
   Alcohol last use: November 2018
   Tobacco Use: Patient denies tobacco use.
      Drug Use: Patient states "steriods"

   REVIEW OF SYSTEMS: REVIEW OF SYSTEMS - MALE:
   Fever, blood in sputum, prolonged cough or night sweats? - No
   Blood in stools or black / tarry stools? - No
    Skin lesions, spider bites, or infections? - No
   Unintentional weight loss more than 10%? - No
   Experiencing penile discharge, itching, lesions or urinary burning? - No
   Lumps or lesions on testicles? - No
   History of prostate cancer? - No

   Any current complaints: No
   Any current injuries?   YES

*Mr. Bailey was Self-Employed with a valid State license through **SUNBIZ** & an online web-based platform known as YouTube, paid by **Google AdSense**.*

Injury Description(s): 05/14/2019: Right wrist x-ray results: acute Fx of the navicular

General Condition:
    40 year old w male free-moving, good hygiene, well developed.
Mental Status:
    Alert and oriented x 3. Cooperative. **Cooperative**
Motor:
    Normal gait and coordination. No tremors noted.
Head/Neck:
    Atraumatic. No lesions or infestations. Neck supple. Thyroid not enlarged.
Eyes, Ears, Nose:
    PERRL. Sclera white. EACs pink and patent. TM's intact and clear. No septal deviation.
Oral:
    Mucosa is pink and moist. Pharynx without lesions or exudate.
Dental:
    No decay, gum disease or absent teeth.
Lymph Nodes:
    No tenderness or enlargement at cervical or axillary nodes.
Breasts:
    No lesions or masses.
Skin:
    Pink, warm and dry. Good turgor. No rashes, lesions or infestations.
Heart:
    RRR without adventitious sounds.
Lungs:
    CTA.
Abdomen:
    Normal bowel sounds. No masses or tenderness noted.
Genitals:
    Deferred.
Back:
    Full ROM. No scoliosis.
Extremities:
    Pedal pulses present and equal bilaterally. No edema or cyanosis noted. Right wrist acute Fx of the navicular per x-ray results -05/14/2019
Special Needs:
    No hearing aids, eyeglasses, canes, intellectual disabilities, etc.

CURRENT MEDICATIONS:
    Acetaminophen 325 mg 325 mg   **Medication Denied**

DENTAL ASSESSMENT:
    Do you have any dental concerns? No
Dental Pain? No

MENTAL HEALTH ASSESSMENT:
Have you been hospitalized in a psychiatric unit?   YES
    2018
Reason(s): Pt states "I don't know"
Have you received outpatient counseling/treatment for emotional/nervous problems?   No
Past Psychiatric Medications?   No
Do you have current emotional problems?   No
Have you ever attempted suicide?   YES

*Mr. Bailey was about to walk through unknown doors, holding other individuals. While being offered "**pain medication**" from staff at West Detention Center Belle Glade.*

How many times have you attempted suicide? 1
When was your last suicide attempt? Several years ago, 2008 per patient
How did you attempt suicide? "Patient states "I didn't have a plan"
Are you thinking about suicide now?   No
Do you ever think of hurting yourself or others?   No
Have you ever been a victim of sexual assault or physical abuse?   No
Have you ever perpetrated sexual assault or physical abuse?   No

PREVENTIVE HEALTH AND EDUCATION:
Immunizations: Received routine childhood vaccinations?   YES
Does patient have any complaints of penile/vaginal discharge or burning? -
No

Is patient 24 years of age OR younger? - No
1) Have you ever received treatment for a positive tuberculosis skin test?
No
2) Have you ever been treated for active tuberculosis?   No
3) TB Skin Test: NO

Why was PPD not planted? Previously planted with a negative result per
patient so patient refused to receive it again

4) Symptom Screening - Are you experiencing:
        a) Unintentional weight loss (> 10 pounds in one month)?   No
        b) Cough (lasting more than 2 weeks)?   No
        c)   Heavy sweats at nighttime?
No
        d) Fevers?   No

5) Disposition: Chest X-Ray ordered.
Tuberculosis Screening (PT-024) completed? Yes

ASSESSMENT:
Acute conditions identified:

TREATMENT/PLAN:
Health education and prevention provided?   Yes, list materials
requested/provided:

ANNUNAL HEALTH MAINTENANCE:
        Date of Incarceration:

Intake weight:
Current weight:
        Reviewed Intake Screening
        Reviewed MH Intake

    Inmate refused TB test
        Provided instructions on accessing health care in the institution.
        Instructed in oral hygiene and provided preventive oral education.
        Follow-up in Sick Call as needed ARMOR CORRECTIONAL HEALTH SERVICES,
INC:

    Electronically Approved by JANNET GOMEZ, LPN on 05-18-2019 05:26:01 PM.

    Electronically Approved by CHADIA WILSON MORCOS, MD MEDICAL DIRECTOR on
05-22-2019 02:16:35 PM.

Height: 6 ft 0 in   Blood Pressure: 102 / 64   Temp: 97.7   Pulse: 57
Respiration: 16
Patient's Condition is Related to

4/19/2021 3:57:21 PM

Current Illness Date   :
1st Date Of Illness   :
Unable to Work Dates   :
Hospitilization Dates :
DIAGNOSES:

PROCEDURES:

Attending Provider: GOMEZ, LPN JANNET,   ARMOR   ID:

End Of Encounter.

5/21/2019

Physician Blandon

Portable Medical Diagnostics, inc.
8080 Belvedere Rd. Ste. 6 West Palm Beach, FL 33411
Phone: 888.387.XRAY Fax: 888.493.1890
pmdxu.com

Radiology Interpretation

PATIENT NAME: BRIAN BAILEY
DATE OF BIRTH: 02/24/1979
ID/MRN: 0403731
PHYSICIAN: BLANDON
FACILITY: West County Detention
DATE OF EXAM: 05/21/2019
HISTORY: R/O TB

Portable Chest X-Ray 1V:
Findings: Chest x-ray is normal. There is no infiltrate effusion or mass. There is no adenopathy. There is no tuberculosis.

IMPRESSION:
1. Normal chest.

Electronically Signed By: Dr. Elliott Wagner M.D. 05/21/2019 13 14:44 EDT
This transmission is proprietary, privileged and confidential. It is intended to be communication only for the use of the addressee; access to this message by anyone else is unauthorized. If you are not the intended recipient and have received this communication in error, please notify us immediately at (888) 387-9729. Any other action taken, including but not limited to the disclosure, copying or distribution of this communication is prohibited by law.
ID: 5ced335b0f29e

5/22/19

5/24/2019
Dr. Louidor Alliance

Dictation : PROVIDER CLINIC VISIT FOLLOW UP - ARMOR CORRECTIONAL HEALTH
SERVICES, INC:

Resident Name: BRIAN DALE BAILEY   **141 lbs**
ID#: 0403731
DOB: 02-24-1979
Location: B W E 01 1 02L B

Allergies: NKDA
Current Problems:
41, LOW BUNK/LOW LEVEL   Low Bunk / Low Level

Current Medications:

DateTime: 05-24-2019 Fri / 13:33

CHIEF COMPLAINT/HPI: **Left Shoulder Pain**
    BRIAN DALE BAILEY, 40 year old W Male complains of left shouldr pain
with radiation to his arm. Pain moderate but worsens with movement or if to
have ti lift something.. Denies Numbness and tingling but has weakness due to
pain. Patient did Physical Therapy while he was outside w/o success he was
scheduled to have surgery. He was rejected y HCD and was not able to have his
procedure done. He gets arrested was able to follow up.
REVIEW OF SYSTEMS:
    Headache: Denied by Palm Beach County Health Care District
        Negative.
    Vision Changes:

---

*At the time, Mr. Bailey was homeless & **Palm Beach County Health Care District** requires a residential address. In order to receive a **"District Cares"** health card for service assistance.*

```
            Negative.
   Chest Pain:
            Negative.
   Shortness of Breath:
            Negative.
   Leg Swelling:
            Negative.
   Abdominal Pain:
            Negative.
   Nausea/Vomiting:
            Negative.
   Diarrhea:
            Negative.
   Constipation:
            Negative.
   Hemoptysis:
            Negative.
   Hematuria:
            Negative.
   Hematochezia:
            Negative.


PHYSICAL EXAM:
       Height:  6 ft.
       Weight:  141 lbs 8 oz
       Temp:  97.6
       B/P:   99/69
       Pulse:  51
       Respiration:  16
       Pulse Ox:    %
   EYES:
       Eyes clear bilaterally.  PERRLA.
   ENT:
       Ears clear bilaterally.  Nares are patent.  No congestion noted.
Pharynx clear.
   NECK:
       Neck supple.  No palpable lymph nodes of head/neck.  No thyromegaly
noted.  No JVD.
   HEART:
        RRR.  No murmur.
   LUNGS:
       Respirations non-labored.  Clear to auscultation.
   ABDOMEN:
       Soft, non-tender.  No CVA tenderness.  Resident walks erect with
steady gait.
   EXT:  Left Shoulder decreased ROM, flexion and etension and rotation.
abduction is also limited

   ASSESSMENT:LEFT SHOULDER PAIN.  Pain

   PLAN:Patient is refusing any medical therapy. He wants to be alert so he
cantrol and protect himself from others rom his cell.
   RTC as aneeded  Mr. Bailey refusing pain medication, due to being in a survival situation.

   Electronically Approved by Louidor Alliance, MD on 05-24-2019 01:46:14 PM.

Weight: 141 lbs 8 oz      Height: 6 ft 0 in    Blood Pressure: 99 / 69    Temp:
97.6   Pulse: 51   Respiration: 16
Patient's Condition is Related to
Current Illness Date  :
```

Mr. Bailey pulse was 51, considered to be, "Bradycaria" this is when the patient's pulse is abnormally slow. Mr. Bailey has always been above average with fitness, creating a low resting heartrate.

BAILEY, BRIAN DALE   **5/28/2019**
05-28-2019 Tue 12:05:00 PM
ENCOUNTER
    Dictation : Signal 73 GENERAL SOAP NOTE - ARMOR CORRECTIONAL HEALTH
SERVICES, INC:

    Patient Name: BRIAN DALE BAILEY
    NO: 0403731
    DOB: 02-24-1979
    Sex: Male
    Date: 05-28-2019 Tue
    Time: 19:40
    Location: B2 W M 01 1 30 B2

    SUBJECTIVE:Arrived. Pt stated," I was on the floor get blues and the next
thing I know the nurse was waking me up. I have been fasting except for water
and coffee since May 11 for religious reason. Nurse Langley said that she
assisted pt to floor from chair.

    OBJECTIVE: AAO x3. Pt laying on Rt side on floor.:Pt transported to medical
via stretcher.
                    Transported to Medical on a stretcher

                              5/28/2019
                          RN Marcia Phillips

4/19/2021 3:57:19 PM

    Date: 05-28-2019 Tue
    Time: 20:07
    Location: B2 W M 01 1 30 B2

    SUBJECTIVE:PT fasting since May 11th for religious reason. Calapse today in
dorm.States that he want to continue until June 23rd (40 days and 40 nights)
           Fasting after becoming a member of Christ Fellowship Church
                         18 Days of No Food
    OBJECTIVE:Resting most of evening. continuing fast, easily awakened.
appetite 0 % for lunch and dinner.

    ASSESSMENT:Nutritional deficit

    PLAN:Encourage fluid and food.

    EDUCATION:Nutrition and hydration.

    CHARGES:

    Electronically Approved by Marcia Phillips, RN on 05-28-2019 08:20:00 PM.

Height: 6 ft 0 in   Blood Pressure: 91 / 59   Temp: 98   Pulse: 79
 Respiration: 18
Patient's Condition is Related to
Current Illness Date :
1st Date Of Illness   :
Unable to Work Dates :
Hospitilization Dates :
DIAGNOSES:
                                                    No Weight Listed
PROCEDURES:

Attending Provider: Phillips, RN Marcia, Armor - BG   ID:

End Of Encounter.

84

BAILEY, BRIAN DALE
05-29-2019 Wed 12:25:15 AM   **Deputy Taylor**
ENCOUNTER
    Dictation : INFIRMARY GENERAL SOAP NOTE - ARMOR CORRECTIONAL HEALTH
SERVICES, INC:

        Patient Name: BRIAN DALE BAILEY
        NO: 0403731
        DOB: 02-24-1979
        Sex: Male
        Date: 05-29-2019 Wed
        Time: 00:26
        Location: B2 W M 01 1 30 B2

    SUBJECTIVE: Deputy Taylor stated that the pt was asking for more gatorade
and then passed out falling back on the bed. Pt stated " I don't know what
happened. I was standing at the door asking the deputy for more gatorade and
then I woke up finding myself looking at the ceiling."

Mr. Bailey Passed Out

    OBJECTIVE:Upon arrival Pt was found sitting at edge of bed in no acute
distress. Denies dizziness. Denies any injury. Pt still refuses to eat.

    ASSESSMENT: VITAL SIGNS: (4)   Blood Pressure: 118/77, Pulse: 94,
Respiration: 18, Pulse Oxygen: 99, Blood Sugar: 176

    PLAN: Gatorade given

    EDUCATION:Encouraged nutrition and fluid intake

    CHARGES:None

    Electronically Approved by Melvia Guillame, RN on 05-29-2019 12:37:10 AM.

Blood Pressure: 118 / 77   Pulse: 94   Respiration: 18
Patient's Condition is Related to
Current Illness Date :
1st Date Of Illness   :
Unable to Work Dates :
Hospitilization Dates :
DIAGNOSES:

PROCEDURES:

Attending Provider: Guillame, RN Melvia, Armor   ID:

RN Melvia Guillame

End Of Encounter.

When this happened, Mr. Bailey was struck by a higher power & was no accident.

5/29/2019
RN Melvia Guillame

Dictation : INFIRMARY GENERAL SOAP NOTE - ARMOR CORRECTIONAL HEALTH SERVICES, INC:

```
Patient Name:        BRIAN DALE BAILEY
NO:                  0403731
DOB:                 02-24-1979
Sex:                 Male
Date:                05-29-2019 Wed
Time:                03:52
Location:            B2  W M 01 1 30 B2
```

SUBJECTIVE: " I feel better."

OBJECTIVE: Pt AAOX3, steady gait. denies dizziness. Ate 90% of breakfast

ASSESSMENT: Nutritional deficit
VITAL SIGNS: (6)   Weight: 139 lbs , Blood Pressure: 118/77, Temperature: 98.3, Pulse: 94, Respiration: 18, Pulse Oxygen: 99

PLAN: continue to monitor

EDUCATION: report signs and symptoms of dizziness. Encourage intake of fluids and food. Pt verbalized understanding.

CHARGES: None

Electronically Approved by Melvia Guillame, RN on 05-29-2019 03:56:24 AM.

Weight: 139 lbs   Blood Pressure: 118 / 77   Temp: 98.3   Pulse: 94
 Respiration: 18
Patient's Condition is Related to
Current Illness Date   :
1st Date Of Illness   :
Unable to Work Dates   :
Hospitilization Dates :
DIAGNOSES:

PROCEDURES:

Attending Provider: Guillame, RN Melvia, Armor   ID:

139 lbs

End Of Encounter.

5/29/2019

RN Ruth Ihinger

Dictation : INFIRMARY GENERAL SOAP NOTE OBS - ARMOR CORRECTIONAL HEALTH SERVICES, INC:

Patient Name:	BRIAN DALE BAILEY
NO:	0403731
DOB:	02-24-1979
Sex:	Male
Date:	05-29-2019 Wed
Time:	09:35
Location:	B2 W M 01 1 30 B2

SUBJECTIVE:Pt. housed for syncopal episodes x 2;
r/t "Not eating solid food since May 11"

No Food 18 Days

Sheriff's Department, "Gifts One Book to Inmates."

OBJECTIVE:Pt. stated "In the bible it says I need to repent"

The Holy Bible

ASSESSMENT:Pt. seem's to want to punish himself by fasting/repent per pt.
for 40 days.   **Repent "NOT" Punish**

PLAN:Cont. to monitor pt.

EDUCATION:Instructed pt. on the importance of eating/ proteins are needed.

Staff demanded Mr. Bailey to eat or be taken to the Emergency Room and given an I.V.

Against his practice of religion at his own out of pocket expense.

Electronic Signature:
Electronically Approved by Ruth Ihinger, RN, CCHP on 05-29-2019 11:40:32
AM.

Height: 6 ft 0 in   Blood Pressure: 89 / 60   Temp: 97.9   Pulse: 79
Respiration: 18
Patient's Condition is Related to
Current Illness Date :

LOST 18 LBS. DUE TO FASTING. THE PT STATED, "I'M REPENTING FOR WHAT I'VE DONE, I'VE DONE THIS BEFORE".THE PT DENIES WANTING TO HARM HIMSELF.
WHILE TALKING TO THE PATIENT HE REQUESTED A VEGAN DIET, HE REPORTS THAT HE DOES NOT EAT PORK. HE C/O FEELING FATIGUE.

VITALS: BP 115/81, T 97.9, P 89, R 18, O2 SAT 98%

OBJECTIVE:
General Appearance:
    Oriented x 3. Steady gait. Speech clear. Hollow cheeks.
Eyes:
    PERRLA. Sunken eyes noted.
Chest:
    Clear bilaterally.
Heart.
    RRR.
Skin:
    Warm, dry, pink, no lesions. Skin drooping.

ASSESSMENT: WEIGHT LOSS   No Weight Listed
                DEHYDRATION
                MALNUTRITION

*The Bible does "**NOT**" say Jesus used an IV to be forgiven for his sins.*

BAILEY, BRIAN DALE
05-29-2019 Wed 11:15:21 AM

5/29/2019

ENCOUNTER
Dictation : INFIRMARY HOUSING GENERAL SOAP NOTE - ARMOR CORRECTIONAL HEALTH
SERVICES, INC:

Mr. Bailey is in the Infirmary

Patient Name:	BRIAN DALE BAILEY
NO:	0403731
DOB:	02-24-1979
Sex:	Male
Date:	05-29-2019 Wed
Time:	12:39
Location:	B2 W M 01 1 30 B2

SUBJECTIVE: THE PT IS CURRENLTY BEING HOUSED IN THE INFIRMARY AFTER SEVERAL
EPISODES OF SYNCOPE. THE PT HAS ALSO

5/29/2019
ARNP Lillian Dent

4/19/2021 3:57:19 PM

Electronically Approved by Lillian Dent, ARNP on 05-29-2019 12:52:44 PM.

Weight: 137 lbs 6 oz   Height: 6 ft 0 in   Blood Pressure: 115 / 81   Temp:
97.9   Pulse: 89   Respiration: 18
Patient's Condition is Related to
Current Illness Date :
1st Date Of Illness   :
Unable to Work Dates :
Hospitilization Dates :   ## 137 lbs
DIAGNOSES:

PROCEDURES:

Attending Provider: Dent, ARNP Lillian, Armor   ID:

End Of Encounter.

BAILEY, BRIAN DALE   # 5/29/2019
05-29-2019 Wed 05:00:00 PM
ENCOUNTER   ## RN Ruth Ihinger
Dictation : Inc. note: Pt. ate 100% of his vegan dinner.
Vegan
Electronic Signature:
Electronically Approved by Ruth Ihinger, RN, CCHP on 05-29-2019 05:17:24
PM.

Patient's Condition is Related to
Current Illness Date :
1st Date Of Illness   :
Unable to Work Dates :
Hospitilization Dates :
DIAGNOSES:

PROCEDURES:

Attending Provider: Ihinger, RN, CCHP Ruth, Armor   ID:

End Of Encounter.

5/30/2019

RN Wanda Baker

ASSESSMENT: alteration in comfort

PLAN: To continue with the current plan of care.

EDUCATION: Pt was told to ask for any needed assistance.

CHARGES: none

Electronically Approved by Wanda Baker, RN on 05-30-2019 02:50:32 PM.

Patient's Condition is Related to
Current Illness Date   :
1st Date Of Illness   :
Unable to Work Dates   :
Hospitilization Dates :
DIAGNOSES:

PROCEDURES:

Attending Provider: Baker, RN Wanda, Armor - BG   ID:

End Of Encounter.

5/30/2019

PLAN: VEGAN DIET
    ENSURE 3X DAILY X 5 DAYS
    WEEKLY Check weight every Saturday or Sunday for 4 weeks
    Collect specimen for CBC with CMP
    MONITOR FOR FOOD INTAKE/OUTPUT

Vegan Diet Plan reported by Medical Staff

EDUCATION: SAFETY, IMPORTANCE OF NUTRITiON, POTENTIAL FOR MUSCLE WASTING
AND POSSIBLE DEATH, INCREASED HYDRATION, S/S TO REPORT

RTC: TOMORROW

CHARGES:

4/19/2021 3:57:18 PM

Dictation : Incidental Note: Lab specimens collected as ordered: (1) gold
tube, (1) lavender tube. Pt tolerated it well.

Electronically Approved by Melvia Guillame, RN on 05-30-2019 06:08:34 AM.

Patient's Condition is Related to
Current Illness Date   :
1st Date Of Illness   :
Unable to Work Dates   :
Hospitilization Dates :
DIAGNOSES:

PROCEDURES:

Attending Provider: Guillame, RN Melvia, Armor   ID:

RN Melvia Guillame

End Of Encounter.

BAILEY, BRIAN DALE
05-30-2019 Thu 06:10:09 AM

5/30/2019
RN Melvia Guillame

ENCOUNTER
    Dictation : incidental note: Ate 100% of breakfast.

Electronically Approved by Melvia Guillame, RN on 05-30-2019 06:10:36 AM.

Patient's Condition is Related to
Current Illness Date :
1st Date Of Illness   :
Unable to Work Dates :
Hospitilization Dates :
DIAGNOSES:

PROCEDURES:

Attending Provider: Guillame, RN Melvia, Armor   ID:

End Of Encounter.

BAILEY, BRIAN DALE
05-30-2019 Thu 09:12:52 AM
                      5/30/2019

ENCOUNTER
    Dictation : INFIRMARY HOUSING GENERAL SOAP NOTE - ARMOR CORRECTIONAL HEALTH
SERVICES, INC:

Patient Name:	BRIAN DALE BAILEY
NO:	0403731
DOB:	02-24-1979
Sex:	Male
Date:	05-30-2019 Thu
Time:	09:35
Location:	B2 W M 01 1 30 B2

SUBJECTIVE: THE PT STATED, "I FEEL BETTER, I'VE BEEN EATING". THE PT DENIES
COMPLAINTS.

VITALS: BP 83/57, T 97.6, P 71, R 18, O2 SAT 98%

OBJECTIVE:
General Appearance:
    Oriented x 3. Steady gait. Speech clear. Hollow cheeks.
Eyes:
    PERRLA. Sunken eyes noted.
Chest:
    Clear bilaterally.
Heart.
    RRR.
Skin:
    Warm, dry, pink, no lesions. Skin drooping.

ASSESSMENT: WEIGHT LOSS   No Weight Listed

90

ARNP Lillian Dent

4/19/2021 3:57:18 PM

DEHYDRATION
MALNUTRITION

PLAN: CONTINUE W/INTAKE MONITORING, WT CHECKS, AND CURRENT NUTRITION PLAN

EDUCATION: SAFETY, IMPORTANCE OF NUTRITION, POTENTIAL FOR MUSCLE WASTING
AND POSSIBLE DEATH, INCREASED HYDRATION, S/S TO REPORT

RTC: TUESDAY TO F/U ON WEIGHT LOSS AND SYNCOPE

CHARGES:

Electronically Approved by Lillian Dent, ARNP on 05-30-2019 09:43:00 AM.

Height: 6 ft 0 in   Blood Pressure: 83 / 57   Temp: 97.6   Pulse: 71
 Respiration: 18
Patient's Condition is Related to
Current Illness Date   :
1st Date Of Illness   :
Unable to Work Dates   :
Hospitilization Dates :
DIAGNOSES: No Weight Listed
PROCEDURES:

Attending Provider: Dent, ARNP Lillian, Armor   ID:

End Of Encounter.

While it is being reported that the patient is suffering from, "Dehydration & Malnutrition" the medical staff has not listed the weight of the patient.

BAILEY, BRIAN DALE   **5/30/2019**
05-30-2019 Thu 02:45:49 PM
ENCOUNTER
    Dictation : GENERAL SOAP NOTE - ARMOR CORRECTIONAL HEALTH SERVICES, INC:

    Patient Name: BRIAN DALE BAILEY
    NO: 0403731
    DOB: 02-24-1979
    Sex: Male
    Date: 05-30-2019 Thu
    Time: 14:47
    Location: B2 W M 01 1 30 B2

    SUBJECTIVE: " I am okay, thank you." Mr. Bailey treating staff with kindness

    OBJECTIVE: Pt was seen today at cellside. Pt was not having any issues
today as far as the food is concern. Pt ate 100% of meals. Pt was seen by
LDent, ARNP. Pt did not voice any complaints or concerns to writer.

5/31/2019

ENCOUNTER
    Dictation : INFIRMARY GENERAL SOAP NOTE - ARMOR CORRECTIONAL HEALTH
SERVICES, INC:

Dr. Louidor Alliance

    Patient Name: BRIAN DALE BAILEY
    NO: 0403731
    DOB: 02-24-1979
    Sex: Male

        Respiration: 16
        Pulse Ox: %
    EYES:
        Eyes clear bilaterally. PERRLA.
    ENT:
        Ears clear bilaterally. Nares are patent. No congestion noted.
Pharynx clear.
    NECK:
        Neck supple. No palpable lymph nodes of head/neck. No thyromegaly
noted. No JVD.
    HEART:
        RRR. No murmur.
    LUNGS:
        Respirations non-labored. Clear to auscultation.
    ABDOMEN:
        Soft, non-tender. No CVA tenderness. Resident walks erect with
steady gait.

    ASSESSMENT:N1 PHYSICAL EXAM

    PLAN:REASSURANCE. DISCHARGE to GP

    Electronically Approved by Louidor Alliance, MD on 06-03-2019 03:33:42 PM.

Weight: 147 lbs 2 oz   Height: 6 ft 0 in   Blood Pressure: 101 / 67   Temp:
 98.1 Pulse: 72 Respiration: 16
Patient's Condition is Related to
Current Illness Date :
1st Date Of Illness   :
Unable to Work Dates :
Hospitilization Dates :
DIAGNOSES:

                                                        147 lbs

PROCEDURES:

Attending Provider: Alliance, MD Louidor, Armor - MJ   ID:

End Of Encounter.

Dr. Louidor Alliance the attending provider weighs Mr. Bailey at 147lbs, which is unhealthy weight gain, 10lbs in 2 days.

4/19/2021 3:57:18 PM

Date: 05-31-2019 Fri
Time: 11:18
Location: B2 W M 01 1 30 B2

SUBJECTIVE:" I am feeling dizzy when I get up"

OBJECTIVE: Pt is AAOx3 ambulatory within cell with a steady gait, skin is
pink, dry and warm to touch, Pt c/o dizziness, denies headache at this time.
Pt ate lunch tray and fluid given. Observed Pt exercising/squating right
after finishing his lunch tray, then pt. was cleaning toilet and making his
bed. Pt. vital signs remain stable at this time.

ASSESSMENT: Alteration in comfort   **Mr. Bailey is exercising**

PLAN: continue with current plan of care

EDUCATION: Encouraged pt to sit up for a few minutes prior getting up and
to rise slowly, continue with his fluid intake and to ask for assistance when
needed. Pt
                    verbalized understanding

CHARGES:

Electronically Approved by Mioche Remy, RN on 05-31-2019 01:45:27 PM.

Weight: 146 lbs 2 oz   Height: 6 ft 0 in   Blood Pressure: 106 / 63   Pulse:
70   Respiration: 17
Patient's Condition is Related to   **Unhealthy Weight Gain**
Current Illness Date   :
1st Date Of Illness   :   **(9 lbs Gained in 2 days)**
Unable to Work Dates   :
Hospitilization Dates :
DIAGNOSES: **146 lbs**

PROCEDURES:

Attending Provider: Remy, RN Mioche, Armor   ID:

End Of Encounter.

The unhealthy weight gain is being documented by showing the weight of the patient. But, none of the medical staff or Sheriff's Department takes notice. Mr. Bailey didn't eat meat or have any meals that were not on the schedule.

BAILEY, BRIAN DALE
06-03-2019 Mon 11:40:00 AM   **6/3/2019**
ENCOUNTER
    Dictation : INFIRMARY GENERAL SOAP NOTE - ARMOR CORRECTIONAL HEALTH
SERVICES, INC:

    Patient Name: BRIAN DALE BAILEY
    NO: 0403731
    DOB: 02-24-1979
    Sex: Male
    Date: 06-03-2019 Mon
    Time: 12:00
    Location: B2 W M 01 1 30 B2

    SUBJECTIVE:Pt. housed for weight loss d/t "Fasting"
                                       (Religious)

    OBJECTIVE:Pt. ate 100% of his lunch; pt. has gained 10 lbs. since 5/29.

BAILEY, BRIAN DALE
06-03-2019 Mon 11:48:45 AM
ENCOUNTER
    Dictation : PROVIDER CLINIC VISIT ROUTINE - ARMOR CORRECTIONAL HEALTH
SERVICES, INC:

    Resident Name: BRIAN DALE BAILEY
    ID#: 0403731
    DOB: 02-24-1979
    Location: B W E 01 1 08M B

    Allergies: NKDA
    Current Problems:
    41, LOW BUNK/LOW LEVEL   Low Bunk / Low Level
    783.21, LOSS OF WEIGHT

    Current Medications:

    DateTime: 06-03-2019 Mon / 15:23

    CHIEF COMPLAINT/HPI: (Pain)
        BRIAN DALE BAILEY, 40 year old W Male complains of none. Has h/o
shoulder lesion was hold on infirmary. due to other PBSO issue

    PAST MEDICAL HISTORY:as above
    REVIEW OF SYSTEMS:
        Headache:
            Negative.
        Vision Changes:
            Negative.
        Chest Pain:
            Negative.
        Shortness of Breath:
            Negative.
        Leg Swelling:
            Negative.
        Abdominal Pain:
            Negative.
        Nausea/Vomiting:
            Negative.
        Diarrhea:
            Negative.
        Constipation:
            Negative.
        Hemoptysis:
            Negative.
        Hematuria:
            Negative.
        Hematochezia:
            Negative.

    PHYSICAL EXAM:
        Height: 6 ft.
        Weight: 147 lbs 2 oz   **147 lbs**
        Temp: 98.1
        B/P: 101/67
        Pulse: 72

6/5/2019

IN THE COUNTY COURT OF THE FIFTEENTH JUDICIAL CIRCUIT
IN AND FOR PALM BEACH COUNTY, FLORIDA - CRIMINAL DIVISION
CIRCUIT/COUNTY COURT
Court Event Form

DEFENDANT: BRIAN DALE BAILEY
CASE NO: 50-2019-MM-005685-AXXX-MB

STATE OF FLORIDA   DATE: 6/5/2019
vs.
DEFENDANT: BRIAN DALE BAILEY   JACKET #:   0403731
CASE NO: 50-2019-MM-005685-AXXX-MB   BOOKING #:   2019015844
DIVISION: B: Cnty Crim - B (County)

PRESIDING JUDGE: COLLINS, JUDGESHERRI L   START TIME: 9:24 AM
ASA: JAEGERS, ROBERT   END TIME: 9:26 AM
ATTORNEY:
PUBLIC DEFENDER: FAGAN, LESLI
CO-COUNSEL: COURT REPORTER   CENTRAL
                                                             RECORDED
DEPUTY CLERK: IR   COURT TYPE: AR   -
                                                             ARRAIGNMENT
COURT ROOM: #1 (West Branch)

Reset For
Court Date Scheduled - CD - CASE DISPOSITION - 6/11/2019 8:30 AM - 2E (Main Branch) MB, 205 N. Dixie
Highway West Palm Beach FL 33401 - JAIL TO TRANSPORT

Other: DEFENDANT PRESENT AND IN CUSTODY

Count 1 - MF TRESPASS AFTER WARNING 810.09(2A)
Plea: NOT GUILTY

96

Filing # 90872101 E-Filed 06/11/2019 07:20:07 AM

IN THE COUNTY COURT OF THE FIFTEENTH JUDICIAL CIRCUIT,
IN AND FOR PALM BEACH COUNTY, FLORIDA
CRIMINAL DIVISION "B"

STATE OF FLORIDA,　　　　　　　　　　CASE NO. 19MM005685AMB

vs.

Brian Dale Bailey,

　　　　Defendant.

DEFENDANT'S WAIVER OF APPEARANCE

The Defendant, Brian Dale Bailey, through undersigned counsel, pursuant to Fla.R.Crim.P. 3.180(a)(3) and 3.220(o), hereby waives presence at all pretrial conferences held in the above-styled case.

Respectfully submitted,

CAREY HAUGHWOUT
Public Defender, 15th Judicial Circuit
421 3rd Street
West Palm Beach, FL 33401
Telephone: (561) 355-7500

Anthony Shih
Assistant Public Defender
Fla. Bar No. 115168

CERTIFICATE OF SERVICE

I HEREBY CERTIFY that a true and correct copy hereof has been served to , Assistant State Attorney, Division "B" OR the Assistant State Attorney currently assigned in STAC at the time of filing, via the STAC case management exchange on this _____ day of June, 2019.

_____
Anthony Shih
Assistant Public Defender

On the date of **6/5/2019**, while in custody at **PBSO - West Detention Center**. That morning Mr. Bailey had court & was still unsure on how to handle the current situation. Making a **Plea** of **Not Guilty** before the court, when only understanding what was taking place from one perspective, which was his own. By now Mr. Bailey was trying to create a routine of reading & praying, after an inmate by the name of **Mr. James Lynch** was kind enough to loan Mr. Bailey his **NIV Holy Bible**. He was on page 1090, & still hitting the words with persistence.

³ ⁴	Reading HB (Pg 860) Fainted + was removed by EMS	(Started vegan) diet Solitare Confinement	Exercise	E
al	4 James Lynch Passed me a New NIV Bible Wrote 2 songs	5 Court in Belle Glade Reading HB (Pg 1090)	6 Reading HB + Exercise wrote 4 Christian Songs	7 E w (
3 HB + 5e	11 Court No Main court House Vegan	12 Reading HB + Law	13 Reading HB + Law +	1 +

6/11/2019

IN THE COUNTY COURT OF THE FIFTEENTH JUDICIAL CIRCUIT
IN AND FOR PALM BEACH COUNTY, FLORIDA - CRIMINAL DIVISION
CIRCUIT/COUNTY COURT
Court Event Form

DEFENDANT: BRIAN DALE BAILEY
CASE NO: 50-2019-MM-005685-AXXX-MB

STATE OF FLORIDA   DATE: 6/11/2019

vs.
DEFENDANT: BRIAN DALE BAILEY   JACKET #:   0403731
CASE NO: 50-2019-MM-005685-AXXX-MB   BOOKING #: 2019015844
DIVISION: B: Cnty Crim - B (County)

PRESIDING JUDGE: HANSER, JUDGELEONARD   START TIME: 10:39 AM
ASA: MYERS, RYAN   END TIME: 10:41 AM
ATTORNEY:
PUBLIC DEFENDER: SHIH, JONELL-ANTHONY
CO-COUNSEL: COURT REPORTER   CENTRAL
                                                                RECORDED
DEPUTY CLERK: SH   COURT TYPE: CD   -   CASE
                                                                DISPOSITION
COURT ROOM: 2E (Main Branch)

Reset For
Court Date Scheduled - PC - PLEA CONFERENCE - 6/18/2019 8:30 AM - 2E (Main Branch) MB, 205 N. Dixie
Highway West Palm Beach FL 33401 - JAIL TO TRANSPORT

Motion - Denied   - DEFENSE TO RELEASE DEFENDANT
Other: DEFENDANT PRESENT AND IN CUSTODY

Count 1 - MF TRESPASS AFTER WARNING 810.09(2A)

Tuesday, June 11, 2019   Page 1 of 1

100

IN THE CIRCUIT/COUNTY COURT OF THE FIFTEENTH JUDICIAL CIRCUIT
IN AND FOR PALM BEACH COUNTY, FLORIDA

STATE OF FLORIDA

-Vs-

Date: 06/11/2019

Case No: 50-2019-MM-005685-AXXX-MB

Division: B: Cnty Crim - B (County)

BRIAN DALE BAILEY
GENERAL DELIVERY
WEST PALM BEACH, FL. 32200

NOTICE OF HEARING

THE DEFENDANT MUST BE PRESENT AT THIS HEARING

For Criminal Charges: Failure to Appear will result in a Bond Forfeiture or
revocation of own recognizance (O.R.) and a Capias/Warrant being issued for your arrest.
For Civil Traffic Charges: Failure to appear may result in the suspension of your driver's license.
IF YOUR CASE IS ON-CALL, CONTACT YOUR ATTORNEY FOR THE TIME TO APPEAR

YOU ARE HEREBY NOTIFIED that this case is scheduled

DATE:	TIME:	HEARING TYPE:	LOCATION:
6/18/2019	8:30 AM	PC - PLEA CONFERENCE	2E (Main Branch) MB, 205 N. Dixie Highway West Palm Beach FL 33401

BE PREPARED TO PAY COURT COSTS AND FINES ASSESSED BY THE COURT AT THIS HEARING
"IF YOU INTEND TO REQUEST THE SERVICES OF THE PUBLIC DEFENDER, YOU MUST FILE AN APPLICATION AT THE CLERK &
COMPTROLLER'S OFFICE AND BE APPOINTED THE PUBLIC DEFENDER BEFORE YOUR COURT DATE. THE APPLICATION FEE IS $50.00."
Civil Traffic Charges are not eligible for a Public Defender.

SHARON R. BOCK,
CLERK & COMPTROLLER
BY: SH

Deft/Atty: DEFENDANT IN CUSTODY

Deputy Clerk

cc: RYAN MYERS
      SHIH, JONELL-ANTHONY

FILED: PALM BEACH COUNTY, FL SHARON R BOCK, CLERK 06/11/2019 10:41:27 AM

IN THE CIRCUIT/COUNTY COURT OF THE FIFTEENTH JUDICIAL CIRCUIT
IN AND FOR PALM BEACH COUNTY, FLORIDA

"If you are a <u>person with a disability</u> who needs any accommodation in order to participate in this proceeding, you are entitled, at no cost to you, to the provision of certain assistance. Please contact Tammy Anton, Americans with Disabilities Act Coordinator, Palm Beach County Courthouse, 205 North Dixie Hwy, West Palm Beach, FL 33401; telephone number (561) 355-4380 at least 7 days before your scheduled court appearance, or immediately upon receiving this notification if the time before the scheduled appearance is less than 7 days; if you are hearing or voice impaired, call 711."

"Si usted es una <u>persona minusválida</u> que necesita algún acomodamiento para poder participar en este procedimiento, usted tiene derecho, sin tener gastos propios, a que se le provea cierta ayuda. Tenga la amabilidad de ponerse en contacto con Tammy Anton, 205 N. Dixie Highway, West Palm Beach, Florida 33401; teléfono número (561) 355-4380, por lo menos 7 días antes de la cita fijada para su comparecencia en los tribunales, o inmediatamente después de recibir esta notificación si el tiempo antes de la comparecencia que se ha programado es menos de 7 días; si usted tiene discapacitación del oído o de la voz, llame al 711."

"Si ou se yon <u>moun ki enfim</u> ki bezwen akomodasyon pou w ka patisipe nan pwosedi sa, ou kalifye san ou pa gen okenn lajan pou w peye, gen pwovizyon pou jwen kèk èd. Tanpri kontakte Tammy Anton, kòòdonatè pwogram Lwa pou ameriken ki Enfim yo nan Tribinal Konte Palm Beach la ki nan 205 North Dixie Highway, West Palm Beach, Florida 33401; telefòn li se (561) 355-4380 nan 7 jou anvan dat ou gen randevou pou parèt nan tribinal la, oubyen imedyatman apre ou fin resevwa konvokasyon an si lè ou gen pou w parèt nan tribinal la mwens ke 7 jou; si ou gen pwoblèm pou w tande oubyen pale, rele 711."

IN THE CIRCUIT/COUNTY COURT OF THE FIFTEENTH JUDICIAL CIRCUIT
IN AND FOR PALM BEACH COUNTY, FLORIDA

STATE OF FLORIDA

-Vs-

Date: 06/05/2019

Case No: 50-2019-MM-005685-AXXX-MB

Division: B: Cnty Crim - B (County)

BRIAN DALE BAILEY
GENERAL DELIVERY
WEST PALM BEACH, FL 32200

NOTICE OF HEARING
THE DEFENDANT MUST BE PRESENT AT THIS HEARING

For Criminal Charges: Failure to Appear will result in a Bond Forfeiture or
revocation of own recognizance (O.R.) and a Capias/Warrant being issued for your arrest.
For Civil Traffic Charges: Failure to appear may result in the suspension of your driver's license.
IF YOUR CASE IS ON-CALL, CONTACT YOUR ATTORNEY FOR THE TIME TO APPEAR
YOU ARE HEREBY NOTIFIED that this case is scheduled

DATE:	TIME:	HEARING TYPE:	LOCATION:
6/11/2019	8:30 AM	CD - CASE DISPOSITION	2E (Main Branch) MB, 205 N. Dixie Highway West Palm Beach Fl. 33401

BE PREPARED TO PAY COURT COSTS AND FINES ASSESSED BY THE COURT AT THIS HEARING
"IF YOU INTEND TO REQUEST THE SERVICES OF THE PUBLIC DEFENDER, YOU MUST FILE AN APPLICATION AT THE CLERK &
COMPTROLLER'S OFFICE AND BE APPOINTED THE PUBLIC DEFENDER BEFORE YOUR COURT DATE. THE APPLICATION FEE IS $50.00."
Civil Traffic Charges are not eligible for a Public Defender.

SHARON R. BOCK,
CLERK & COMPTROLLER
BY: JR

Deft/Atty: DEFENDANT IN CUSTODY

Deputy Clerk

cc: ROBERT JAEGERS
      FAGAN, LESLI KAREN

FILED: PALM BEACH COUNTY, FL SHARON R BOCK, CLERK 06/05/2019 09:26:11 AM

IN THE CIRCUIT/COUNTY COURT OF THE FIFTEENTH JUDICIAL CIRCUIT
IN AND FOR PALM BEACH COUNTY, FLORIDA

"If you are a person with a disability who needs any accommodation in order to participate in this proceeding, you are entitled, at no cost to you, to the provision of certain assistance. Please contact Tammy Anton, Americans with Disabilities Act Coordinator, Palm Beach County Courthouse, 205 North Dixie Hwy, West Palm Beach, FL 33401; telephone number (561) 355-4380 at least 7 days before your scheduled court appearance, or immediately upon receiving this notification if the time before the scheduled appearance is less than 7 days; if you are hearing or voice impaired, call 711."

"Si usted es una persona minusválida que necesita algún acomodamiento para poder participar en este procedimiento, usted tiene derecho, sin tener gastos propios, a que se le provea cierta ayuda. Tenga la amabilidad de ponerse en contacto con Tammy Anton, 205 N. Dixie Highway, West Palm Beach, Florida 33401; teléfono número (561) 355-4380, por lo menos 7 días antes de la cita fijada para su comparecencia en los tribunales, o inmediatamente después de recibir esta notificación si el tiempo antes de la comparecencia que se ha programado es menos de 7 días; si usted tiene discapacitación del oído o de la voz, llame al 711."

"Si ou se yon moun ki enfim ki bezwen akomodasyon pou w ka patisipe nan pwosedi sa, ou kalifye san ou pa gen okenn lajan pou w peye, gen pwovizyon pou jwen kèk èd. Tanpri kontakte Tammy Anton, kòòdonatè pwogram Lwa pou ameriken ki Enfim yo nan Tribinal Konte Palm Beach la ki nan 205 North Dixie Highway, West Palm Beach, Florida 33401; telefòn li se (561) 355-4380 nan 7 jou anvan dat ou gen randevou pou parèt nan tribinal la, oubyen imedyatman apre ou fin resevwa konvokasyon an si lè ou gen pou w parèt nan tribinal la mwens ke 7 jou; si ou gen pwoblèm pou w tande oubyen pale, rele 711."

On the date of **6/11/2019**, Mr. Bailey had to be up early for court in the Main Court house, held downtown West Palm Beach, FL. This means as an inmate he'll be on a bus in chains, heading to the main jail to pick-up any other inmates that have a court date. Then being transported to the **Main Court house** & spending only, "**three minutes**" on this case. The motion was denied, meaning Mr. Bailey wasn't being released & the courts didn't accept the Plea of Not Guilty.

Then resetting the court for a later date & another hearing. After court & being held in the basement, there was **No Vegan** meal for Mr. Bailey. Interrupting the current diet, he was on due to religious reasons. By now, he had read the complete **NIV Holy Bible**, including the **New Testament** located in the back. While he was in medical, he completely read the **Department of Correction Handbook** & was now reading **West's Florida Law**, on page 150.

2 Medical Reading Corrects! Handbook	3 Medical	4 James Lynch Passed me a new NIV Bible wrote 2 songs	5 Court in Belle Glade Reading HB (Pg 1040)	6 Reading + Exercise wrote 4 Christian S
9 Bible study 9:00 AM E-1 Reading Law (Pg 20-70)	10 Reading HB + Law + Exercise (Pg 125)	11 Court No Main court Vegan House Reading HB + Law (Pg 150)	12 Reading HB + Law (Called Attorney Twice) (Pg 140)	13 Reading + Law Exerc (Pg
16 Reading HB + Law + Exercise (Pg 35A)	17 Reading HB + Law + Exercise (Pg 384)	18 Court Main Court House Reading HB + Law + Exercise (Pg 110)	19 Reading HB + Law Volume II Exercise (Pg 22)	20 Reading + Law vol Exercise (Pg

IN THE COUNTY COURT OF THE FIFTEENTH
JUDICIAL CIRCUIT, CRIMINAL DIVISION
IN AND FOR PALM BEACH COUNTY, FLORIDA

CASE NO.2019MM005685AMB   DIVISION "B"

STATE OF FLORIDA

vs.

BRIAN DALE BAILEY

ANSWER TO DEMAND FOR DISCOVERY;
DEMAND FOR RECIPROCAL DISCOVERY AND
DEMAND FOR NOTICE OF ALIBI

       The State of Florida, by and through the undersigned Assistant State Attorney, hereby responds to the **Demand for Discovery** made on behalf of the Defendant, pursuant to Rule 3.220(a)&(b), Florida Rules of Criminal Procedure. The State hereby demands a **Reciprocal Discovery Exhibit** and all disclosure required by the Defendant, pursuant to Rule 3.220(a)(c)&(d), Florida Rules of Criminal Procedure. Further, the State hereby demands **Notice of Alibi** pursuant to Rule 3.200, Florida Rules of Criminal Procedure.

       NOTICE IS HEREBY GIVEN that all information and material as defined by Rule 3.220(a), Florida Rules of Criminal Procedure, within the State's possession or control has been disclosed by providing copies of all reports and statements in the State Attorney's file to the Attorney for the Defendant.

       The Attorney for the Defendant, PUBLIC DEFENDER - DIVISION B, is hereby granted permission to inspect, copy, test, and photograph the information and material described in supplied reports which are attached to this answer, if prior notice has been given to the undersigned of any such inspection, copying, testing, or photographing.

Respectfully submitted,
DAVID ARONBERG
STATE ATTORNEY

/s/

By: RYAN G MYERS
      Assistant State Attorney
      Florida Bar No. 0124446
      E-Service E-Mail: CCDIVB@SA15.ORG

DEFENDANT: BRIAN DALE BAILEY
CASE NUMBER: 2019MM005685AMB
AGENCY: PALM BEACH COUNTY SHERIFF'S OFFICE
AGENCY CASE NO: 06-19-070132

LIST OF PERSONS KNOWN TO HAVE INFORMATION
ALL WITNESSES ARE CLASSIFIED AS CATEGORY A UNLESS OTHERWISE NOTED

WITNESS CATEGORY A

DS JOSHUA CARMENATE #30553
PALM BEACH COUNTY SHERIFF'S OFFICE
3228 GUN CLUB RD
WEST PALM BEACH, FL 33406

GERALD CHARLES
C/O CHRIST FELLOWSHIP CHURCH SECURITY
9905 SOUTHER BLVD
ROYAL PALM BEACH, FL 33411

DS ROBERT PEITZ #6432
PALM BEACH COUNTY SHERIFF'S OFFICE
3228 GUN CLUB RD
WEST PALM BEACH, FL 33406

WITNESS CATEGORY B

CHRIST FELLOWSHIP CHURCH
C/O GREGORY READE (YOUTH MINISTRIES)
9905 SOUTHERN BLVD.
ROYAL PALM BEACH, FL 33411

WITNESS CATEGORY C

DEFENDANT: BRIAN DALE BAILEY
CASE NUMBER: 2019MM000608AMB
AGENCY: PALM BEACH COUNTY SHERIFF'S OFFICE
AGENCY CASE NO: 06-18450132

YES	NO		
☑	☐	STATEMENTS OF WITNESSES (per all police reports & video/audio recordings)	
		• CIVILIAN WRITTEN - AUDIO STATEMENTS	
☑	☐	STATEMENTS OF DEFENDANT (per all police reports, video/audio recordings, witness statements)	
☐	☑	STATEMENTS OF CO-DEFENDANT(S)	
☐	☑	CERTIFIED COPIES OF DEFENDANT'S CONVICTIONS (to be supplemented before trial)	
☐	☑	DEFENDANT'S DRIVING RECORD	
☐	☑	SUPPL. OFFENSE/REPORTING OFK. ___	
☐	☑	PROPERTY SECURITIES	
☑	☐	ADDITIONAL EVIDENCE	

☑	Arrest Report		Narcotics (In evidence)		Def. Booking Photo
☑	Probable Cause Affidavit		Paraphernalia (In evidence)		Miranda Card
	Accident Report		Photos (Total =)		Cert. Copy of Injunction & Proof of Service
	911 Tape		Surveillance Video		Photo Line Up - Areas
	A20 Report		Citations (Total =)		Photocopy of Defendant's D.L.
	OTHER				

	DUI				
☑	Roadside Video		DUI Testing Facility Task Report		Blood Test Affidavit
	BAT Video		BAT Testing Facility Information Sheet		Blood (Drunk) Cert Forms
	Roadside Tasks		Breath Test Affidavit		Blood (6.1) Vials (in evidence)
	Implied Consent Card		Intoxilyzer Certifications		Toxicology Report (Blood / urine)
	Refusal Affidavit		Operation / Permits		Expert T.X.
	Operator Viewer Form		Maintenance Records Tags		Booking Slip
	OTHER				

	Miscellaneous	

All witnesses' statements / evidence listed in police reports and disclosed during depositions.
Copies of all recordings are to be obtained from the appropriate police department.

Statue Violations: 837.05 False reports to law enforcement authorities. 490.009 Discipline

After reviewing the report, Mr. Bailey found **insufficient evidence** & **false reporting** to law enforcement. Never had he been **DUI** while on the property of the **Christ Fellowship Church**, nor had Mr. Bailey ever been arrested or charge with **DUI** in the history of his lifetime. After having a history of stomach Ulcers, drinking alcoholic beverages was not a choice Mr. Bailey usually makes.

Palm Beach County Sheriff's Office, FL
Palm Beach West Detention
38811 James Wheeler Way
Belle Glade , FL 33430

Progress Notes

✚ **wellpath**™

Patient Name	Patient Number	Booking Number	Birth Date	Date Of Service
BRIAN DALE BAILEY	0403731	20190512050	2/24/1979	6/14/2019

Orders:

No Applicable Data Found For Patient

Patient Problems:

Observed Date	Category	Type	Problem	Confirmed By
06-08-2019	Acute	Symptoms	Abnormal weight loss	

Patient Allergies:

Observed Date	Type	Allergy	Reaction
06-06-2019	Allergy Items	No Known Drug Allergies	

☐ *Vital Signs Taken*

Patient Vitals:

Observed Date	BP	Pulse	Resp	Temp	Pulse Ox	Weight	BMI	PF#1	PF#2	PF#3	Waist

---

Notes / History: ○ *Free Text* ◉ *SOAPE*

S:

Added 06/14/2019 04:40 PM CST by NLangley LPN

I'm observing Passover for religious reasons. I am eating tomorrow.

O:

Added 06/14/2019 04:40 PM CST by NLangley LPN

Pt looked slightly dry but mucous moist

A:

Added 06/14/2019 04:40 PM CST by NLangley LPN

b/p 105/69 P53 T 97.7 pulse 53 pso2 100%

Palm Beach County Sheriff's Office, FL
Palm Beach West Detention
38811 James Wheeler Way
Belle Glade, FL 33430

Progress Notes

wellpath

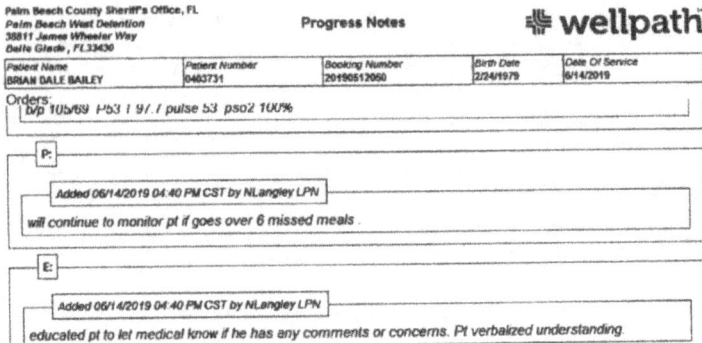

Patient Name	Patient Number	Booking Number	Birth Date	Date Of Service
BRIAN DALE BAILEY	0403731	20190512050	2/24/1979	6/14/2019

Orders:
b/p 105/69 P53 T 97.7 pulse 53 pso2 100%

P:

Added 06/14/2019 04:40 PM CST by NLangley LPN

will continue to monitor pt if goes over 6 missed meals .

E:

Added 06/14/2019 04:40 PM CST by NLangley LPN

educated pt to let medical know if he has any comments or concerns. Pt verbalized understanding.

110

6/18/2019

IN THE COUNTY COURT OF THE FIFTEENTH JUDICIAL CIRCUIT
IN AND FOR PALM BEACH COUNTY, FLORIDA - CRIMINAL DIVISION
CIRCUIT/COUNTY COURT
Court Event Form

DEFENDANT: BRIAN DALE BAILEY
CASE NO: 50-2019-MM-005685-AXXX-MB

STATE OF FLORIDA   DATE: 6/18/2019
vs.
DEFENDANT: BRIAN DALE BAILEY   JACKET #:   0403731
CASE NO: 50-2019-MM-005685-AXXX-MB   BOOKING #: 2019015844
DIVISION: B: Cnty Crim - B (County)

PRESIDING JUDGE: HANSER, JUDGELEONARD   START TIME: 10:39 AM
ASA: MYERS, RYAN   END TIME: 10:41 AM
ATTORNEY:
PUBLIC DEFENDER: SHIH, JONELL-ANTHONY
CO-COUNSEL: COURT REPORTER
DEPUTY CLERK: SH   COURT TYPE: PC - PLEA
                                                                CONFERENCE
COURT ROOM: 2E (Main Branch)

Reset For
Court Date Scheduled - CC - CALENDAR CALL - 7/2/2019 8:30 AM - 2E (Main Branch) MB, 205 N. Dixie
Highway West Palm Beach FL 33401 - JAIL TO TRANSPORT

Other: DEFENDANT PRESENT AND IN CUSTODY

Count 1 - MF TRESPASS AFTER WARNING 810.09(2A)

IN THE CIRCUIT/COUNTY COURT OF THE FIFTEENTH JUDICIAL CIRCUIT
IN AND FOR PALM BEACH COUNTY, FLORIDA

STATE OF FLORIDA

-Vs-

Date: 06/18/2019

Case No: 50-2019-MM-005685-AXXX-MB

Division: B: Cnty Crim - B (County)

BRIAN DALE BAILEY
GENERAL DELIVERY
WEST PALM BEACH, FL 32200

NOTICE OF HEARING
THE DEFENDANT MUST BE PRESENT AT THIS HEARING

*For Criminal Charges: Failure to Appear will result in a Bond Forfeiture or
revocation of own recognizance (O.R.) and a Capias/Warrant being issued for your arrest.
For Civil Traffic Charges: Failure to appear may result in the suspension of your driver's license.
IF YOUR CASE IS ON-CALL, CONTACT YOUR ATTORNEY FOR THE TIME TO APPEAR*
YOU ARE HEREBY NOTIFIED that this case is scheduled

DATE:	TIME:	HEARING TYPE:	LOCATION:
7/2/2019	8:30 AM	CC - CALENDAR CALL	2E (Main Branch) MB, 205 N. Dixie Highway West Palm Beach FL 33401

BE PREPARED TO PAY COURT COSTS AND FINES ASSESSED BY THE COURT AT THIS HEARING
*"IF YOU INTEND TO REQUEST THE SERVICES OF THE PUBLIC DEFENDER, YOU MUST FILE AN APPLICATION AT THE CLERK &
COMPTROLLER'S OFFICE AND BE APPOINTED THE PUBLIC DEFENDER BEFORE YOUR COURT DATE. THE APPLICATION FEE IS $50.00."*
Civil Traffic Charges are not eligible for a Public Defender.

SHARON R. BOCK,
CLERK & COMPTROLLER
BY: SH

Deft/Atty: DEFENDANT IN CUSTODY

Deputy Clerk

cc: RYAN MYERS
       SHIH, JONELL-ANTHONY

Page 1 of 2

IN THE CIRCUIT/COUNTY COURT OF THE FIFTEENTH JUDICIAL CIRCUIT
IN AND FOR PALM BEACH COUNTY, FLORIDA

"If you are a person with a disability who needs any accommodation in order to participate in this proceeding, you are entitled, at no cost to you, to the provision of certain assistance. Please contact Tammy Anton, Americans with Disabilities Act Coordinator, Palm Beach County Courthouse, 205 North Dixie Hwy, West Palm Beach, FL 33401; telephone number (561) 355-4380 at least 7 days before your scheduled court appearance, or immediately upon receiving this notification if the time before the scheduled appearance is less than 7 days; if you are hearing or voice impaired, call 711."

"Si usted es una persona minusválida que necesita algún acomodamiento para poder participar en este procedimiento, usted tiene derecho, sin tener gastos propios, a que se le provea cierta ayuda. Tenga la amabilidad de ponerse en contacto con Tammy Anton, 205 N. Dixie Highway, West Palm Beach, Florida 33401; teléfono número (561) 355-4380, por lo menos 7 días antes de la cita fijada para su comparecencia en los tribunales, o inmediatamente después de recibir esta notificación si el tiempo antes de la comparecencia que se ha programado es menos de 7 días; si usted tiene discapacitación del oído o de la voz, llame al 711."

"Si ou se yon moun ki enfim ki bezwen akomodasyon pou w ka patisipe nan pwosedi sa, ou kalifye san ou pa gen okenn lajan pou w peye, gen pwovizyon pou jwen kèk èd. Tanpri kontakte Tammy Anton, kòòdonatè pwogram Lwa pou ameriken ki Enfim yo nan Tribinal Konte Palm Beach la ki nan 205 North Dixie Highway, West Palm Beach, Florida 33401; telefòn li se (561) 355-4380 nan 7 jou anvan dat ou gen randevou pou parèt nan tribinal la, oubyen imedyatman apre ou fin resevwa konvokasyon an si lè ou gen pou w parèt nan tribinal la mwens ke 7 jou; si ou gen pwoblèm pou w tande oubyen pale, rele 711."

113

On the date of **6/18/2019**, one week later after visiting the Main Court house, Mr. Bailey was back again, only to see time lost. Due to **lack of integrity** on the bases of the court system. The system needing to have Mr. Bailey present in the courthouse, while his presence in the courthouse is unnecessary. While needing officer to transport & escort him around in chains, unable to change the current events taking place around the environment he's being held in.

Only to be brought into a courtroom to watch & listen, while the case is being pushed back again for another calendar call, all taking less than three minutes. Meanwhile back at the **Belle Glade – West Detention Center** Mr. Bailey was still in review & continuing bible study, using the **NIV Holy Bible**. Now on page 404 of the West's Florida Law book & exercising most days. While being incarcerated mental stimulation is key & at times it can be difficult to see the light and stay focused.

9 Bible study 9:00 am E-1 Reading Law (Pg 20-70)	10 Reading HB + Law + Exercise (Pg 125)	11 Court No Main court Vegan House Reading HB + Law (Pg 150)	12 Reading HB + Law (Called Attorney twice) (Pg 110)	13 Reading HB + Law + Exercise (Pg 238)
16 Reading HB + Law + Exercise (Pg 358)	17 Reading HB + Law + Exercise (Pg 384)	18 Court Main court House Reading HB + Law Exercise (Pg 404)	19 Reading HB + Law volume II Exercise (Pg 22)	20 Reading HB + Law volume II Exercise (Pg 50)
23 Reading HB + Law volume I Exercise 1000 squats (Pg 500)	24 Reading HB + Law volume I Exercise (writing Devil at 40) 1000 squats (Pg 539)	25 Reading HB + Law volume I Exercise 1000 squats (Pg 575)	26 Reading HB + Law volume I Exercise 1000 squats (Pg 605)	27 Reading HB + Law volume I Exercise (writing music) church 600 squats (Pg 615)
30 Reading HB CERT				

Filing # 91384101 E-Filed 06/20/2019 08:16:26 AM

IN THE COUNTY COURT OF THE FIFTEENTH
JUDICIAL CIRCUIT, CRIMINAL DIVISION
IN AND FOR PALM BEACH COUNTY, FLORIDA

CASE NO. 2019MM005685AMB   DIVISION: "B"

STATE OF FLORIDA

vs.

BRIAN DALE BAILEY,

    Defendant.

_____/

SUPPLEMENTAL DISCOVERY
PURSUANT TO RULE 3.220(f)

    COMES NOW the State of Florida, by and through its undersigned Assistant State Attorney, and, pursuant to Florida Rules of Criminal Procedure, Rule 3.220(f), files the following supplemental discovery:

    OFFENSE REPORT BY OFC PEITZ

    I HEREBY CERTIFY that a true and correct copy of the foregoing Supplemental Discovery has been furnished to PUBLIC DEFENDER - DIVISION B, 421 3RD STREET, WEST PALM BEACH, FL 33401 at STAC EXCHANGE by E-SERVICE this 20th day of June, 2019.

        Respectfully submitted,

        DAVID ARONBERG
        STATE ATTORNEY

    /s/

By: RYAN G MYERS
       Assistant State Attorney
       Florida Bar No. 0124446
       E-Service E-Mail: CCDIVB@SA15.ORG

*** FILED: PALM BEACH COUNTY, FL SHARON R BOCK, CLERK. 06/20/2019 08:16:26 AM ***

IN THE COUNTY COURT OF THE FIFTEENTH
JUDICIAL CIRCUIT, CRIMINAL DIVISION
IN AND FOR PALM BEACH COUNTY, FLORIDA

CASE NO. 2019MM005685AMB DIVISION: B

STATE OF FLORIDA

vs.

BRIAN DALE BAILEY,

     Defendant.

_____/

SUPPLEMENTAL LIST OF WITNESSES
PURSUANT TO RULE 3.220(f)

Comes now the State of Florida, by and through its undersigned Assistant State Attorney

and files this Supplemental List of Witnesses pursuant to Florida Rules of Criminal Procedure,

Rule 3.220(f) in the above-styled cause as follows:

DON EDWARD HELVEY
9905 SOUTHERN BLVD.
ROYAL PALM BEACH, FL 33411

    I HEREBY CERTIFY that a true and correct copy of the foregoing Supplemental Witness

List has been furnished to PUBLIC DEFENDER - DIVISION B at STAC EXCHANGE by E-

SERVICE this 20th day of June, 2019.

               Respectfully submitted,

               DAVID ARONBERG
               STATE ATTORNEY

               /s/

    By: RYAN G MYERS
           Assistant State Attorney

116

Florida Bar No. 0124446
E-Service E-Mail: CCDIVB@SA15.ORG

On the date of **6/20/2019**, supplemental discovery pursuant to rule 3.220(f) comes to the **State of Florida** from Officer Peitz. The definition for rule **3.220(f)** any tangible papers or objects that were obtained from or belonged to the **defendant**. This requires a search or seizure of property in order to review. While being detained Mr. Bailey was never made aware of any of the discovery & requested a number of times for the discovery.

On the date of **6/20/2019**, Mr. Bailey was sticking to his pod area where the four different bunks would revolve with different inmates. Not releasing much information about himself, while some inmates are more talkative than others. Still reviewing the **NIV Holy Bible**, understanding that the issue our world is facing today has evolved to extreme levels that might not have been present in history, due to evolution of technology & science. Creating a more difficult world for law, moving at tremendous rate of creating the human race & artificial intelligence.

The **West's Florida Law** book Mr. Bailey was reading, was now loaned to another inmate. So, he made a decision to continue reading the next volume II **West's Florida Law** & was on page number 50. While exercising when able, meaning when allowed by Sheriff's Department & having an area where there's not as much hostility. People are being powered to make mistakes in this world.

✓	Law Called Attorney Twice) (pg 110)	Exercise (Pg 238)	+ Law + Exercise (Passover) (Pg 291)	+ Law Exer
3+ 50)				
Law+ .04)	19 Reading HB + Law Volume II Exercise (Pg 22)	20 Reading HB + Law Volume II Exercise (Pg 50)	21 Reading HB + Law Volume II Exercise Drawing Art (Pg 95)	22 f HB + Volum Writti Money Drawn
HB +1	26 Reading HB + Law Volume I Exercise	27 Reading HB + Law Volume I Exercise (writing music)	28 Reading HB + Law Volume I Pg 635 Volume II pg 115	29 Re + Law Exer

6/27/2019

Health Care District
of Palm Beach County
1515 N. Flagler Dr. Suite 101
West Palm Beach, FL 33401-3429
(866) 930-0035

06/27/2019   Coverage Denied

BRIAN BAILEY
3200 SUMMIT BLVD STE 15532
WEST PALM BEACH, FL 33416

MEMBER NO.: 1000315673 - 01
SUBJECT: DISTRICT CARES COVERAGE DENIED

Dear BRIAN BAILEY:

Your application for health care coverage has been denied. Enrollment
in our program is based on meeting four eligibility guidelines. Based
on the information you submitted, your application has been denied for
the following reasons:

ID
Residence
Income
Other
Note:

Your application for District Cares program, has been denied because
you did not complete the application process. We did not receive the
requested information.

If your situation should change, you can apply again. Call
Customer Service, Monday through Friday, 8:00 am to 5:00 pm, at
1-866-930-0035 (toll free) to have an application sent to you,or
visit our website at www.hcdpbc.org to download an application.

Although you do not qualify for District Cares coverage,the
doctors at C.L. Brumback Primary Care Clinics are available
regardless of your ability to pay. If you need to see a doctor
call 561-642-1000.

Sincerely,
Eligibility Department
Letter 4   ms
Si-w bezwen moun ede-w an kreyol, tanpri rele 1-866-930-0035.
Si necesita asistencia en espanol, favor de llamar al 1-866-930-0035.

*The **Palm Beach County Health Care District** has
guidelines that I was unable to meet after finding
myself injured & unable to continue affording housing.
While still Self-Employed & collecting a source of low-
income.*

IN THE COUNTY COURT OF THE FIFTEENTH JUDICIAL CIRCUIT
IN AND FOR PALM BEACH COUNTY, FLORIDA - CRIMINAL DIVISION
CIRCUIT/COUNTY COURT
Court Event Form

DEFENDANT: BRIAN DALE BAILEY
CASE NO: 50-2019-MM-005685-AXXX-MB

STATE OF FLORIDA   DATE: 7/2/2019
vs.
DEFENDANT: BRIAN DALE BAILEY   JACKET #: 0403731
CASE NO: 50-2019-MM-005685-AXXX-MB   BOOKING #: 2019015844
DIVISION: B: Cnty Crim - B (County)

PRESIDING JUDGE: HANSER, JUDGELEONARD   START TIME: 12:04 PM
ASA: MYERS, RYAN   END TIME: 12:07 PM
ATTORNEY:
PUBLIC DEFENDER: BURNS, RAYMON
CO-COUNSEL: COURT REPORTER
DEPUTY CLERK: ME   COURT TYPE: CC
    CALENDAR
    CALL

COURT ROOM: 2E (Main Branch)

Reset For
Court Date Scheduled - JT - JURY TRIAL - 7/24/2019 8:30 AM - 2E (Main Branch) MB, 205 N. Dixie Highway
West Palm Beach FL 33401

Other: DEFENDANT PRESENT AND IN CUSTODY

Count 1 - MF TRESPASS AFTER WARNING 810.09(2A)

Tuesday, July 02, 2019   Page 1 of 1
FILED: PALM BEACH COUNTY, FL SHARON R BOCK, CLERK 07/02/2019 12:07:23 PM

On the document above titled **County Court of the Fifteenth Judicial Circuit** in and for **Palm Beach County, Florida - Criminal Division** Circuit / County Court. The professional business title for Assistant Public Defender Raymon A. Burns is listed as: **Public Defender**. This is misleading & needs to be titled **Assistant Public Defender**, with the head of the circuit listed next to the **APD**. ADP Raymon A. Burns has, "**NOT**" been a member in good standing with **The Florida Bar for the preceding 5 years**.

Violating Statutes 27.50 Public defender; qualifications; election. - For each judicial circuit, there shall be a public defender who shall be, & shall be & shall have been for the preceding 5 **years, a member in good standing** of **The Florida Bar**.

121

IN THE CIRCUIT/COUNTY COURT OF THE FIFTEENTH JUDICIAL CIRCUIT
IN AND FOR PALM BEACH COUNTY, FLORIDA

STATE OF FLORIDA

-Vs-

Date: 07/02/2019

Case No: 50-2019-MM-005685-AXXX-MB

Division: B: Cnty Crim - B (County)

BRIAN DALE BAILEY
GENERAL DELIVERY
WEST PALM BEACH, FL 32200

NOTICE OF HEARING
THE DEFENDANT MUST BE PRESENT AT THIS HEARING

For Criminal Charges: Failure to Appear will result in a Bond Forfeiture or
revocation of own recognizance (O.R.) and a Capias/Warrant being issued for your arrest.
For Civil Traffic Charges: Failure to appear may result in the suspension of your driver's license.
IF YOUR CASE IS ON-CALL, CONTACT YOUR ATTORNEY FOR THE TIME TO APPEAR
YOU ARE HEREBY NOTIFIED that this case is scheduled

DATE:	TIME:	HEARING TYPE:	LOCATION:
7/24/2019	8:30 AM	JT - JURY TRIAL	2E (Main Branch) MB, 205 N. Dixie Highway West Palm Beach FL 33401

"*BE PREPARED TO PAY COURT COSTS AND FINES ASSESSED BY THE COURT AT THIS HEARING*"
"*IF YOU INTEND TO REQUEST THE SERVICES OF THE PUBLIC DEFENDER, YOU MUST FILE AN APPLICATION AT THE CLERK &
COMPTROLLER'S OFFICE AND BE APPOINTED THE PUBLIC DEFENDER BEFORE YOUR COURT DATE. THE APPLICATION FEE IS $50.00."*
Civil Traffic Charges are not eligible for a Public Defender.

SHARON R. BOCK,
CLERK & COMPTROLLER
BY: _ME_

Deft/Atty: DEFENDANT IN CUSTODY   Deputy Clerk

cc: RYAN MYERS
       BURNS, RAYMON A

Page 1 of 2

FILED: PALM BEACH COUNTY, FL SHARON R BOCK, CLERK 07/02/2019 12:07:23 PM

"If you are a person with a disability who needs any accommodation in order to participate in this proceeding, you are entitled, at no cost to you, to the provision of certain assistance. Please contact Tammy Anton, Americans with Disabilities Act Coordinator, Palm Beach County Courthouse, 205 North Dixie Hwy, West Palm Beach, FL 33401; telephone number (561) 355-4380 at least 7 days before your scheduled court appearance, or immediately upon receiving this notification if the time before the scheduled appearance is less than 7 days; if you are hearing or voice impaired, call 711."

"Si usted es una persona minusválida que necesita algún acomodamiento para poder participar en este procedimiento, usted tiene derecho, sin tener gastos propios, a que se le provea cierta ayuda. Tenga la amabilidad de ponerse en contacto con Tammy Anton, 205 N. Dixie Highway, West Palm Beach, Florida 33401; teléfono número (561) 355-4380, por lo menos 7 días antes de la cita fijada para su comparecencia en los tribunales, o inmediatamente después de recibir esta notificación si el tiempo antes de la comparecencia que se ha programado es menos de 7 días; si usted tiene discapacitación del oído o de la voz, llame al 711."

"Si ou se yon moun ki enfim ki bezwen akomodasyon pou w ka patisipe nan pwosedi sa, ou kalifye san ou pa gen okenn lajan pou w peye, gen pwovizyon pou jwen kèk èd. Tanpri kontakte Tammy Anton, kòòdonatè pwogram Lwa pou ameriken ki Enfim yo nan Tribinal Konte Palm Beach la ki nan 205 North Dixie Highway, West Palm Beach, Florida 33401; telefòn li se (561) 355-4380 nan 7 jou anvan dat ou gen randevou pou parèt nan tribinal la, oubyen imedyatman apre ou fin resevwa konvokasyon an si lè ou gen pou w parèt nan tribinal la mwens ke 7 jou; si ou gen pwoblèm pou w tande oubyen pale, rele 711."

Filing # 92002227 E-Filed 07/02/2019 01:41:28 PM

IN THE COUNTY COURT OF THE FIFTEENTH
JUDICIAL CIRCUIT, CRIMINAL DIVISION
IN AND FOR PALM BEACH COUNTY, FLORIDA

CASE NO. 2019MM005685AMB   DIVISION: "B"

STATE OF FLORIDA

vs.

BRIAN DALE BAILEY,

      Defendant.

_____/

SUPPLEMENTAL DISCOVERY
PURSUANT TO RULE 3.220(f)

COMES NOW the State of Florida, by and through its undersigned Assistant State Attorney, and, pursuant to Florida Rules of Criminal Procedure, Rule 3.220(f), files the following supplemental discovery:

CERTIFIED CONVICTIONS

I HEREBY CERTIFY that a true and correct copy of the foregoing Supplemental Discovery has been furnished to PUBLIC DEFENDER - DIVISION B, 421 3RD STREET, WEST PALM BEACH, FL 33401 at STAC EXCHANGE by E-SERVICE this 2nd day of July, 2019.

Respectfully submitted,

DAVID ARONBERG
STATE ATTORNEY

/s/

By: RYAN G MYERS
       Assistant State Attorney
       Florida Bar No. 0124446
       E-Service E-Mail: CCDIVB@SA15.ORG

*** FILED: PALM BEACH COUNTY, FL SHARON R BOCK, CLERK. 07/02/2019 01:41:28 PM ***

On the date of **7/2/2019**, Mr. Bailey was transported to the **Main Jail house**, located in West Palm Beach, FL. Then transported back to the Main courthouse downtown West Palm Beach. Now, while Mr. Bailey sits in the courtroom and listens to **Judge Leonard Hanser** share that the case is being rescheduled for a trial at a later date, taking all of three minutes.

When arriving in the basement, & making a request for a Vegan meal, which He had been assigned by the authority within the system. Yet again, there was, **"No Vegan"** meal available for Mr. Bailey. Once arriving back to the **Belle Glade – West Detention Center**. He continued the rest of his day with a routine of bible study, and still reading **West's Florida Law** - Volume I on page 718. Then exercising throughout the day, coming to a total of 800 squats.

Reading HB Law volume I exercise 10 squts (pg 500)	24 Reading HB + Law volume I Exercise (writing Devil of 40) (1000 squats)	25 Reading HB + Law volume I Exercise (1000 squats) (pg 575)	26 Reading HB + Law volume I Exercise (1000 squats) (pg 605)	27 Reading HB + Law volume I Exercise (writing music) church (600 squats) (pg 618)
Reading HB Law volume I exercise (50 Days) (Pg 675)	Jul 1 **CERT** Reading HB + Law Volume I Exercise 1000 (Pg 710)	2 Court (No Vegan Bag) main court House Reading HB + Law pg 718 (800)	3 Reading HB + Law + Exercise Waiting Defense (7/2/2019) (Court room)	4 Reading HB + Law + Exercise Called Public Defense 4 times 12:30-4 waiting Defense case
Reading HB exercise writing only bag squats 200	8 Reading HB writing letter for Court Canceled trial + defense attorney is rescheduled	9 Called Public defender (re-sched) Reading HB + Law writing (Money Bag) Exercise pg 745 squats 500	Read HB + Law 10 60 Days (Indigent Packing) Received pg 755 Exercise (New representation) Sent Letters to the judge 500	1000 squats Church + Bible study Reading HB Exercise Apologize for Her 600 squat
Passover	No Bread	No Bread	No Bread	

Case # 50-2019-MM-005685-AXXX-MB

While in custody on 7/2/2019, I was walked into the courtroom by Sheriff's department, then seated while cases were in session. I was approached by a Mr. Rayown Burns, who advised that he would be handling my case. Mr. Burns asked me a few questions in regards to case number 50-2019-MM-005685-AXXX-MB. Towards the end of our conversation, I was asked to make a decession, either take a plea offer or trial. I decided to take the case to trial, and that was the end of our conversation. A few minutes later, Mr. Burns came back over to where I was sitting and informed me, that his supervisor would be coming to speak with me.

Sometime passed and a woman appeared in the courtroom, she then approached me and asked "Are you Brian Bailey"? I replied "Yes". Her name is Ms. Ilana Marcus, I had never seen her before this, and didn't know her position title at this time. Ms. Marcus claimed that she had some concerns about my competence. This eased my level of concern, because I had never met Ms. Marcus before, how could she judge my level of competence? Ms. Ilana Marcus who never showed her professional title with me, started asking me questions like.

Do I think the state attorney is my friend? I replied "that would be based upon opinion". Ms. Marcus then asked "do I know what the prosecutors job is"? I replied "that is not my line of work". At this point I was bothered by the intent of her questions. Ms. Marcus went on to make a statement, by saying "Well you have history with the system, you should know"! I replied "I will only be speaking to Mr. Burns" my appointed representation. Ms. Marcus then walked away and asked Mr. Burns to step outside the courtroom and that was the last time I saw Ms. Ilana Marcus.

When Mr. Burns returned, I asked him for her full name and title position, along with some questions regarding his experience as a public defender with the state. On a yellow piece of paper (with writing in black ink), Mr. Burns wrote the answers down, and gave me this yellow sheet of paper. After seeing the answers, I realized that they were not detailed into a timeline. I asked Mr. Burns "what is the timeline, on your one hundred cases? Is it annual or monthly? And are they open or closed"? Mr. Burns replied (laughing not sure what to answer) "he would have to look it up and get back to me". (Mr. Burns seemed confused.) On the yellow sheet of paper Mr. Burns wrote down Ms. Ilana Marcus title position as Assistant Public Defender.

→

Not long after was the case was called before the judge. I stood up and both the state prosecutor, public defender and judge agreed upon a trial date. The end result on July 2, 2019 was there would be a jury trial on July 24, 2019.

Statue Violation

1) s. 27.18 Assistant to state Attorney
The state attorney, by and with the consent of court may procure the assistance of any member of the bar when the amount of the state business renders it necessary, either in the grand jury room to advise them upon legal points and framing indictments, or in the court to prosecute criminal; but such assistants shall not be authorized to sign any indictments or administer any oaths, or to perform any other duty except the giving of legal advice, drawing up of indictments, and the prosecuting of criminals in open court. His or her compensation shall be paid by the state attorney and not by the state.

2) s. 393.17(1) Behavioral program; certification of behavior analysts

3) s. 393.18 Comprehensive transitional education program

4) s. 490.005   Licensure by examination

Respectfully,
B. B.

In the courtroom on 7/2/2019

Case# 50-2019-MM-005685-AXXX-MB

While in custody on 7/2/2019, Mr. Bailey was walked into the courtroom by Sheriff's Department, then seated while cases were in session. He was approached by a **APD Raymon A. Burns**, who advised that he would be handling Mr. Bailey's case. APD Burns asked Mr. Bailey a few questions in regards to case number 50-2019-MM-005685-AXXX-MB. Towards the end of their conversation, Mr. Bailey was asked to make a decision, either take a plea offer or trial. Mr. Bailey decided to take the case to trial, & that was end of their conversation.

A few minutes later, APD Burns came back over to where Mr. Bailey was sitting & informed him, that his supervisor would be coming over to speak with him. Sometime passed & a woman appeared in the courtroom, she then approached Mr. Bailey & asked, "Are you Brian Bailey"? He replied, "Yes". Her name is **Assistant Public Defender Ilana Felice Marcus**. Mr. Bailey had never seen her before this and didn't know her professional position & title at this time, nor did she offer that information. APD Marcus claimed that she had some concerns about Mr. Bailey's, "competence." This raised his level of concern, because he had never met APD Marcus before, how could she judge his level of competence?

APD Ilana Marcus who never shared her professional title with Mr. Bailey, started asking Mr. Bailey questions like; Do you think the state attorney is your friend? He replied, "that would be based upon opinion". APD Marcus then asked, "Does Mr. Bailey know what the prosecutor job is"? he replied, "That is not my line of work". At this point he was bother by the intent of her questions. APD Marcus went on to make a statement, by saying, "Well you have history with the system, you should know"! He replied, "I will only be speaking with APD Burns" his appointed representation.

APD Marcus then walked away & asked APD Burns to step outside the courtroom & that was the last time Mr. Bailey saw APD Ilana Marcus. When APD Burns returned, Mr. Bailey asked him for her full name & title position, along with some questions regarding his experience as a public defender with the State. On a yellow piece of paper with writing in black ink, APD Burns wrote the answers down & gave Mr. Bailey this yellow sheet of paper.

*After seeing the answers, realizing that they were not detailed with a timeline. Mr. Bailey asked APD Burns, "What is the timeline on your hundred cases"? Is it annual or monthly? And are they open or closed"? APD Burns replied (humbling not sure what to answer) "he would have to look it up & get back to Mr. Bailey". (APD Burns seemed unsure) On the yellow sheet of paper APD Burns wrote down APD Ilana Marcus's title position as Assistant Public Defender. Not long after this case was called before the Judge. Mr. Bailey stood up & both the State prosecutor, Public defender & Judge decided upon a trial date. The end result on **July 2, 2019,** was there would be a jury trial on **July 24,2019.***

Listed below are the Statutes Violated by **Assistant Public Defender Ilana Felice Marcus:** When, "Not" acting as an Assistant Public Defender & turning the case as a prosecuting State Attorney.

Assistant Public Defenders are Attorney's working for the State, licensed through **The Florida Bar**, creating a State Attorney.

Statute violation: **27.18 Assistant to State Attorney**

The State Attorney, by & with the **consent of court** may procure the assistance of any member of the bar when the amount of the state business renders it necessary, either in the grand jury room to advise them upon legal points & framing indictments, or in the court to prosecute criminals; but such Assistant shall **NOT be authorized** to sign any indictments or administer any oaths, or to **perform any other duty** except the giving of legal advice, drawing up of indictments, & the prosecuting of criminals **in open court**. His or her compensation shall be paid by the State Attorney & not by the State.

1) Statute violation: **393.17 (1) Behavior program; certification of behavior analysts**

2) Statute violation: **393.18 Comprehensive transitional education program**

3) Statute violation: **490.005 Licensure by examination**

Below is the page that has been created, that has been typed for the purpose of distribution, while on the inside of a jail cell before court the previous day.

The date was **7/2/2019**, when Mr. Bailey created a list of questions for the **Assistant Public Defender,** that would be brought into the courtroom the very next day.

State Public Defender (Information)

Case# 50-2019-MM-005685-AXXX-MB

1) How long has APD Raymon A. Burns been a public defender for the state?
   > **Answer:** Since **August of 2018** to present / **less than One - year**
2) How many cases does APD Raymon A. Burns have currently?
   > **Answer:** Current case load 100
3) How many cases did APD Raymon A. Burns have dropped or dismissed since starting as a Public Defender for the State of Florida?
   > **Answer:** One not guilty and one guilty (Having only two trial cases)
4) How many Trespass cases has APD Raymon A. Burns had?
   > **Answer:** Didn't have a number of Trespass cases
5) How many hours have been spent on case number 50-2019-MM-005685-AXXX-MB?
   > **Answer:** Unaswered as of 7/2/2019 – **"I don't know"** was on **7/8/2019**
6) Are APD Raymon A. Burns going to record the hours on case number 50-2019-MM-0056685-MB?
   > **Answer:** "I don't know" then it was crossed out.
   > **Answering:** "There is no system to record hours" was on **7/8/2019**
   > (Yet from the inside of my cell I have a complete log of all hours spent on this case.)
7) What is the timeline that prosecution has after request to produce evidence?
   > **Answer:** Not set-in stone
8) Are APD Raymon A. Burns going to interview the witness?
   > **Answer:** Wasn't going to depose witness, until I requested, they be interviewed.

These next two question were created after being visited by APD Ilana Felice Marcus in the courtroom

9) Does Assistant Public Defender Ilana Felice
Marcus have any Degree, Certificate or Licenses
for mental illness?
Answer: ADP Burns wasn't sure **7/8/2019**

10) Does Assistant Public Defender Ilana Felice
Marcus have at least one-year of experience in
providing behavior analysis services for
individuals in developmental disabilities?
Answer: APD Burns wasn't sure **7/8/2019**

Yet, Assistant Public Defender Raymon A. Burns,
Mr. Bailey's **appointed representation attorney,** who allowed
Assistant Public Defender Ilana Felice Marcus to interview his
client in the courtroom without knowing her qualifications at
the time of interview. Hired by the **State of Florida** &
considered to be a professional attorney.

133

Brian Bailey   7/2/2019
                    State Public Defender
                    (Information)

Case # 50-2019 MM-005685-AXXR-MB

1) How long has Mr. Raymon Burns been a public defender for the state?
Answer: Since August of 2018 to present / less than one year

2) How many cases does Mr. Raymon Burns have currently?
Answer: Current case load 100.

3) How many cases did Mr. Raymon Burns have dropped or dismissed since starting as a public defender for the state of florida?
Answer: One not guilty and one guilty, only 2 trial cases (7/8/2019) BB

4) How many trespass cases has Mr. Raymon Burns had?
Answer: Didn't have a number of trespass cases (7/8/2019) BB

5) * How many hours have been spent on case number 50-2019-MM-005685-AXXR-MB?
Answer: (Unanswered as of 7/2/2019)   I don't know (7/8/2019 BB)

6) Are (Mr. Raymon Burns) going to record the hours on case number 50-2019-MM-005685-AXXR MB?
Answer: I Don't know   There is no system to record hours (7/8/2019) BB

7) What is the timeline that prosecution has after request to produce evidence? And the state
Answer: Couldn't answer with a timeline

8) Are (Mr. Raymon Burns) going to interview the witness?
Answer: Wasn't going to depose witness, until I requested to have the witness interviewed
                    (Ms. Ilana Marcus)

9) Does Assistant Public Defender Ilana Marcus have any Degree, Certificate or licenses for mental health?
Answer: Mr. Burns wasn't sure (7/8/2019) BB

10) Does Assistant Public Defender Ms. Ilana Marcus have at least 1 year of experience in providing behavior analysis services for individuals with developmental disabilities?
Answer: Mr. Burns wasn't sure (7/8/2019) BB

Regional Counsel: — (561) 847-5417
Bailey Colson Regional: (561) 994-4830
Public Defender: (561) 355-7500
Mr. Raymon Burns: —   (561) 355-7748

                                              Pg 5

*Here is a list of **statutes violated** by the court, after ADP Raymon A. Burns has answered the questions to the best of his knowledge. Statute Title (Public Defenders, State Attorneys)*

1) Statute violation: **27.40 (9) Court-appointed counsel; circuit registries; minimum requirements; appointment by court.** Any interested person may advise the court of any circumstance affecting the **quality of representation.**

2) Statute violation: **27.40 (b) 1.** The attorney shall **maintain appropriate documentation,** including contemporaneous and **detailed hourly accounting of time spent representing the client.** If the attorneys fail to maintain such contemporaneous and detailed hourly records, the attorney waives the Right to seek compensation in excess of the flat fee estabished in s. **27.5304 and General Appropriations Act.**

3) Statute violation: **27.50 Public defender; qualifications; election.** For each judicial circuit, there shall be a public defender who shall be, and shall have been for the preceding **5 years, a member in good standing of The Florida Bar.**

4) Statute violation: **27.405 (1) Court-appointed counsel; Justice Administration Commission tracking & reporting**

(Question 5)

The commission shall prepare & issue on a quarterly basis a statewide report comparing actual year-to-date expenditures to budget amounts for each of the judicial circuits. The commission shall prepare & issue on an annual basis a statewide report comparing performance measures for each of the judicial circuits. The commission shall distribute copies of the quarterly & annual reports to the Governor, the Chief Justice of the Supreme Court, the President of the Senate, & the Speaker of the House of Representatives.

IN THE COUNTY COURT OF THE FIFTEENTH JUDICIAL CIRCUIT,
IN AND FOR PALM BEACH COUNTY, FLORIDA
CRIMINAL DIVISION "B"

State of Florida,   CASE NO.: 19MM005685AMB
vs.

Brian Dale Bailey,
    Defendant
_____/

Motion to Appoint Experts
to Evaluate Defendant For Competency

The Public Defender for the Fifteenth Judicial Circuit, through the Assistant Public Defender, moves this Court, pursuant to Section 916.12, Florida Statutes (2019) and Florida Rule of Criminal Procedure 3.210(b), to issue an Order appointing experts to evaluate Brian Dale Bailey for competency to proceed with any material stage of the proceeding and to stay further proceedings pending the further order of this Court.

Grounds for Motion

Bailey does not appear to appreciate the range and nature of possible penalties. Bailey does not appear able to testify relevantly in his defense. He also does not seem to understand the adversarial nature of the legal process.

Relief Requested

For these reasons, counsel requests the Court immediately enter an Order Appointing Experts to determine Brian Dale Bailey's mental condition and competency to proceed.

Certificate of Good Faith

Counsel certifies that this motion is made in good faith and on reasonable grounds to believe that Brian Dale Bailey is incompetent to proceed.

Respectfully submitted,

CAREY HAUGHWOUT
Public Defender, 15th Judicial Circuit
421 3rd Street
West Palm Beach, FL 33401
Telephone: (561) 355-7500

_____
Raymon Burns
Assistant Public Defender
Fla. Bar No.: 1012306

CERTIFICATE OF SERVICE

I certify that I served this motion to Ryan Meyers, Assistant State Attorney, Division "B"

or the Assistant State Attorney currently assigned in STAC at the time of filing, via the STAC case

management exchange on this __2___ day of July, 2019.

_____
Raymon Burns
Assistant Public Defender

7/3/2019

Filing # 92039751 E-Filed 07/03/2019 08:20:07 AM

IN THE COUNTY COURT OF THE FIFTEENTH JUDICIAL CIRCUIT,
IN AND FOR PALM BEACH COUNTY, FLORIDA
CRIMINAL DIVISION "B"

STATE OF FLORIDA,   CASE NO. 19MM005685AMB

vs.

Brian Dale Bailey,
        Defendant.
_____/

NOTICE OF HEARING

PLEASE TAKE NOTICE that the Public Defender will call up the Motion to Appoint Experts before the Honorable LEONARD HANSER on Monday July 08, 2019 at 8:30 AM in COURTROOM 2E, of the Palm Beach County Courthouse, 205 N. Dixie Highway, West Palm Beach, Florida.

___X_____ Movant's attorney has spoken in person or by telephone with the attorney(s) for all parties who may be affected by the relief sought in the motion in a good faith effort to resolve or narrow the issues raised.

_____ Movant's attorney has attempted to speak in person or by telephone with the attorney(s) for all parties who may be affected by the relief sought in the motion.

_____One or more of the parties who may be affected by the motion are self represented.

Respectfully submitted,

CAREY HAUGHWOUT
Public Defender, 15th Judicial Circuit
421 3rd Street
West Palm Beach, FL 33401
Telephone: (561) 355-7500

If you are a person with a disability who needs any accommodation in order to participate in this proceeding, you are entitled, at no cost to you, to the provision of certain assistance. Please contact the ADA Coordinator in the Administrative Office of the Court, Palm Beach County Courthouse, 205 N. Dixie Highway, Room 5.2500, West Palm Beach, FL 33401; telephone (561)355-4380 within two (2) working days of your receipt of this Notice; if you are hearing or voice impaired, call 1-800-955-8771.

FILED: PALM BEACH COUNTY, FL, SHARON R. BOCK, CLERK, 07/03/2019 08:20:07 AM

Raymon Burns
Assistant Public Defender
Fla. Bar No. 1012306

CERTIFICATE OF SERVICE

I HEREBY CERTIFY that a true and correct copy hereof has been served to Ryan Myers, Assistant State Attorney, Division "B" OR the Assistant State Attorney currently assigned in STAC at the time of filing, via the STAC case management exchange on this __2__ day of July, 2019.

Raymon Burns
Assistant Public Defender

Brian Bailey — Time sheet   7/3/2019

Case # C-50-2019-MM-005685-AXXX-MB

Date	Time - in	Time - out	Hours	Total	
5/12/2019 - 7/1/2019	back pace	—	1	1 Hr	1
7-2-2019	Back pace	—	3	4 Hr	2
7-3-2019	12:20 PM	4:20 PM	4	8 Hr	3
7-3-2019	4:45 PM	9:45 PM	5	13 Hr	4
7-4-2019	1:00 PM	3:00 PM	2	15 Hr	5
7-4-2019	6:00 PM	7:15 PM	1:15	16.25 Hr	6
7-4-2019	8:00 PM	9:30 PM	1:30	17.75 Hr	7
7-5-2019	1:45 PM	4:15 PM	3:30	20.25 Hr	8
7-6-2019	2:30 PM	3:30 PM	1	21.25 Hr	9
7-8-2019	9:15 PM	12:15 Am	3	24.25 Hr	10
7-9-2019	4:20 AM	5:00 AM	:30	24.75 Hr	11
7-9-2019	5:00 AM	8:00 AM	3	27.75 Hr	12
7-15-2019	12:00 PM	2:30 PM	2:30	30.25 Hr	13
7-15-2019	6:00 PM	7:15 PM	1:15	31.50 Hr	14
7-17-2019	12:00 PM	3:30 PM	3:30	35 Hr	15
7-18-2019	11:45 PM	2:15 PM	2:30	37.50 HR	16
7-18-2019	7:15 PM	9:30 PM	2:15	39.75 HR	17
7-19-2019	5:30 AM	7:00 AM	1:30	41.25 Hr	18
7-19-2019	12:30 PM	1:15 PM	:45	42 Hr	19
7-22-2019	3:00 PM	3:30 PM	:30	42.50 Hr	20
7-22-2019	6:00 PM	8:30 PM	2:30	45 Hr	21
7-24-2019	7:00 PM	9:15 PM	2:15	47.25 Hr	22
7-27-2019	6:30 PM	7:45 PM	1:15	48.50 Hr	23
7-29-2019	7:00 PM	7:15 PM	:15	48.75 HR	24
7-30-2019	4:45 PM	6:30 PM	1:45	50.50 HR	25
7-30-2019	7:30 PM	9:00 PM	2	52.50 Hr	26
8-2-2019	2:15 PM	4:15 PM	2	54.50 HR	27
8-3-2019	12:30 PM	3:30 PM	3	57.50 HR	28
8-7-2019	6:30 PM	10:30 PM	4	61.50 HR	29
8-8-2019	12:00 PM	3:30 PM	3:30	65 Hr	30
8-9-2019	12:15 PM	4:00 PM	3:45	68.75 Hr	31
8-10-2019	No clock	—	—		32
8-11-2019	1:15 PM	5:00 PM	3:45	72.50 HR	33
8-11-2019	6:30 PM	8:00 PM	1:30	74 Hr	34
8-15-2019	7:30 PM	8:00 PM	:30	74.50 HR	35
8-16-2019	8:30 PM	9:00 PM	:30	75 HR	36
8-19-2019	1:45 PM	5:15 PM	4:30	79.50 HR	37
8-21-2019	2:00 PM	3:00 PM	1	80.50 Hr	38

On the date **7/3/2019**, while being held at the **West Detention Center**, Belle Glade, while being locked in a cell, Mr. Bailey created his **Defense for case # 50-2019-MM-005685-AXXX-MB**

Hello & my name is **Brian Bailey**, born on 2/24/1979. I'm here today because I have been charged with **1 count of Misdemeanor Trespass after warning**. Over the last serval months dating into last-year, I've been serving for the **Christ Fellowship Church, Royal Palm Beach campus** in **Florida**. Looking to grow with our community by attending church & being enrolled at a state college. I started out serving as a greeter, then moved to the Production Team. As time passed, I jumped in wherever I was needed. Leading me to the coffee shop & Traffic Team.

On the morning of **5/5/2019**, I was heading into the church to serve & worship, when I was struck by an SUV at a high rate of speed, while riding my bicycle. Fracturing my right wrist & wrecking the bicycle I was riding. Once the Sheriff's Department arrived, I called Mr. Gary Borge, one of the brothers of Christ Fellowship Church & asked if he would mind picking me up, then giving me a ride to the church. He gladly showed up to the scene, putting my bicycle in his truck & carried me to the church. When arriving I headed into the area called, "The Traffic Cubby" located in the back of the church. I did my usual routine, grabbing a radio off of a charger.

I started off to the front parking area. When I saw one of the youth group members who I had a gift for, it was a Yo-yo. Wanting to give him this gift I turned around & headed back inside to ask Mr. Gary Borge for his truck keys. After locating Mr. Borge & him locating the key, then passing them to me. I went off to the back-parking lot, opened the truck & located the gift. Locking the truck & heading through the back doors of the church. I was intercepted by security & asked to go with them. I followed him into an office, where the room quickly filled with Pastor Oscar & serval other men.

Pastor Oscar started speaking about a previous conversation that had taken place. Where he asked me not to hug ladies in the front & rather to the side. I had done as he requested in that conversation. Now with these other men in the room he claimed that I was chasing women around our church & was questioning my behavior in the church. He then brought up my prayer card I filled out, asking for help with my medical conditions. Embarrassing me & sharing my private prayers amongst other men.

While I was under the impression prayer cards were to write down your prayers & hopes, while in need of help & having dreams. I was never chasing any women in our church, nor have I ever given or asked for any female's telephone number or emails for personal relationships. After Pastor Oscar stop speaking, another man started speaking who was wearing a polo shirt, I don't know his name or position held. He shared some words with me & asked if I had anything that belong to the church. After being hit by an SUV automobile only a few hours earlier, I don't recall the details of who or what was said in the office.

Now, I was being escorted outside to the front parking lot. Standing in front of a Sheriff's Department's automobile, I was met by two of Christ Fellowship security team. One of which I serve with in the morning setting up the cones named, "Floyd". He asked, "where can I take you"? Since my bicycle was damaged & not ridable. I replied, "Let me call my Aunt Brenda Taft & ask her if you can drop me off there". Then calling her by telephone, she picked up & I asked could I go to her house, she said yes. Then the two men dropped me off in Lake Worth.

Later that day, Mr. Borge met up with me & dropped off the bicycle repaired and ridable. He also handed me twenty dollars, which I didn't ask for & tried giving it back to him, but he wouldn't accept it, I deposited it into the bank & transferred the funds to Christ Fellowship online. Now one week later on Sunday **5/12/2019**, I arrived at Christ Fellowship, Royal Palm Beach to **worship & pray.**

When arriving, I walked to the front of the chapel, when I saw Pastor Oscar, I said, "I'm here" & smiled. Pastor Oscar Soto then quickly left his position & guided me outside to the eastside of the building. We were met outside by security & Sheriff's Department. Pastor Oscar Soto, "unsure" of what to have the Sheriff's Department do. We stood outside waiting for him to be advised. I then heard him say to the Sheriff's Department, "He's Going". At that time, I was placed in the back of a Sheriff's cruiser and taken to Belle Glade's West Detention Center, controlled by **Palm Beach County Sheriff's Office** - Department of Corrections.

Now serving a total of 102 days in custody with a fractured right wrist & left shoulder needing a total reconstructive surgery. Being punished for attempting to grow with our community by serving, worshiping, praying, tithing & living in an unstable environment at times, while studying for Palm Beach State College.

Defense
(5/5/2019 — 5/12/2019)

Case #   50-2019-MM-005685-AXXX-MB

Hello and my name is Brian Bailey, born on 2/24/1979. I'm here today because I have been charged with 1 count of Misdemeanor Trespass after warning. Over the last several months dating into last year, I've been serving for the Christ Fellowship Church, Royal Palm Beach, Florida Campus. Looking to grow with our community by attending church and college. I started out serving as a greeter, then moved up to the Production Team. As time passed I jumped in where given I was needed, leading me to the coffee shop and Traffic Team.

On the morning of May 5, 2019, I was heading into the church to serve and worship, when I was struck by an SUV while riding my bicycle. Faceting my right wrist and wreathing my bicycle. Once the Sheriff's department arrived, I called Gary Bange, one of the brothers of Christ Fellowship Church, and asked if he would mind picking me up, then giving me a ride to the church. He gladly showed up to the scene, putting my bicycle in his trunk and carried me to the church.

When arriving I headed into the area called the Traffic lobby, located in the back of the church. I did my usual routine, grabbing a radio off of a charger. I started off to the front parking area. When I saw one of the youth group members who I had a gift for. Wanting to give him this gift, I turned around and headed back inside to ask Mr. Gary Bange for his truck keys. After locating Mr. Bange and him locating the keys, then passing them to me. I went off to the back parking lot, opened the trunk and located the gift. Locking the trunk and heading through the back doors of the church.

I was intercepted by security, and asked to go with them. I followed him into an office, where the room quickly filled with Pastor Oscar and several other men. Pastor Oscar started speaking about a previous conversation that had taken place. Where he asked me not to hug ladies in the front and rather to the side. I had done as he requested in that conversation. Now with three other men in the room he claimed that I was chasing women around our church, and was questing my behavior in the church. He then brought up my prayer card I filled out, asking for help with my medical conditions. Embarrassing me and sharing my private prayers amongst other men. While I was under the aggression, prayers chairs were to write down your prayers and hopes while in need of help. I was never chasing any women in our church, nor have I ever given or asked for any females telephone numbers or emails for personal relationships.

Pg 1.2

145

After Pastor Oscar stop speaking, another man started speaking who was wearing a polo shirt, I don't know his name or position held. He shared some words with me, and ask if I had anything that belong to the church. After being hit by an SUV automobile only a few hours ealier I don't recall the details of who or what was said in the office. Now I was being escorted outside to the front parking lot. Standing in front of a Sheriffs car, I was met by two of Christ fellowship security team. One of whom I serve with in the morning setting up the cones named "Floyd". He asked "where can I take you? Since my bicycle was damaged and not rideable. I replied "let me call my Aunt Brenda and ask if you can drop me off there". Then calling her by telephone, she picked up and I asked could I go to her house, she said yes. The two men dropped me off in the town of Lantana.

Later that day, Gary Banga met up with me and dropped off the bicycle repaired and rideable. He also handed me twenty dollars, which I didn't ask for and tried giving it back to him, but he wouldn't accept it, I deposited it into the bank and transfered the funds to Christ fellowship office. Now one week later on Sunday May 12, 2019, I arrived at Christ fellowship, Royal Palm Beach to ~~worship and~~ ~~pray~~. When arriving I walked to the front of the chapel, when I saw Pastor Oscar Andy, I said "I'm here" and smiled. Pastor Oscar then quickly left his position and guided me outside to the east side of the building. We were met outside by security and Sheriff's department.

Pastor Oscar unsure of what to have the Sheriff's department do. We stood outside waiting for him to be advised. I then heard him say to the Sheriff's department "he's going". At that time I was placed in the back of a Sheriff's cruiser and taken to Belle Glade's west detention center, controlled by Palm Beach County Sheriff's Office department of Corrections. Now serving a total of 102 days in custody with a fractured right wrist and left shoulder needing a reconstructive surgery. Being punished for attemping to give with his community by serving, worshipping, praying, and tithing. (STOP READING)!!

Thank you for taking the time to listen to my story.

God Bless!

Brian Brant

Brian Bailey   8/21/2019

Notes: On 7-4-2019 when attempting to reach the
state appointed public defender, an
alteration broke out between to inmates
in block E-1. In return this shut down
the block and and all inmates return
to there bunks. I was unable to attemp
to reach the state appointed public defender.

Timesheet
CASE # 50-2019-MM-005685-AXXX-MB

Date	Time-in	Time-out	Hours	Total

On the date of 7/4/2019, Mr. Bailey created an information request form, for the Assistant Public Defender in Case# 50-2019-MM-005685-AXXX-MB

1) Does Assistant Public Defender Ilana Felice Marcus have a doctorate degree, certification or license with a primary focus in behavior analyst from an accredited university? In certified behavior analyst pursuant to s. 393.17

    Answer: Unanswered (Never given the opportunity to ask this question)

If the answer is no, then **Statute 393.17** has been violated by the Assistant Public Defender Ilana Felice Marcus. Creating hurdles in the case that need not be there. This Statute states, for the record.

Statute **393.17 Behavioral programs; certification of**

behavior analysts

1) The agency may establish a certification process for behavior analysts in order to ensure that only qualified employees and service providers provide behavioral analysis services to clients. The procures must be established by rule and must include criteria for scope of practice, qualifications for certification, including training and testing requirements, continuing education requirements for ongoing certification, and standard performance. The procedures must also include decertification procedures that may be used to determine whether an individual continues to meet the qualifications for certification or the professional performance standards and, if not, the procedures necessary to decertify an employee or service provider.

Statute 393.18 Comprehensive transitional education program

1) A comprehensive transitional education program serves individuals who have developmental disabilities, severe maladaptive behaviors, severe maladaptive behaviors & co-occurring complex medical conditions, or a dual diagnosis of developmental disability & mental illness. Services provided by the program must be temporary in nature & delivered in a manner designed to achieve the primary goal of incorporating the principles of self-determination & person-centered planning to transition individuals to the most appropriate, least restrictive community living option of their choice which is not operated as a comprehensive transitional education program. The supervisor of the clinical director of the program licensee must hold a doctorate degree with a primary focus in behavior analysis from an accredited university, be a certified behavior analyst pursuant to s. 393.17, & have at least one-year of experience in providing behavior analysis services for individuals in developmental disabilities. The staff must include behavior analyst and teachers, as appropriate, who must be available to provide services in each component center or unit of the program. A behavior analyst must be certified pursuant to s.393.17

Brian Bailey   7/4/2019
                    Assistant Public Defender
                    (information request)

Case # 50-2019-mm-005685-AXKX-mB

1) Does Assistant Public Defender Ms. Ilana Marcus have
a doctorate degree, certificate or licenses with a
primary focus in behavior analyst from an accredited
university? In certified behavior analyst pursuant to s. 393.17
Answer:

2) Does Assistant Public Defender Ms. Ilana Marcus have
at least one year of experience in providing behavior
analysis services for individuals in developmental
disabilities?
Answer:

393.17 - Behavioral programs; certification of behavior analysts
    (1) The agency may establish a certification process for behavior analysts
    in order to ensure that only qualified employees and service providers
    provide behavioral analysis services to clients. The procedures must
    be established by rule and must include criteria for scope of
    practice, qualifications for certification, including training and testing
    requirements, continuing education requirements for ongoing
    certification, and standard performance. The procedures must
    also include decertification procedures that may be used to
    determine whether an individual continues to meet the
    qualifications for certification or the professional performance
    standards and, if not, the procedures necessary to
    decertify an employee or service provider.

393.18 - Comprehensive transitional education program
    A comprehensive transitional education program serves individuals
    who have developmental disabilities, severe maladaptive
    behaviors, severe maladaptive behaviors and co-occurring complex
    medical conditions, or a dual diagnosis of developmental disability
    and mental illness. Services provided by the program must be temporary
    in nature and delivered in a manner designed to achieve the primary
    goal of incorporating the principles of self-determination and
    person-centered planning to transition individuals to the most appropriate,
    least restrictive community living option of their choice which is not
    operated as a comprehensive transitional education program. The
    supervisor of the clinical director of the program licensee must hold
    a doctorate degree with a primary focus on behavior analysis from an
    accredited university, be a certified behavior analyst pursuant to
    s. 393.17, and have at least 2 years of experience in providing
    behavior analysis services for individuals in developmental disabilities.
    The staff must include behavior analysts and teachers, as appropriate,
    who must be available to provide services in each component center or units
    of the program. A behavior analyst must be certified pursuant to s. 393.17   Pg 4

Case # 50-2019-MM-005085-AXXX-MB

Violation

1) s. 27.18 Assistant to state attorney

The state attorney, by and with the consent of court, may procure the assistance of any member of the bar when the amount of the state business renders it necessary, either in the grand jury room to advise them upon legal points and framing indictments, or in court to prosecute criminals; but, such assistant shall not be authorized to sign any indictments or administer any oaths, or to perform any other duty except the giving of legal advice, drawing up of indictments and the prosecution of criminals in open court. His or her compensation shall be paid by the state attorney and not by the state.

On the date of 7/4/2019, while Mr. Bailey was still creating a defense & mind stimulating by reading the *NIV Holy Bible*, *West's Florida Law & Exercising,* pumping out 1000 squats, while having two arms with injuries. He made an attempt to contact the Public Defenders office more than one time. Unable to reach the Assistant Public Defender, working the open case. During this time, an altercation broke out between a couple of inmates. Locking down the Block E-1 & requiring everyone to return to their pod area or bunk. While Sheriff's Department defused the situation & provided safety for the inmates.

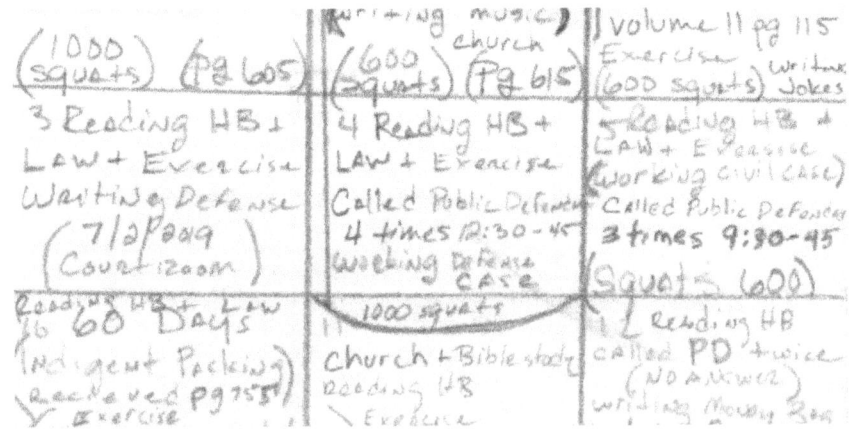

On the date of **7/5/2019**, Mr. Bailey created a page with a number of Statutes relating to **Evidence Code**. While waiting to hear from the Public Defender's office, in regard to what evidence was being brought forward to prosecute.

Evidence Code

Case# 50-2019-MM-005685-AXXX-MB

1) Statute **90.105 Preliminary questions**
   (1) When the relevancy of evidence depends upon the existence of a **preliminary fact**, the court shall admit the proffered evidence when there is prima facie evidence sufficient to support a finding of the **preliminary fact**. If prima facie evidence **is not introduced** to support a finding of the preliminary fact, the court may admit the proffered evidence subject to the subsequent introduction of prima facie evidence of the preliminary fact.

2) Statute **90.202 Matters which may be judicially Noticed**

   (12) Facts that are not subject to dispute because they are capable of accurate & ready determination by resort to sources whose accuracy cannot be questioned.

3) Statute **90.202 Compulsory judicial notice upon request**

A court shall take judicial notice of any matter in s. 90.202 when a party request it and:

(1) Gives each adverse party timely written notice of the request, proof of which is filed with the court, to enable the adverse party to prepare to meet the request.

(2) Furnishes the court with sufficient information to enable it to take judicial notice of the matter.

4) Statute **90.302 Classification of rebuttable presumptions**

Every rebuttable presumption is either:

(1) A presumption affecting the burden of producing evidence and requiring the trier of fact to assume the existence of the presumed fact, unless creditable evidence sufficient to sustain a finding of the nonexistence of the presumed fact shall be determined from the evidence without regards to the presumption; or

(2) A presumption affecting the burden of proof that imposes upon the party against whom it operates the burden of proof concerning the nonexistence of the presumed fact.

CASE # 50-2019-MM-005685-AXXX-MB

1) s. 90.105 Preliminary questions
   (2) When the relevancy of evidence depends upon the existence
        of a preliminary fact, the court shall admit the proffered
        evidence when there is prima facie evidence sufficient to
        support a finding of the preliminary fact. If prima facie
        evidence is not introduced to support a finding of the
        preliminary fact, the court may admit the proffered
        evidence subject to the subsequent introduction of prima
        facie evidence of the preliminary fact.

2) s. 90.202 Matters which may be judicially noticed
   (12) Facts that are not subject to dispute because they
         are capable of accurate and ready determination by
         resort to sources whose accuracy cannot be questioned.

3) s. 90.203 Compulsory judicial notice upon request
         A court shall take judicial notice of any matter in
         s. 90.202 when a party requests it, And:
   (1) Gives each adverse party timely written notice of the
        request, proof of which is filed with the court, the
        enable the adverse party to prepare to meet the request.

   (2) Furnishes the court with sufficient information to
        enable it to take judicial notice of the matter.

4) s. 90.302 Classification of rebuttable presumptions
         Every rebuttable presumption is either:
   (1) A presumption affecting the burden of producing evidence and requiring
        the trier of fact to assume the existence of the presumed fact,
        unless credible evidence sufficient to sustain a finding of the
        nonexistence of the presumed fact is introduced, in which event
        the existence or nonexistence of the presumed fact shall
        be determined from the evidence without regard to the
        presumption; or

   (2) A presumption affecting the burden of proof that imposes
        upon the party against whom it operates the burden of proof
        concerning the nonexistence of the presumed fact.

*Below is a list of Statutes that revolve around the **power of confidentially**, in this it refers to:*

(Prayer Card)

Statute violations:

1) Statute **27.151 Confidentiality of specified executive orders; criteria**

   (1) *If the Governor provides in an executive order issued pursuant to s. 27.14 or s. 27.15 that the order or a portion thereof is **confidential**, the order or portion so designated, the application of the Governor to the Supreme Court and all proceedings thereon, and the order of the Supreme Court shall be **confidential** & exempt from the provisions of s. 119.07 (1)*

   (2) *The Governor shall base his or her decision to make an executive order **confidential** on the criteria set forth in s. 119.14*

   (3) *To maintain the **confidential** of the executive order, the state attorney, upon entering the circuit court of assignment, shall immediately have the executive order sealed by the court prior to filing it with the clerk of the circuit court, The Governor may make public any executive order issued pursuant to s. 27.14 or s. 27.15 by a subsequent executive order, and at the expiration of a confidential executive order or any extensions thereof, the executive order & all associated orders and reports shall be open to the public pursuant to chapter 119 unless the information contained in the executive order is confidential pursuant to the provisions of chapter 39, chapter 415, chapter 984, or chapter 985.*

Statute violations by **Pastor Oscar Soto** *include:*

1) *Statute* **836.05 Threats; extortion**
   *Whoever, either verbally or by a written or printed communication, maliciously threatens to accuse another of any crime or **offense** or by such communication maliciously threatens an injury to the person, property or **reputation** of another, or maliciously threatens to **expose another to disgrace**, or to **expose any secret** affecting another, or to impute any deformity or **lack of chastity** to another, with intent thereby to extort money or any pecuniary advantage whatsoever, or with intent to compel the person so threatened, or any other person, to do any act of refrain from doing any act against his or her will, shall be guilty of a felony of the second degree, punishable as provided in s. 775.082, s.775.083 or s. 775.084*

Case # 50-2019-MM-005685-AXXX-MB

• Violations

(Prayer Card)

1) s. 27.151 Confidentiality of specified executive orders; criteria

(1) If the Governor provides in an executive order issued pursuant to s. 27.14 or s.27.15 that the order or a portion thereof is confidential, the order or portion so designated, the application of the Governor to the Supreme Court and all proceedings thereon, and the order of the Supreme Court shall be confidential and exempt from the provisions of s. 113.07(1)

(2) The Governor shall base his or her decision to make an executive order confidential on the criteria set forth in s. 119.14

(3) To maintain the confidential of the executive order, the state attorney, upon entering the circuit of assignment, shall immediately have the executive order sealed by the court prior to filing it with the clerk of the circuit court. The Governor may make public any executive order issued pursuant to s. 27.14 or s.27.15 by a subsequent executive order, and at the expiration of a confidential executive order or any extension thereof, the executive order and all associated orders and requests shall be open to the public pursuant to chapter 119 unless the information contained in the executive order is confidential pursuant to the provisions of chapter 39, chapter 415, chapter 984, or chapter 985.

2) s. 836.05 Threats; extortion

Whoever, either verbally or by a written or printed communication, maliciously threatens to accuse another of any crime or offense, or by such communication maliciously threatens an injury to the person, property or reputation of another, or maliciously threatens to expose another to disgrace, or to expose any secret affecting another, or to impute any deformity or lack of chastity to another, with intent thereby to extort money or any pecuniary advantage whatsoever, or with intent to compel the person so threatened, or any other person, to do any act or refrain from doing any act against his or her will, shall be guilty of a felony of the second degree, punishable as provided in s. 775.082, s. 775.083 or s. 775.084

On the date of **7/8/2019**, things seamed busy on both ends of the court system. Both on the inside, while Mr. Bailey was turning into an administrator creating paperwork on the daily bases & on the outside witness were being subpoena. It was time he writes a letter to the Judge in regard to his disappointment with the Public Defender's office. Spending quite a bit of time going through the notes written down on scrap pieces of paper & then creating paper with lines. Mr. Bailey was to the point of requesting a new appointed attorney, while watching the Circuit Court continue to make mistakes & violate statutes, while being held in custody.

Just before the trial date, the courts canceled trial. Prolonging the case, defeating the purpose of, **"Right to a Speedy Trial"** blocking Mr. Bailey from getting back to **Palm Beach State College**, & continuing to gain a Higher Education. Just after taking Government Loans with financial aid & living outside. Now, claiming that he had to see a doctor for competence, after putting all the necessary paperwork together & not with the help from any county assistance. Competence wasn't the issue here & the court were using the tricks of Law, combined with **The Fifteenth Judicial Circuit / County Court** in and for **Palm Beach County, Florida.**

7/8/2019

IN THE COUNTY COURT OF THE FIFTEENTH JUDICIAL CIRCUIT
IN AND FOR PALM BEACH COUNTY, FLORIDA - CRIMINAL DIVISION
CIRCUIT/COUNTY COURT
Court Event Form

DEFENDANT: BRIAN DALE BAILEY
CASE NO: 50-2019-MM-005685-AXXX-MB

STATE OF FLORIDA   DATE: 7/8/2019
vs.
DEFENDANT: BRIAN DALE BAILEY   JACKET #:   0403731
CASE NO: 50-2019-MM-005685-AXXX-MB   BOOKING #: 2019015844
DIVISION: B: Cnty Crim - B (County)

PRESIDING JUDGE: HANSER, JUDGELEONARD   START TIME: 8:49 AM
ASA: MYERS, RYAN   END TIME: 8:52 AM
ATTORNEY:
PUBLIC DEFENDER: BURNS, RAYMON
CO-COUNSEL: COURT REPORTER
DEPUTY CLERK: SH   COURT TYPE: MH - MOTION
                                                                     HEARING

COURT ROOM: 2E (Main Branch)

Reset For
Court Date Scheduled - STCK - STATUS CHECK - 7/24/2019 8:30 AM - 2E (Main Branch) MB, 205 N. Dixie
Highway West Palm Beach FL 33401 - RE COMPETANCY
Court Date Cancelled - JT - JURY TRIAL - 7/24/2019 8:30 AM - 2E (Main Branch) MB

Motion - Granted   - DEFENSE TO APPOINT EXPERT WITNESS RE: COMPETANCY - ORDER FILED
Other: DEFENDANT NOT PRESENT

Count 1 - MF TRESPASS AFTER WARNING 810.09(2A)

160

7/8/2019

IN THE CIRCUIT/COUNTY COURT OF THE FIFTEENTH JUDICIAL CIRCUIT
IN AND FOR PALM BEACH COUNTY, FLORIDA

STATE OF FLORIDA

-Vs-

BRIAN DALE BAILEY
GENERAL DELIVERY
WEST PALM BEACH, FL 32200

Date: 07/08/2019

Case No: 50-2019-MM-005685-AXXX-MB

Division: B: Cnty Crim - B (County)

NOTICE OF HEARING
THE DEFENDANT MUST BE PRESENT AT THIS HEARING

For Criminal Charges: Failure to Appear will result in a Bond Forfeiture or
revocation of own recognizance (O.R.) and a Capias/Warrant being issued for your arrest.
For Civil Traffic Charges: Failure to appear may result in the suspension of your driver's license.
IF YOUR CASE IS ON-CALL, CONTACT YOUR ATTORNEY FOR THE TIME TO APPEAR
YOU ARE HEREBY NOTIFIED that this case is scheduled

DATE:	TIME:	HEARING TYPE:	LOCATION:
7/24/2019	8:30 AM	STCK - STATUS CHECK	2E (Main Branch) MB, 205 N. Dixie Highway West Palm Beach FL 33401

BE PREPARED TO PAY COURT COSTS AND FINES ASSESSED BY THE COURT AT THIS HEARING
"IF YOU INTEND TO REQUEST THE SERVICES OF THE PUBLIC DEFENDER, YOU MUST FILE AN APPLICATION AT THE CLERK &
COMPTROLLER'S OFFICE AND BE APPOINTED THE PUBLIC DEFENDER BEFORE YOUR COURT DATE. THE APPLICATION FEE IS $50.00."
Civil Traffic Charges are not eligible for a Public Defender.

SHARON R. BOCK,
CLERK & COMPTROLLER
BY: SH

Deft/Atty: MAILED TO DEFENDANT

Deputy Clerk

cc: RYAN MYERS
        BURNS, RAYMON A

IN THE CIRCUIT/COUNTY COURT OF THE FIFTEENTH JUDICIAL CIRCUIT
IN AND FOR PALM BEACH COUNTY, FLORIDA

"If you are a <u>person with a disability</u> who needs any accommodation in order to participate in this proceeding, you are entitled, at no cost to you, to the provision of certain assistance. Please contact Tammy Anton, Americans with Disabilities Act Coordinator, Palm Beach County Courthouse, 205 North Dixie Hwy, West Palm Beach, FL 33401; telephone number (561) 355-4380 at least 7 days before your scheduled court appearance, or immediately upon receiving this notification if the time before the scheduled appearance is less than 7 days; if you are hearing or voice impaired, call 711."

"Si usted es una <u>persona minusválida</u> que necesita algún acomodamiento para poder participar en este procedimiento, usted tiene derecho, sin tener gastos propios, a que se le provea cierta ayuda. Tenga la amabilidad de ponerse en contacto con Tammy Anton, 205 N. Dixie Highway, West Palm Beach, Florida 33401; teléfono número (561) 355-4380, por lo menos 7 días antes de la cita fijada para   su comparecencia en los tribunales, o inmediatamente después de recibir esta notificación si el tiempo antes de la comparecencia que se ha programado es menos de 7 días; si usted tiene discapacitación del oído o de la voz, llame al 711."

"Si ou se yon <u>moun ki enfim</u> ki bezwen akomodasyon pou w ka patisipe nan pwosedi sa, ou kalifye san ou pa gen okenn lajan pou w peye, gen pwovizyon pou jwen kèk èd. Tanpri kontakte Tammy Anton, kòòdonatè pwogram Lwa pou ameriken ki Enfim yo nan Tribinal Konte Palm Beach la ki nan 205 North Dixie Highway, West Palm Beach, Florida 33401; telefòn li se (561) 355-4380 nan 7 jou anvan dat ou gen randevou pou parèt nan tribinal la, oubyen imedyatman apre ou fin resevwa konvokasyon an si lè ou gen pou w parèt nan tribinal la mwens ke 7 jou; si ou gen pwoblèm pou w tande oubyen pale, rele 711."

162

IN THE COUNTY COURT OF THE FIFTEENTH JUDICIAL CIRCUIT,
IN AND FOR PALM BEACH COUNTY, FLORIDA
CRIMINAL DIVISION "B"

STATE OF FLORIDA   CASE NO. 19MM005685AMB

vs.

Brian Dale Bailey,
        Defendant.

_____

ORDER GRANTING EXAMINATION
OF DEFENDANT'S COMPETENCY

THIS CAUSE having come to be heard upon the Defendant's written motion in the above-styled cause, requesting a determination of the competency of the defendant to stand trial, and the Court being otherwise fully advised, it is

ORDERED AND ADJUDGED

1. That said motion is hereby Granted.

2. The following expert(s) is appointed to examine the defendant whose name, address and phone number is:

Dr. Lisa Faraldo 140 JFK Drive, Suite 146, Atlantis, FL 33462, (954) 812-0900

3. If the defendant is in custody, the Sheriff of Palm Beach County shall permit the above-named expert(s) to enter the Palm Beach County Jail to conduct the foregoing evaluation of the defendant upon presentment of this Order. If the defendant is not in custody, the expert is to contact defense counsel, or pro se defendant, for scheduling.

4. The expert is to give timely notice to the parties of the date and place of the examination.

5. A copy of the order serves as authorization for the expert to inspect and copy any discoverable information relating to the Defendant maintained by the defense counsel, Clerk of this Court, State Attorney's Office, any hospital, doctor, or any health care provider, therapist, psychiatrist, psychologist, counselor, or any mental health provider, or other social or human services agency without the necessity of written consent by Defendant.

6. This cause is scheduled for a hearing on the issue of the defendant's competency to proceed on, Wednesday, July 24, 2019 at 8:30 AM.

7. The expert shall submit a written evaluation of the defendant's mental condition to this Court with copies to the Assistant State Attorney and the Attorney for the Defendant on or before the _19_ day of _July_, 20_19_, which shall include but is not limited to:

a. **Competence to Proceed** (See Fla.R.Crim.P. 3.211(a), F.S. §§916.115, 916.301). Whether the defendant has sufficient present ability to consult with counsel with a reasonable degree of rational understanding and whether the defendant has a rational, as well as factual,

SCANNED

JUL 08 2019

FILED

JUL 08 2019

understanding of the pending proceedings. In considering the issue of competence to proceed, the examining expert shall consider and include in their report, the following factors, and any other factors deemed relevant by the experts, as they pertain to the defendant's capacity and/or ability to:

1. Appreciate the charges or allegations against him;
2. Appreciate the range and nature of possible penalties which may be imposed against him;
3. Understand the adversary nature of the legal process;
4. Disclose to his attorney facts pertinent to the proceedings at issue;
5. Manifest appropriate courtroom behavior;
6. Testify relevantly;

b. **Recommend Treatment** (See Fla.R.Crim. P. 3.211(b)). Should the appointed expert find that the defendant is incompetent to proceed, then the expert shall determine whether the defendant meets the criteria for involuntary hospitalization and report on any recommended treatment for the defendant to attain competence to proceed. The expert's report and recommendations shall include consideration of the following:

1. The mental illness or intellectual disability causing the incompetence;
2. The treatment or treatments appropriate for the mental illness or intellectual disability of the defendant and an explanation of each of the possible treatment alternative in order of choices;
3. The availability of acceptable treatment, including whether the treatment is available in the community and whether the treatment involves community or residential facilities or inpatient or outpatient settings;
4. The likelihood of the defendant attaining competence under the recommended treatment, an assessment of the probable duration of the treatment required to restore competence, and the probability that the defendant will attain competence to proceed in the foreseeable future;

8. All written reports submitted by the expert shall contain the following:

a. A list of the specific matters referred for evaluation;
b. A description of the evaluation procedure, techniques and tests used in the examination and purpose for each;
c. The expert's clinical observations, findings, and opinions on each issue referred for evaluation by the Court, and specific identification of those issues which the expert could not give an opinion;
d. An identification of the sources of information used by the expert and a presentation of the factual basis for the expert's clinical findings and opinions.

All information contained in the motion to determine competency of the defendant or in any report submitted under this order, insofar as the information relates solely to the issues of competency to proceed or to commitment, shall be used only in determining the mental competency to proceed or the commitment or other treatment of the defendant.

SCANNED

JUL 08 2019

When Mr. Bailey was interviewed by WDC Mental Health Associate Ms. Mary Foss. She did **NOT** comply with (8)a,b,c,d, before having Mr. Bailey Q15 as a suicidal inmate.

Violating multiply statutes in the court of Law.

9. If an order is entered for the determination of competence, the appointed expert shall be paid in accordance with his or her current contract with the responsible party, or in the absence of a contract, the current Administrative Order regarding payment of appointed experts. Evaluations that include both competency and sanity will be proportionately paid for by the responsible parties.

10. Payment for competency evaluations to determine competence to proceed or to determine recommended treatment for competence to proceed shall be made by the Court in accordance with the contract between the Court and the expert, or if no contract exists, then in accordance with the current Administrative Order regarding payment of appointed experts. The expert shall submit the bill and appropriate invoice with an attached copy of this Order Directing Examination of the Defendant's Competency to the Court at:

> Court Administration
> Administrative Office of the Courts
> 205 North Dixie Highway, 5th Floor
> West Palm Beach, FL 33401

When a request is made for an evaluation of the defendant to determine the defendant's sanity or as an aid for sentencing, the requesting party shall pay. Payment shall be made in accordance with the contract between the responsible party and the expert, or if no contract exists, then in accordance with the current Administrative Order regarding payment of appointed experts.

DONE AND ORDERED in Chambers at West Palm Beach, Palm Beach County, Florida this _8_ day of July, 2019.

LEONARD HANSER
County Court Judge

Copies furnished:
Expert, Dr. Lisa Faraldo 140 JFK Drive, Suite 146, Atlantis, FL 33462, (954) 812-0900 lwretzel@gmail.com
Palm Beach County Sheriff's Office – Belle Glade
3228 Gun Club Road West Palm Beach, FL 33406 Email: IMDCOURTORDERS@PBSO.ORG
Ryan Meyers, Assistant State Attorney, Division B
401 N Dixie Hwy, West Palm Beach, FL 33401, Email: rmeyers@sa15.org
Raymon Burns, Assistant Public Defender, Division B
421 3rd Street west Palm Beach, FL 33401, Email: rburns@pd15.org;jmechetti@pd15.org
Paulina Pasquarelli, Court Administration, 205 N. Dixie Highway, 5th Floor, West Palm Beach, FL 33401 email PPasquarelli@pbcgov.org

SCANNED
JUL 0 8 2019

Details of what happened in the court room on 7/8/2019

On the date of 7/8/2019, Mr. Bailey was walked into the courtroom in custody by Sheriff's Department & guided in the third seat. Unsure why he was there before the trial date of 7/24/2019. Assistant Public Defender Raymon A. Burns his appointed counsel walked over to where he was seated. Assistant Public Defender Raymon A. Burns started off by greeting Mr. Brian Bailey & he replied with a greeting. Then leading into the reason, he had Mr. Bailey transported to the courthouse. APD Raymon A. Burns replied, "my supervisor has requested that you visit with a doctor". APD Raymon A. Burns is referring to a behavior analyst expert.

This was to Mr. Bailey surprise, because on 7/2/2019, Mr. Bailey was interrogated by, Assistant Public Defender Ilana F. Marcus. Followed up by the State Attorney, Public Defender & Judge scheduling a trial date on the docket. After Assistant Public Defender Raymon A. Burns informed Mr. Bailey of this new information & him unaware of his rights & options as a civilian. Mr. Bailey only continued to listen to what he had to say. When Assistant Public Defender Raymon A. Burns stopped speaking, Mr. Bailey said, "Can you answer some questions for me"?

Then pulling out the questions Mr. Bailey had written down on one sheet of paper. As Mr. Bailey asked the questions Assistant Public Defender Raymon A. Burns answered, when Mr. Bailey finished reading the questions to Assistant Public Defender Raymon A. Burns, Mr. Bailey then asked him to write the answers down on that same sheet of paper. Assistant Public Defender Raymon A. Burns complied by writing these answers to the questions. A few minutes later the Sheriff's Department walked over to Mr. Bailey after seeing Assistant Public Defender Raymon A. Burns walk away from where Mr. Bailey was sitting.

The officer handed me four papers from the clerk of the court, with what had just taken place. With no time to review this information, Mr. Bailey was then placed back in handcuffs & escorted out of the courtroom. Then transported back to Belle Glade West Detention Center. Approximately one hour after arriving back in jail. Mr. Bailey made an attempt to speak with the Assistant Public Defender. By using the telephone inside the jail. While waiting on hold for two minutes, the commanding officer requested the inmates return to their bunks, Mr. Bailey then asked the officer if he could stay on the telephone while on hold. The officer named, "Mc Williams" replies, "No". Mr. Bailey then returned to the bunk area & wrote my report. This took place at (approximately 3:30 pm - 3:35pm)

Below is a list of questions Mr. Bailey created on 7/8/2019, after speaking with Assistant Public Defender Raymon A. Burns, in the courtroom earlier that day.

1) Who covers the cost of a behavior analyst expert doctor?
   Answer: Public Defender's office (7/17/2019)

2) Are, "Assistant Public Defender Raymon A. Burns" going to be there to represent Mr. Bailey during interview?
   Answer: Yes (7/17/2019)

3) Did the State prosecutor request a behavior analyst doctor?
   Answer: No (7/17/2019)

4) As Mr. Bailey's representation, how does having a behavior analyst expert, help the defense in this case?
   Answer: It doesn't help with defending the case (7/17/2019)

5) What is, "APD Raymon A. Burns" professional business title?
   Answer: Assistant Public Defender (7/17/2019)

6) What is, "APD Raymon A. Burns" direct telephone number?
   Answer: (561) 355-7543 (7/17/2019)

7) How long has, "Assistant Public Defender Raymon A. Burns" been in good standing with The Florida Bar?
   Answer: November 2018 (7/17/2019)

Brian Bailey   7/8/2019

State Public Defender
(New Information)

1) Who covers the cost of a behavior analyst expert doctor?
   Answer: Public Defender's office   7-17-2019

2) Are (Mr. Raymon Burns) going to be there to represent Mr. Bailey
   during interview?
   Answer: Yes   7-17-2019

3) Did the state prosecutor request a behavior analyst doctor?
   Answer: No   7-17-2019

4) As Mr. Bailey's representation, how does having a behavior
   analyst expert, help the defense in this case?
   Answer: It doesn't help with defending the case.   7-17-2019

5) What is (Mr. Raymon Burns) professional business title?
   Answer: Assistant Public Defender   7-17-2019

6) What is (Mr. Raymon Burns) direct telephone number?
   Answer: 561 355 7543   7-17-2019

7) How long has Mr. Raymon Burns been in good standing with the
   Florida Bar? November 2018   7-17-2019

Statements for Mr. Raymon Burns

1) I would like you to represent me as my legal advisor,
   while visiting with a behavior analyst expert.
   Answer:

Times called:
7/9/2019 1:35-1:40 PM (No Answer)
7/11/2019 12:50-1:00 PM (LM)
7/12/2019 12:30-12:35 (No Answer)
7/14/2019 9:50-9:55 (LM with Assistant) Assistant stated Mr. Burns was available till Friday, out late Sunday,
                                                                    then taking a vacation.

Mr. Raymon Burns   -   (561) 966-4880
                         (561) 355-7500

169

Letter to Judge Hanser Leonard, created on 7/8/2019

Brian Bailey
0403731 - Case# 50-2019-MM-005685-AXXX-MB
Inmate in custody
West Detention Center
38811 James Wheeler Way
Belle Glade, FL 33430

Attention Judge:
Hanser, Judge Leonard
Palm Beach County - Fifteenth Judicial Circuit
205 North Dixie Highway
West Palm Beach, FL 33401

Dear Judge Hanser,

I bring this letter to your attention today, due to a conflict of interest between myself and my appointed representation Assistant Public Defender Raymon A. Burns. I'm requesting new representation for the reason of Statute **27.40 (9) & 27.50**. Due to Assistant Public Defender Raymon A. Burns qualifications in representation, number of cases that have been to trial and lack of experience in trespass cases. Also, allowing Assistant Public Defender Ilana F. Marcus to interrogate me while being held in the courtroom. Not introducing Assistant Public Defender Ilana F. Marcus or sharing her professional position, that Ms. Ilana F. Marcus holds with the court. I've also been unable to reach Assistant Public Defender Raymon A. Burns by telephone, **not one time**.

Assistant Public Defender Raymon A. Burns allowed this integration to take place not only without advising during this interrogation, but without knowing if Assistant Public Defender Ilana F. Marcus holds in current and good standing the proper qualifications, certifications or doctorate degree from an accredited university and having at least one-year experience in providing behavior analysis services for individuals in developmental disabilities.
Following Statutes: **393.17 & 393.18**
Thank you for your time.
God Bless

(Original for Records)

Brian Bailey   7/8/2019
0403731 - Case # 50-2019-MM-005685-AXXX-MB
Inmate in custody
West Detention Center
38811 James Wheeler Way
Belle Glade, Florida

Attention Judge:
Hanzee, Judge Leonard
Palm Beach County - Fifteenth Judicial Circuit
205 North Dix Highway
West Palm Beach, Fl
33401

        Dear Judge Hanzee,

        I bring this letter to your attention today, due to a
conflict of interest between myself and my appointed
representation Mr. Raymon Burns. I'm requesting new representation
for the reason of statue 27.40(9) s/ 27.50. Due to Mr. Burns
qualifications in representation, number of cases that have been to
trial and lack of experience in trespass cases. Also
allowing Assistant Public Defender, Ms. Ilana Marcus to interrogate
me while being held in the courtroom. Not introducing Ms. Marcus
or sharing her professional position, that Ms. Marcus holds
with the court. I've also been unable to reach Mr. Burns by
telephone on 1 time.

        Mr. Raymon Burns allowed this interrogation to take place
not only without advising during this interrogation, but
without knowing if Ms. Ilana Marcus holds in current
and good standing the proper qualifications, certifications or
doctorate degree from an accredited university and having at
least one year experience in providing behavior analysis
services for individuals in developmental disabilities. Following
statues 393.17 (1) s. 393.18

        Thank you for your time.
        God Bless

Brian Brlong - Inmate in custody   7/8/2019
0403731 - case # 50-2019-MM-005685-AXXX-MB
West Detention Center
38811 James Wheeler Way
Belle Glade, Florida

Attention Judge:
Hanson, Judge Leonard
Palm Beach County - Fifteenth Judicial Circuit
205 North Dixie Highway
West Palm Beach, FL 33401

        Dear Judge Hanser,

        I bring this letter to your attention today, due to a conflict
of interest between myself and my appointed representation
Mr. Raymon Burns. I'm requesting new representation for the
reason of status 27.40(9) and 827.56. Due to Mr. Burns
qualifications in representation, number of cases that have been
to trial and lack of experience in trespass cases. Also
allowing Assistant Public Defender Ms. Ilene Marcus to interrogate
me while being held in the courtroom. Not introducing Ms. Marcus
or sharing her professional position, that Ms. Marcus holds with
the court before interrogation. I've also been unable to reach Mr. Burns
by telephone, not one time.

        Mr. Raymon Burns allowed this interrogation on 7/2/2019 to
take place not only without advising during this interrogation,
but without knowing if Ms. Ilene Marcus holds in character
and good standing the proper qualifications, certifications
or doctorate degree from an accredited university and
having at least one year experience in providing behavior
analysis services for individuals in developmental
disabilities. following statues 393.17(1), and s.393.18

        Thank you for your time while reviewing this situation.
        God Bless!
        Respectfully,
        Brian Brong

IN THE COUNTY COURT OF THE FIFTEENTH
JUDICIAL CIRCUIT, CRIMINAL DIVISION
IN AND FOR PALM BEACH COUNTY, FLORIDA

TO: CHRIST FELLOWSHIP CHURCH
C/O GREGORY READE (YOUTH MINISTRIES)
9905 SOUTHERN BLVD.
ROYAL PALM BEACH, FL 33411
00

CASE NO. 2019MM005685AMB
DIVISION: "B"
Police Case No 06-19-070132
ME. No.

STATE OF FLORIDA
vs.
BRIAN DALE BAILEY

JURY TRIAL
2 WEEK DOCKET - REMAIN ON CALL
COUNTY COURT - DIVISION B

You are commanded to appear at the Palm Beach County Courthouse, 205 North Dixie
Highway, West Palm Beach, FL 33401, COURTROOM 2E, beginning at 8:30 AM, on
07/24/2019. PLEASE DO NOT APPEAR BEFORE CALLING: (561) 355-7413 (or 1-(800)
353-3859 7413 if out of the area) to verify if you will be needed for the trial.

Failure to appear will subject you to contempt of Court. This subpoena is binding day to
day and week to week until the case is closed.

RYAN G MYERS
Assistant State Attorney
Fla. Bar No.0124446

July 2, 2019

I received this subpoena on the ___8___ day of ___July___, 2019, and executed the same on the ___9___ day
of ___July___, 2019, in Palm Beach County, Florida.

SHERIFF, PALM BEACH COUNTY

By:_____ 7835

Deputy Sheriff

If you are a person with a disability who needs any accommodation in order to participate
in this proceeding, you are entitled, at no cost to you, to the provision of certain assistance.
Please contact the ADA Coordinator in the Administrative Office of the Court, Palm
Beach County Courthouse, 205 North Dixie Highway, Room 5.2500, West Palm Beach,
Florida, 33401; telephone number (561) 355-4380 at least 7 days before your scheduled
court appearance, or immediately upon receiving this notification if the time before the
scheduled appearance is less than 7 days; if you are hearing or voice impaired, call 1-800-
955-8771.

FILED: PALM BEACH COUNTY, FL, SHARON R. BOCK, CLERK. 7/11/2019 3:17:00 PM

IN THE COUNTY COURT OF THE FIFTEENTH
JUDICIAL CIRCUIT, CRIMINAL DIVISION
IN AND FOR PALM BEACH COUNTY, FLORIDA

TO: GERALD CHARLES
C/O CHRIST FELLOWSHIP CHURCH SECURITY
9905 SOUTHER BLVD
ROYAL PALM BEACH, FL 33411
PALM BEACH

CASE NO. 2019MM005685AMB
DIVISION: "B"
Police Case No 06-19-070132
ME. No.

STATE OF FLORIDA
vs.
BRIAN DALE BAILEY

JURY TRIAL
2 WEEK DOCKET - REMAIN ON CALL
COUNTY COURT - DIVISION B

You are commanded to appear at the Palm Beach County Courthouse, 205 North Dixie
Highway, West Palm Beach, FL 33401, COURTROOM 2E, beginning at 8:30 AM, on
07/24/2019. PLEASE DO NOT APPEAR BEFORE CALLING: (561) 355-7413 (or 1-(800)
353-3859 7413 if out of the area) to verify if you will be needed for the trial.

Failure to appear will subject you to contempt of Court. This subpoena is binding day to
day and week to week until the case is closed.

RYAN G MYERS
Assistant State Attorney
Fla. Bar No.0124446

July 2, 2019

I received this subpoena on the _8_ day of _July_, 2019, and executed the same on the _9_ day
of _July_, 2019, in Palm Beach County, Florida.

SHERIFF, PALM BEACH COUNTY

By:_____
Deputy Sheriff

SCANNED
JUL 12 2019

If you are a person with a disability who needs any accommodation in order to participate
in this proceeding, you are entitled, at no cost to you, to the provision of certain assistance.
Please contact the ADA Coordinator in the Administrative Office of the Court, Palm
Beach County Courthouse, 205 North Dixie Highway, Room 5.2500, West Palm Beach,
Florida, 33401; telephone number (561) 355-4380 at least 7 days before your scheduled
court appearance, or immediately upon receiving this notification if the time before the
scheduled appearance is less than 7 days; if you are hearing or voice impaired, call 1-800-
955-8771.

IN THE COUNTY COURT OF THE FIFTEENTH
JUDICIAL CIRCUIT, CRIMINAL DIVISION
IN AND FOR PALM BEACH COUNTY, FLORIDA

TO: DON EDWARD HELVEY   CASE NO. 2019MM005685AMB
9905 SOUTHERN BLVD.   DIVISION: "B"
ROYAL PALM BEACH, FL 33411   Police Case No 06-19-070132
PALM BEACH   ME. No.

STATE OF FLORIDA   JURY TRIAL
vs.   2 WEEK DOCKET - REMAIN ON CALL
BRIAN DALE BAILEY   COUNTY COURT - DIVISION B

You are commanded to appear at the Palm Beach County Courthouse, 205 North Dixie
Highway, West Palm Beach, FL 33401, COURTROOM 2E, beginning at 8:30 AM, on
07/24/2019. <u>PLEASE DO NOT APPEAR BEFORE CALLING: (561) 355-7413 (or 1-(800)
353-3859 7413 if out of the area) to verify if you will be needed for the trial.</u>

Failure to appear will subject you to contempt of Court. This subpoena is binding day to
day and week to week until the case is closed.

RYAN G MYERS
Assistant State Attorney
Fla Bar No.0124446

July 2, 2019
* *
I received this subpoena on the ___8___ day of ___July___, 2019, and executed the same on the ___9___ day
of ___July___, 2019, in Palm Beach County, Florida.

July 9
11:02

                    SHERIFF, PALM BEACH COUNTY   SCANNED

                    By:_____ 7885   JUL 1 2 2019
                         Deputy Sheriff

If you are a person with a disability who needs any accommodation in order to participate
in this proceeding, you are entitled, at no cost to you, to the provision of certain assistance.
Please contact the ADA Coordinator in the Administrative Office of the Court, Palm
Beach County Courthouse, 205 North Dixie Highway, Room 5.2500, West Palm Beach,
Florida, 33401; telephone number (561) 355-4380 at least 7 days before your scheduled
court appearance, or immediately upon receiving this notification if the time before the
scheduled appearance is less than 7 days; if you are hearing or voice impaired, call 1-800-
955-8771.

FILED: PALM BEACH COUNTY, FL, SHARON R. BOCK, CLERK. 7/11/2019 3:17:00 PM

IN THE COUNTY COURT OF THE FIFTEENTH
JUDICIAL CIRCUIT, CRIMINAL DIVISION
IN AND FOR PALM BEACH COUNTY, FLORIDA

SUBPOENA DUCES TECUM

STATE OF FLORIDA
vs.
BRIAN DALE BAILEY

Case No: 2019MM005685AMB
Division: "B"
Agency: PALM BEACH COUNTY SHERIFF'S OFFICE
Agency No: 06-19-070132
Arr/Inv Officer: DS JOSHUA CARMENATE

To: CHRIST FELLOWSHIP CHURCH
C/O GREGORY READE (YOUTH MINISTRIES), 9905
SOUTHERN BLVD., ROYAL PALM BEACH, FL
33411

Pursuant to Section 27.04, Florida Statutes (2014), YOU ARE HEREBY COMMANDED TO PRODUCE
the following items by email, mail or personal delivery on or before JULY 22, 2019 to the [undersigned
Assistant State Attorney] listed below:

1. Original Business Record Certification signed and notarized
2. SURVEILLANCE VIDEO ON 5/12/19 @ APPROX.: 11:30 AM – 12:30 PM AND ON 5/5/19 @
APPROX.: 7:45 AM – 9:00 AM.

Failure to produce these items may subject you to contempt of Court. Fla. R. Crim. P. 3.830

As per F.S. 934.43 you are not to disclose the existence of this request. Any such disclosure could
obstruct and impede the prosecution being conducted and thereby interfere with the enforcement of the
law.

DAVID ARONBERG
State Attorney

BY
RYAN G MYERS
Assistant State Attorney
401 N. Dixie Highway
West Palm Beach, Fl 33401
Fla. Bar # 0124446
(561)355-7100
E-mail: rmyers@sa15.org

SCANNED
JUL 12 2019

Pursuant to Florida Statute 92.153 any costs incurred may be reimbursed by the State Attorney's office at no more
than 15 cents per page and $10.00 per hour for search and retrieval. Any search or retrieval costs exceeding one hour
must be accompanied by sworn affidavit detailing actual hours spent.
****

Executed on the ___9___ day of ___July___, 2019, by personal service ( ) certified mail ( ) or fax ( ) to
the above names witness.

By:_____ 7855

SAO Filed Case-Subpoena 9/2014

Joy P.
11:02

On the date of **7/9/2019**, while still being held at Belle Glade - West Detention Center in Block E-1. During the day Mr. Bailey attempted to contact the Public Defender's office & was unable to make contact. Continuing to read the Holy Bible & West's Florida Law up to page 745. At times, Mr. Bailey felt the need to exercise, & on this day, he counted out 500 squats. Then writing a book to be creative & think outside the box. Using his imagination to develop & build through writing about some reality that Mr. Bailey had already lived through. While creating an extension that involved increased security & difficulty, while trying to achieve financial success as one individual.

Law Ø Volume 1	House 5 Bag	Writing Defense
Exercise (1000 Squats) (Pg 710)	Reading HB + Law Pg 718 (800 Squats)	(7/2 Pg 09) (Court Zoom)
8 Reading HB & Writing letter for Court Judge	9 Called - Public defender (no answer) Reading HB + Law Writing (Money Bag) Exercise Pg 745	Reading HB + Law 10 60 Days Indigent Packing Reviewed Pg 755 Exercise
Canceled Trial + defense attorney is scheduling doctor		New represent Sent Letters + the Judge sgn
15 No Bread	16 No Bread	17 No Bread 500
Reading HB + (Meeting with) (Doctor Lisa Franco)	Reading HB + Law Writing (Money Bag) Pg 8 Axi	Reading HB Conference Call (Public Defender)

Loss of Henry P. Hall on 7/11/2019

Case: 50-2019-MM-005685-AXXX-MB

While incarcerated in West Detention Center, Belle Glade his brother **Justin P. Bailey** made **Mr. Brian Bailey** aware of the loss of his grandfather, **Henry P. Hall** at the age 93, on the date of 7/11/2019, Mr. Hall had died, while Mr. Bailey was being detained. In return missing the funeral of man he enjoyed spending his time with on many visits throughout his years. Here is a man that lost his life to the Church of the Nazarene, coming from hard labor. Only knowing the work of hands gets it done.

There was a time in his life when he would trim the grass of the neighbors. Through this type of exercise, he was alive and felt that he was doing a solid for another man. Him not being established with a Florida State business license created hurdles for Mr. Hall & others in our family, while contributing to community services. All while donating to churches & offering the talents of the family. Mr. Hall didn't believe in donating 10% of his earnings, but was more than willing to offer what his labor to assist in community needs. Our family visiting a church in South Florida created a loss of income for my grandparents. In return the power of our father struck him, pulling him from the exercise he knew that keep in good spirit. Removing him from using small equipment and having him slowly degenerate.

On the date of **7/11/2019**, Mr. Bailey was exercising by completing 600 squats, reading the Holy Bible & visiting with a religious group held within the jail & applied for a county assisted Health Insurance for inmates.

3 Reading HB + LAW + Exercise Writing Defense (7/2/2019 Court Zoom)	4 Reading HB + LAW + Exercise Called Public Defender 4 times 12:30-45 Working Defense case	5 Reading HB + LAW + Exercise (working civil case) Called Public Defender 3 times 9:30-45 Squats 600
Reading HB + Law 10 60 Days (Indigent Packing) Received pg 755 Exercise New representation Sent Letters to the Judge squats 500	11 1000 squats church + Bible study Reading HB Exercise Applied for Health Insurance (600 squats)	12 Reading HB Called PD twice (NO ANSWER) writing Money Bag LAW Pg 765 Exercise (Squats 1000)
17 No Bread	18 No Bread	19 No Bread
Reading HB conference call (Public Defender) (working on case)	Visitor — PD + Doctor Lisa Faraldo working on case Reading HB/Church	Reading HB, Law Exercise Pg810 (working on case) (Boat Names 110)
24 (CANCELED Court) (working on case) Waukegan Nelson.	25 Law (Church) Reading HB + Law	26 (Visit Doctor) (Bag lunch) Reading HB writing Moreck

Meeting with Doctor Lisa Faraldo, 7/15/2019

Case# 50-2019-MM-005685-AXXX-MB

On the date of **7/15/2019**, Mr. Brian Bailey was alerted by Sheriff's Department while in custody of Belle Glade – West Detention Center, that he had a visitor. Then walking in the visiting area & greeting Dr. Faraldo, she then introduced herself as Dr. Lisa Faraldo, & started explaining why this meeting was taking place. Dr. Faraldo shared that her job was to understand that he knew what he was being charged with & that it is a misdemeanor offense. Dr. Faraldo also explaining that she would be passing her report to both State Attorney prosecutor & Public Defender.

She let him know numerous times, that she is not an attorney or a behavior analyst expert. Her titled position name is Clinical Psychologist with a degree in Clinical Psychology. He shared with Dr. Faraldo that without representation present he wouldn't be comfortable moving forward with there meeting. Dr. Faraldo replies, "I would feel the same way" She then closed her folder on the table & politely discussed how she would go about setting a second meeting. Followed by asking, "Are you taking any mental health medication"?

Mr. Bailey replied, "No mam" Dr. Faraldo mention that question, relating to requesting his medical records, stating she wouldn't need them due to him not taking any mental health medication. Dr. Lisa Faraldo then asked, if there were any questions that she might be able to answer or was there any questions that Mr. Bailey would like to ask the Public Defender & that she would get it to them. Mr. Bailey declined & explained that he had sent a request to the judge by letter, while having a conflict of interest with my appointed representative.

Mr. Bailey asked Dr. Faraldo, "Do you speak directly to the judge"? Dr. Faraldo replies, "No I usually don't, I speak with the State Attorney & Public Defender"? She then asked, "If I can get APD Raymon A. Burns to meet with us, would you move forward"? He replied, I would, but I would prefer the new representative, if the judge allows one to be appointed". Dr. Faraldo mentioning that she would move on this matter, not wanting him to have to sit in jail. That she would attempt to get this complete before 7/24/2019, the trial date. Mr. Bailey mentioned the trial date had been canceled, when a doctor for competence was requested. Dr. Faraldo then mentioned she would contact the attorneys & they said their goodbyes.

By APD Raymon A. Burns, "Not" fulfilling his professional position, lacking knowledge & performance in this case, creates a turn in the case. Developing APD Raymon A. Burns into a prosecuting state attorney.

Statute violation by **Assistant Public Defender Raymon A. Burns** include:

1) Statute **27.16 Appointment of Acting State Attorney** Whenever there shall be vacancy in the office of the State Attorney in any of the judicial circuits of this state, either by nonappointment or otherwise, or if a State Attorney shall not be present at any regular or special term of the courts of his or her circuit or, being present, shall from any cause be unable to perform the duties of office or shall be disqualified to act in any particular case, the circuit judge of his or her judicial circuit shall have full power to appoint a prosecuting officer from among the members of the bar, with the consent of the member so appointed, to whom shall be administered an oath to faithfully discharge the duties of State Attorney, & who shall have as full & complete authority, & whose acts shall be in all respects as valid as a regularly appointed State Attorney. He or she shall sign all indictments & other documents as, "Acting State Attorney". The power of the appointee shall cease upon the cessation of the inability or disqualification of the State Attorney or the completion of the appointee's duties in any particular case.

Brian Bailey   7/15/2019

(Dr. Lisa Faraldo)

Case # 50-2019-MM-005685-AYLK-MB

On 7/15/2019 I (Brian Bailey) was alerted by Sheriff's Department, while in custody of Belle Glade, West Detention Center, that I had a visitor. Then walking in the visiting area and greeting Dr. Faraldo, she then introduced herself as Dr. Lisa Faraldo, and started explaining why this meeting was taking place. Dr. Faraldo shared that her job was to understand that I know what I was being charged with and that it is a misdemeanor offense. Dr. Faraldo also explaining that she would be passing her report to both State Attorney Prosecutor and public defender. She let me know numerous times, that she is not an Attorney or a behavior Analyst. I repeat. Her titled position wise is Clinical Psychologist with a degree in Clinical Psychology. I shared with Dr. Faraldo that without representation present, I wouldn't be comfortable moving forward with our meeting. Dr. Faraldo replies "I would feel the same way". She then placed her folder on the table and politely discussed how she would go about setting a second meeting.

Followed by asking "Are you taking any mental health medication"? I replied "No ma'am". Dr. Faraldo mention that question, relating to requesting my medical records status, she wouldn't need them due to me not taking any mental health medication. Then asked if there was any questions that she might be able to answer, or was there any questions that I would like to ask the public defender and that she would get it to them. I declined, and explained that I had sent a request to the judge by letter, having a conflict of interest with my appointed representative. I asked Dr. Faraldo "Do you speak directly to the judge"? Dr. Faraldo replies "No I usually don't, I speak with the state attorney and public defender". She then asked "If I can get Mr. Raymon Burns to meet with us, would you move forward"? I replied "I would, but I would prefer the new representative if the judge allows one to be appointed". Dr. Faraldo mentioning that she would move on this matter, not wanting me to have to sit in jail.

That she would attempt to get this complete before 7/24/2019, the trial date. I mentioned the trial date had been canceled, when a doctor for competence was requested. Dr. Faraldo then mentioned she would contact the attorneys and we said our goodbyes.

183

On the date of **7/15/2019**, while reading the Holy Bible & continuing to exercise. Also, practicing new religious things he was learning, like not eating bread during **Passover**.

7 Reading HB Exercise Writing Money bag Squats 200	8 Reading HB writing letter for Court the Judge Canceled Trial + defense attorney is rescheduled to doctor	9 Called - Public defender (No answer) Reading HB + Law writing (Money Bag) Exercise Pg 745 Squats 500)
4 Passover	15 No Bread	16 No Bread
reading HB + LAW + writing (Money bag) exercise squats	Reading HB + (Meeting with) (Doctor Lisa Fernando) working case squats Exercise	Reading HB + Law Writing (Money Bag) Pg 800 Exercise Squats
No Bread The Nazirite called IA + reading HB + Law Exercise requesting EMS	22 Reading HB (Law) Exercise + (Pg 830) (Planet Moon) (Designing Logo) (working) on case (NVD)	23 Reading HB + Law (300 writing squat) (Money bag Exercise Reading HB + Law

184

Video Call with
APD Raymon A. Burns, 7/17/2019
Case# 50-2019-MM-005685-AXXX-MB

On the date of 7/17/2019, Mr. Brian Bailey was alerted by Sheriff's Department while in custody of Belle Glade – West Detention Center, that he had a video call. This took place at 12:30pm, after waiting a few minutes Assistant Public Defender Raymon A. Burns appeared on the screen. Mr. Bailey picked up the telephone then greeting APD Raymon A. Burns. He asked, "What questions did you have for me"? Mr. Bailey then picked up a piece of paper that had the questions for Assistant Public Defender Raymon A. Burns.

Which Mr. Bailey reviewed with him in the courtroom on 7/2/2019, APD Raymon A. Burns couldn't remember what they reviewed, nor find what he wrote down. APD Raymon A. Burns then asking, "Can you remind me of the questions"? Mr. Bailey then shared the questions from 7/2/2019 that he asked APD Raymon A. Burns to answer. APD Raymon A. Burns answered most of questions, to the best of his knowledge. Mr. Bailey then asked if any discovery had shown up for the case? APD Raymon A. Burns explained, only what the State prosecutor had already shared. Mr. Bailey said, "What about the Prayer Card"? APD Raymon A. Burns replied, "No".

Having to use the internet to locate one of the answers, which was, how long has APD Raymon A. Burns been in good standing with the Florida Bar? While APD Raymon A. Burns was looking to find his answer, he asked. Do you have any other questions for me? Mr. Bailey reached to pick up another piece of paper off the table. With questions that he had written down since their last visit in the courtroom on 7/2/2019. On this paper was seven questions & one statement for APD Raymon A. Burns. Mr. Bailey then asked each question one at time, while writing each answer that APD Raymon Burns gave. APD Raymon A. Burns replied, with the answers to his questions and when doing so, he found the answer regarding a timeline with the Florida Bar.

Once he was finished speaking, Mr. Bailey then shared with Assistant Public Defender Raymon A. Burns that he would like new representation. This decision was based on how the case was being handled & Assistant Public Defender Raymon A. Burns qualifications as a Public Defender. Immediately saying to Assistant Public Defender Raymon A. Burns, "I would like you to cancel the up-and-coming appointment with Dr. Lisa Faraldo, until after Mr. Bailey has been appointed new representation. Assistant Public Defender Raymon Burns said that he needed to speak with a supervisor. Mr. Bailey replied, "I would like you to get me to the judge, so that I can pass him a letter regarding representation".

Assistant Public Defender Raymon A. Burns shared, "Because Mr. Bailey was **indigent**, he was the appointed representation & that the judge wouldn't hear him, till after a competence doctor had seen him. Mr. Bailey replied, "I have the right to see the judge & want you to set a date on the docket, so that I can pass him a letter." Assistant Public Defender Raymon A. Burns shares with him there's already a date set of **7/24/2019**. Mr. Bailey replied, "I was under the impression that this date was for trial & had already been canceled according to the paperwork I had received?"

Assistant Public Defender Raymon A. Burns then changing the previous date he had just given. Now claiming it was on **7/26/2019**. Mr. Bailey had not received any information on the updated docket. Mr. Bailey then requested for Assistant Public Defender Raymon A. Burns to schedule us for a sooner date on the docket. Assistant Public Defender Raymon A. Burns replied, "I'll see what I can do". After this they ended the video call.

In relation with Assistant Public Defender Raymon A. Burns bringing up me being **indigent:**
Verse: Leviticus: 19:15

Do not pervert justice; do not show partially to the poor or favoritism to the great, but judge your neighbor fairly.

Case # 50-2019-MM-005695-AXXX-MB

On 7/17/2019 I (Brian Bailey) was alerted by Sheriff's Department while in custody of Belle Glade West Detention Center, that I had a video call. This took place at 12:10 P.M. After waiting a few minutes Mr. Raymon Burns appeared on the screen. I pick up the telephone then greeting Mr. Burns. He asked "what questions did you have for me"? I then pulled up a piece of paper that had the questions for Mr. Burns. What I reviewed with him in the courtroom on 7/2/2019. Mr. Burns couldn't remember what we reviewed, also that what he wrote down. Mr. Burns then asking "Can you remind me of the questions"? I then scored the questions from 7/2/2019 that I asked Mr. Burns to answer. Mr. Burns answered most of the questions to the best of his knowledge. I then asked if any discovery had shown up on the case? Mr. Burns replied only that the State Prosecutor had showed, snored. I said "What about the police reports"? Mr. Burns replied "no".

Having to use the internet to locate one of the answers, which was How long has Mr. Raymon Burns been in good standing with the Florida Bar? While Mr. Burns was looking to find his answer, he asked Do you have any more questions for me? I needed to pick up other piece of paper off of the table. With questions that I had written down this one last week in the courtroom on 7/2/2019. On this paper was seven questions, and one statement for Mr. Raymon Burns. I then asked each question one at a time, while writing each answer that Mr. Burns gave. Mr. Burns replied with the answers to my questions and when done, say, I found the answer regarding a timeline with the Florida Bar. Once he was finished speaking, I then shared with Mr. Burns that I would like new representation and he would no longer be representing me.

This discussion was based on how the case was being handled and Mr. Raymon Burns qualifications as a public defender. Immediately, saying to Mr. Burns "I want to cancel the in our coming appointment with Dr. Lisa Camaldo, until after I have been appointed new representation. Mr. Burns said that he needed to speak with his supervisor. I replied "I want you to get me in writing, so that I can get a new letter requesting representation. Mr. Burns shared "Burns, I was indigent he was the appointed representation. And how the judge wouldn't let me, till after I completed some steps had seen me." I replied "I have the right to see the judge and want you to set a date on the docket so that I can pass him a letter. Mr. Burns shared with me already have a date of 7/24/2019. I replied "I was under the impression that this date was for trial and had already been canceled regarding to take paperwork I had received". Mr. Burns then clearing the previous date he had just given. Now clearing, it was on 7/26/2019. I had not accessed any information on the updated docket.

I then requested for Mr. Burns to schedule us for a sooner date on the docket. Mr. Burns replied "I'll see what I can do". After this we ended the video call.

In relation with Mr. Ryan Burns bringing up me being indigent:

Verse: Leviticus: 19:15

Do not pervert justice; do not show partiality to the poor or favoritism to the great, but judge your neighbor fairly.

7/18/2019

Meeting with APD Raymon A. Burns
& Dr. Lisa Faraldo

Case# 50-2019-MM-005685-AXXX-MB

On the date of **7/18/2019,** Mr. Bailey was alerted by Sheriff's Department while in custody of Belle Glade - West Detention Center, that he had visitor. The time was 10:20am, he was not expecting any visitors today, after the video call with Assistant Public Defender Raymon A. Burns the day before.

1) Statute **27.40 (9) - Any interested person may advise the court of any circumstance affecting the quality of representation.**

Explaining that they have a conflict of interest & that he would like to see the judge. Requesting new appointed representation for this case. On **7/17/2019,** Mr. Bailey told Assistant Public Defender Raymon A. Burns on that video call that he would no longer be representing him & that he needed to cancel Dr. Lisa Faraldo's appointment for the following day. To his surprise at 10:25am Mr. Bailey approached the visitation area, to find Assistant Public Defender Raymon A. Burns sitting & waiting at a table by himself.

He walked into the room & greeted Assistant Public Defender Raymon A. Burns, then waited for his reply. Assistant Public Defender Raymon A. Burns greeting him in return & then bringing up Statute **27.50** which he couldn't remember the correct Statute number, that he claims to have reviewed the day before.

2) Statute **27.50 – Public Defender; qualifications; election.** For each judicial circuit, there shall be, & shall have been for the preceding **5 years**, a **member in good standing of the Florida Bar.**

Assistant Public Defender Raymon A. Burns stating that in reference to Statute 27.50, there is **only one Public Defender, named Carey Haughwout**, that is qualified under Statute 27.50 & that has been with the Florida Bar for five-years in good standing. Then Assistant Public Defender Raymon A. Burns continues by saying, "Everyone in a Assistant Public Defender under Carey Haughtout". That is misleading, on all the Judicial Circuit Court documents, Assistant Public Defender Raymon A. Burns Professional Business title shows, "**Public Defender**".

It doesn't show anywhere on any of my documents provided by the Judicial Circuit Court, *"Assistant Public Defender"*.

3) Statute 90.401 - **Definition of relevant evidence.** Relevant evidence is evidence tending to **prove or disprove a material fact.**

Which means, Mr. Bailey *"**never**" actually met with a **Public Defender qualified by Statute 27.50**, since he'd been in custody. Then Assistant Public Defender Raymon A. Burns informed him there was still a doctor coming out to meet with them. Mr. Bailey explained, we have a conflict of interest & you will no longer be my representation. Assistant Public Defender Raymon A. Burns asking, "What is the conflict of interest"?*

Mr. Bailey replied, "On two different occasions you allowed another person to interview me without representation. Once in the courtroom with Dr. Lisa Faraldo". Assistant Public Defender Raymon A. Burns corrects him, "You mean ADP Ilana Marcus"? Mr. Bailey replied, "Yes, I meant Assistant Public Defender Ilana Marcus, & with Dr. Lisa Faraldo at Belle Glade - West Detention Center."

Mr. Bailey continues speaking to Assistant Public Defender Raymon A. Burns, "you have done this without knowing their qualifications or if they are holding a valid license in practice." He continued explaining, "You are not doing what I asked, I said yesterday, for you to cancel the doctor's meeting & get me to the judge. You have not done what I've asked". (Then there was a pause) Mr. Bailey continued by saying, "I did not want to waste your time spinning your wheels to come out here or the doctor's". That was the last thing Mr. Bailey said to APD Raymon A. Burns, before exiting the room.

Then returning to the pod area, where the bunk he was using at the time was located. A few minutes there after the Sheriff's Department alerted him to come back to the front desk area. When arriving he see Dr. Faraldo through the window. One of the Commanding Officers opened the door at block E-1's entrance, Mr. Bailey put half his body out between the door & frame, then Dr. Faraldo requesting to start a meeting. He replied, "APD Raymon Burns & I have a conflict of interest. I told him yesterday to cancel this appointment, so that you would not waste your time spinning your wheels coming out here". Dr. Faraldo replied, "Would you give me five minutes"? He replied, "Talk to Mr. Burns" then closing the door to block E-1, then returning to his pod area, with sleeping quarters.

4) *Statute **92.525** (1)(A)(4)(A)(B)(C) –*
*(**Prima Facie Evidence**) Verification of Documents; perjury by false written declaration penalty*

(1) If authorized or required by law, by rule of an administrative agency, or by rule order of court
that a document by verified by a person, the verification may be accomplished in the following manner:

(A)   Under oath or affirmation taken or administered before an officer authorized under s. 92.50 to administer oath.

(1) As used in this section:

(A)The term, "administrative agency" means any department or agency of the state or any county, municipality, special district, or other political subdivision.

(B) The term, "document" means any writing including, without limitation, any form, application, claim, notice, tax return, inventory, affidavit, pleading or paper.

(C) The requirement that a document be verified means that the document must be signed or executed by a person and that the person must state under oath or affirm that the facts or matters stated or recited in the document are true, or words of that import or effect.

Bron Bailey

7/3/2019

Details of what happened
In the courtroom on 7/2/2019

CASE # 50-2019-MM-005685-AXXX-MB

While in custody on 7/2/2019, I was walked into the courtroom by Sheriff's department, then seated while cases were in session. I was approached by Mr. Raymon Burns, who advised that he would be handling my case. Mr. Burns asked me a few questions in regards to case number 50-2019-MM-005685-AXXX-MB. Towards the end of our conversation, I was asked to make a decission, either take a plea offer or trial. I decided to take the case to trial, and that was the end of our conversation. A few minutes later, Mr. Burns came back over to where I was sitting and informed me, that his supervisor would be coming to speak with me.

Sometime passed and a woman appeared in the courtroom, she then approached me and asked "Are you Bron Bailey"? I replied "Yes". Her name is Ms. Ilene Marcus, I had never seen her before this, and didn't know her position/title at this time. Ms. Marcus claimed that she had some concerns about my competencies. This raised my level of concern, because I had never met Ms. Marcus before, how could she judge my level of competence? Ms. Ilene Marcus who never shared her professional business title with me, starting asking me a question like?

"Do I think the state attorney is my friend? I replied "that would be based upon opinion". Ms. Marcus then asked "do I know what the prosecutors job is"? I replied "that is not my line of work". At this point I was bothered by the intent of her questions. Ms. Marcus went on to make a statement, By saying "Well you have history with the system you should know"[1] I replied that "I will only be speaking to Mr. Burns" my appointed representative. Ms. Marcus then walked away and asked Mr. Burns to step outside the courtroom and that was the last time I saw Ms. Ilene Marcus.

When Mr. Burns returned, I asked him for her full name and title/position, along with some questions regarding his experience as a public defender with the states. On a yellow piece of paper with writing in black ink Mr. Burns wrote the answers down and gave me this yellow sheet of paper. After seeing the answers, I realized that they were not detailed with a timeline. I asked Mr. Burns "what is the timeline as you are one hundred cases is it Annual or Monthly? And are they open or closed"? Mr. Burns replied (Humbling not sure what to answer) he would have to look it up and get back to me". (Mr. Burns seemed unsure) On the yellow sheet of paper, Mr. Burns wrote down Ms. Ilene Marcus's title/position as Assistant Public Defender.

Not long after this the case was called before the judge. I stood up and both the state prosecutor, public defender and judge decided upon trial date. The end result on July 2, 2019 was there would be a jury trial on July 24, 2019.

195

Statue violation:

1) S. 27.18 Assistant to state attorney

The state attorney, by and with the consent of court, may procure the assistance of any member of the bar when the amount of the state business renders it necessary, either in the grand jury room to advise them upon legal points and framing indictments, or in the court to prosecute criminals; but such assistant shall not be authorized to sign any indictments or administer any oaths, or to perform any other duty except the giving of legal advice, drawing up of indictments, and the prosecution of criminals in open court. His or her compensation shall be paid by the state attorney and not by the state.

Respectfully,

B. Bailey

Question created on 7/22/2019
for the Psychologist
Case# 50-2019-MM-005685-AXXX-MB

1) What is your professional business title & name?

Answer:

2) How many years of experience have you had in school for psychology?

Answer:

3) How many year's supervised by an individual who is a licensed school psychologist?

Answer:

4) Are you currently licensed as a psychologist?

Answer:

5) What is your business title name under, Department of Business Professional Regulations?

Answer:

These questions were never asked due to,
"Lack of Opportunity".

In the courtroom on 7/24/2019

Case# 50-2019-MM-005685-AXXX-MB

While in custody on **7/24/2019**, Mr. Bailey was walked into the courtroom by Sheriff's Department, with the courtroom quiet & no cases in session. He was approached by APD Raymon A. Burns, they greeted each other, then APD Raymon A. Burns said, "Do you have any questions for me"? Mr. Bailey replied? "No sir" he then continued by saying, "I would like to get these letters to the Judge". In reference to new appointed representation. APD Raymon A. Burns asking to see the letters, Mr. Bailey allowed, & ADP Burns only took a quick glance before his attention was guided back to APD John Rivera.

APD Raymon A. Burns handed him back the letters & made his way over to APD John Rivera, standing in another location of the courtroom. Mr. Bailey then spoke out to a nearby bailiff, saying, "Excuse me, how can I get these letters to the Judge"? Can you do it or do I need to go through the attorney? He shared that he was unable to assist & directed him back in the direction of his appointed representation. APD Raymon A. Burns returned, asking what would Mr. Bailey like to take place? Mr. Bailey wanting a new appointed Public Defender, explained I would like to get these letters to the Judge & speak directly to him.

Then a APD John Rivera approached & stood next to APD Raymon A. Burns, introducing himself. Then continued by saying, I wanna make sure you understand what is taking place, he also had some concerns regarding his cooperation with the competence doctor. Asking, if Mr. Bailey understood? He nodded his head without speaking as a reply. After this they all stood before Judge Hanser, it was APD Raymon A. Burns, APD John Riviera, ASA Ryan Myers & (Defendant) Mr. Bailey Requesting a, **"Nelson Hearing"** in regard to appointing new representation. Judge Hanser asking the court if we could return at a later time on the same day at 10:30am. Everyone in the courtroom agreed to this & they were dismissed by the Judge.

Then holding on to his letters regarding representation. Being placed in handcuffs & removed from the courtroom, by Sheriff's Department to a holding cell below the court. When it was close to the return time, Sheriff's Department removed him from the holding cell, placing him back in handcuffs, & escorted him back up to the courtroom. His handcuffs were removed, & he was seated. Mr. Bailey then started retrieving the letters that he had written for his records. That he would like to share with the Judge. The hearing was about to start in the presence of Judge Hanser & they all stood. With the Judge directing his attention to both APD Raymon A. Burns & APD John Rivera sharing details of what was about to take place.

When their conversation was complete the Judge swore Mr. Bailey in, & he introduced himself to the court. Now sharing the first letter, details of what happened in the courtroom on 7/2/2019. When complete he moved to the second letter, which he mailed to the Judge, but he didn't read because this was still an open case. The third letter Mr. Bailey read for the court, was questions he had for APD Raymon A. Burns & on the backside of that page was Statute violations effected by representation. The fourth letter was regarding a letter about what had taken place at the Belle Glade - West Detention Center, between APD Raymon A. Burns, & Dr. Lisa Faraldo & when Mr. Bailey was done reading the Judge spoke, saying after hearing your reason for new appointed representation.

I find that there are no grounds for new representation after what I have heard. I will continue to allow your current counsel to continue representing you. Mr. Bailey was disappointed but tried not showing it & wanted to save the relationship between APD Raymon A. Burns & himself. With the Judges permission there was a short break, where both APD John Rivera & APD Raymon A. Burns came over to speak with Mr. Bailey in regard to moving forward with Ms. Faraldo. APD John Rivera confirming his cooperation with the doctor, then sharing the timeline & other location besides Belle Glades - West Detention Center.

Then coming to an agreement, & the Judge returned. The court then setting the date on the docket for **8/2/2019**. Then being dismissed by Judge Hanser, the Sheriff's Department handing documentation for the next hearing, then placing Mr. Bailey back in handcuffs. When exiting from the courtroom he saw Brenda Taft sitting in the court, with a grim look on her face. He nodded his head as he passed by. Then being escorted by two female officers to the holding block area.

When arriving downstairs in the basement, the officers looked for his vegan /rad bag lunch, but were unable to find it, claiming the kitchen in Belle Glade - West Detention Center had not sent it. Then offering juice, but not having that either. Mr. Bailey requested a regular bag lunch to at least eat the bread. He was also offered a milk bag, but he kindly denied. Explaining that he was practicing **The Nazirite from the Holy Bible**. He was currently practicing Christian religion, by fasting, starting a vegan diet, & reading the Holy Bible daily, sharing the **Word of God**.

(No Vegan Meal)
Statute violation: **950.04 Penalty for neglect of duty in keeping prisoners of the United States.**

Sheriff's Department was advised by Medical staff after finding Mr. Bailey malnutrition & dehydrated, that he would receive vegan meals. Sheriff's Department, "**NOT** "complying.

7/24/2019

IN THE COUNTY COURT OF THE FIFTEENTH JUDICIAL CIRCUIT
IN AND FOR PALM BEACH COUNTY, FLORIDA - CRIMINAL DIVISION
CIRCUIT/COUNTY COURT
Court Event Form

DEFENDANT: BRIAN DALE BAILEY
CASE NO: 50-2019-MM-005685-AXXX-MB

STATE OF FLORIDA

DATE: 7/24/2019

vs.
DEFENDANT: BRIAN DALE BAILEY
CASE NO: 50-2019-MM-005685-AXXX-MB
DIVISION: B: Cnty Crim - B (County)

JACKET #: 0403731
BOOKING #: 2019015844

PRESIDING JUDGE: HANSER, JUDGELEONARD
ASA: MYERS, RYAN
ATTORNEY:
PUBLIC DEFENDER: BURNS, RAYMON
CO-COUNSEL:
DEPUTY CLERK: SH

START TIME: 9:11 AM
END TIME: 9:12 AM

COURT REPORTER

COURT TYPE: STCK - STATUS
CHECK

COURT ROOM: 2E (Main Branch)

Reset For
Court Date Scheduled - HRNG - Hearing - 7/24/2019 10:30 AM - 2E (Main Branch) MB, 205 N. Dixie Highway
West Palm Beach FL 33401 - NELSON HEARING

Other: DEFENDANT PRESENT AND IN CUSTODY
Other: STAND IN ATTORNEY ASA KERN PRESENT
Other: ADVISED OF RIGHTS
Other: DEFT ADDRESS COURT REGARDING REPRESENTATION
Other: CASE RESET LATER SAME DAY FOR NELSON HEARING

Count 1 - MF TRESPASS AFTER WARNING 810.09(2A)

Wednesday, July 24, 2019

Page 1 of 1

FILED: PALM BEACH COUNTY, FL SHARON R BOCK, CLERK 07/24/2019 09:12:15 AM

7/24/2019

IN THE COUNTY COURT OF THE FIFTEENTH JUDICIAL CIRCUIT
IN AND FOR PALM BEACH COUNTY, FLORIDA - CRIMINAL DIVISION
CIRCUIT/COUNTY COURT
Court Event Form

DEFENDANT: BRIAN DALE BAILEY
CASE NO: 50-2019-MM-005685-AXXX-MB

STATE OF FLORIDA
vs.

DATE: 7/24/2019

DEFENDANT: BRIAN DALE BAILEY
CASE NO: 50-2019-MM-005685-AXXX-MB
DIVISION: B: Cnty Crim - B (County)

JACKET #: 0403731
BOOKING #: 2019015844

PRESIDING JUDGE: HANSER, JUDGELEONARD
ASA: MYERS, RYAN
ATTORNEY:
PUBLIC DEFENDER: BURNS, RAYMON
CO-COUNSEL:
DEPUTY CLERK: SH

START TIME: 10:29 AM
END TIME: 11:15 AM

COURT REPORTER
COURT TYPE: STCK - STATUS
CHECK

COURT ROOM: 2E (Main Branch)

Reset For
Court Date Scheduled - STCK - STATUS CHECK - 8/2/2019 8:30 AM - 2E (Main Branch) MB, 205 N. Dixie
Highway West Palm Beach FL 33401 - RE COMPETANCY

Motion - Denied   - DEFENDANT'S MOTION TO DISCHARGE THE PUBLIC DEFENDERS OFFICE AND
APPOINT NEW COUNSEL
Other: DEFENDANT PRESENT AND IN CUSTODY
Other: STAND IN ATTORNEY ASA KERN PRESENT
Other: DEFENSE COUNSEL J RIVERA AND R BURNS PRESENT
Other: DEFENDANT SWORN AND TESTIFIED
Other: NELSON HEARING HELD AT THE REQUEST OF THE DEFENDANT
Trial Notes Were Added

Count 1 - MF TRESPASS AFTER WARNING 810.09(2A)

FILED: PALM BEACH COUNTY, FL SHARON R BOCK, CLERK 07/24/2019 11:15:18 AM

IN THE CIRCUIT/COUNTY COURT OF THE FIFTEENTH JUDICIAL CIRCUIT
IN AND FOR PALM BEACH COUNTY, FLORIDA

STATE OF FLORIDA

-Vs-

Date: 07/24/2019

Case No: 50-2019-MM-005685-AXXX-MB

Division: B: Cnty Crim - B (County)

BRIAN DALE BAILEY
GENERAL DELIVERY
WEST PALM BEACH, FL 32200

NOTICE OF HEARING
THE DEFENDANT MUST BE PRESENT AT THIS HEARING
For Criminal Charges: Failure to Appear will result in a Bond Forfeiture or
revocation of own recognizance (O.R.) and a Capias/Warrant being issued for your arrest.
For Civil Traffic Charges: Failure to appear may result in the suspension of your driver's license.
IF YOUR CASE IS ON-CALL, CONTACT YOUR ATTORNEY FOR THE TIME TO APPEAR
YOU ARE HEREBY NOTIFIED that this case is scheduled

DATE:	TIME:	HEARING TYPE:	LOCATION:
7/24/2019	10:30 AM	HRNG - Hearing	2E (Main Branch) MB, 205 N. Dixie Highway West Palm Beach FL. 33401
8/2/2019	8:30 AM	STCK - STATUS CHECK	2E (Main Branch) MB, 205 N. Dixie Highway West Palm Beach FL. 33401

BE PREPARED TO PAY COURT COSTS AND FINES ASSESSED BY THE COURT AT THIS HEARING
"IF YOU INTEND TO REQUEST THE SERVICES OF THE PUBLIC DEFENDER, YOU MUST FILE AN APPLICATION AT THE CLERK &
COMPTROLLER'S OFFICE AND BE APPOINTED THE PUBLIC DEFENDER BEFORE YOUR COURT DATE. THE APPLICATION FEE IS $50.00."
Civil Traffic Charges are not eligible for a Public Defender.

SHARON R. BOCK,
CLERK & COMPTROLLER
BY: SH

Deft/Atty: DEFENDANT IN CUSTODY

Deputy Clerk

cc: RYAN MYERS
      BURNS, RAYMON A

IN THE CIRCUIT/COUNTY COURT OF THE FIFTEENTH JUDICIAL CIRCUIT
IN AND FOR PALM BEACH COUNTY, FLORIDA

"If you are a person with a disability who needs any accommodation in order to participate in this proceeding, you are entitled, at no cost to you, to the provision of certain assistance. Please contact Tammy Anton, Americans with Disabilities Act Coordinator, Palm Beach County Courthouse, 205 North Dixie Hwy, West Palm Beach, FL 33401; telephone number (561) 355-4380 at least 7 days before your scheduled court appearance, or immediately upon receiving this notification if the time before the scheduled appearance is less than 7 days; if you are hearing or voice impaired, call 711."

"Si usted es una persona minusválida que necesita algún acomodamiento para poder participar en este procedimiento, usted tiene derecho, sin tener gastos propios, a que se le provea cierta ayuda. Tenga la amabilidad de ponerse en contacto con Tammy Anton, 205 N. Dixie Highway, West Palm Beach, Florida 33401; teléfono número (561) 355-4380, por lo menos 7 días antes de la cita fijada para   su comparecencia en los tribunales, o inmediatamente después de recibir esta notificación si el tiempo antes de la comparecencia que se ha programado es menos de 7 días; si usted tiene discapacitación del oído o de la voz, llame al 711."

"Si ou se yon moun ki enfim ki bezwen akomodasyon pou w ka patisipe nan pwosedi sa, ou kalifye san ou pa gen okenn lajan pou w peye, gen pwovizyon pou jwen kèk èd. Tanpri kontakte Tammy Anton, kòòdonatè pwogram Lwa pou ameriken ki Enfim yo nan Tribinal Konte Palm Beach la ki nan 205 North Dixie Highway, West Palm Beach, Florida 33401; telefòn li se (561) 355-4380 nan 7 jou anvan dat ou gen randevou pou parèt nan tribinal la, oubyen imedyatman apre ou fin resevwa konvokasyon an si lè ou gen pou w parèt nan tribinal la mwens ke 7 jou; si ou gen pwoblèm pou w tande oubyen pale, rele 711."

DEFENDANT: BRIAN DALE BAILEY

CASE NO: 50-2019-MM-005685-AXXX-MB

DATE: 07/24/2019

DIVISION:B: Cnty Crim - B (County)

TRIAL / HEARING NOTES

10:37:19 AM - JUDGE L HANSER PRESIDING

10:37:29 AM - DEPUTY CLERK S HESS PRESENT

10:37:44 AM - STATE ATTORNEY C KERN PRESENT

10:38:01 AM - DEFENSE COUNSEL R BURNS AND J RIVERA PRESENT

10:38:14 AM - HEARING CENTRALLY RECORDED

10:38:24 AM - NELSON HEARING HELD

10:40:52 AM - DEFENDANT READS LETTER PREVIOUSLY SENT TO JUDGE HANSER REGARDING COUNSEL IN OPEN COURT

10:53:16 AM - DEFENSE OFFERS RESPONSE TO DEFENDANT'S LETTER

10:56:39 AM - DEFENDANT'S MOTION IS DENIED

10:56:42 AM - COURT IN RECESS

11:13:24 AM - COURT RECONVENES

7/24/2019

IN THE CIRCUIT/COUNTY COURT OF THE FIFTEENTH JUDICIAL CIRCUIT
IN AND FOR PALM BEACH COUNTY, FLORIDA

STATE OF FLORIDA

-Vs-

BRIAN DALE BAILEY
GENERAL DELIVERY
WEST PALM BEACH, FL 32200

Date: 07/24/2019

Case No: 50-2019-MM-005685-AXXX-MB

Division: B: Cnty Crim - B (County)

NOTICE OF HEARING
THE DEFENDANT MUST BE PRESENT AT THIS HEARING

For Criminal Charges: Failure to Appear will result in a Bond Forfeiture or
revocation of own recognizance (O.R.) and a Capias/Warrant being issued for your arrest.
For Civil Traffic Charges: Failure to appear may result in the suspension of your driver's license.
IF YOUR CASE IS ON-CALL, CONTACT YOUR ATTORNEY FOR THE TIME TO APPEAR
YOU ARE HEREBY NOTIFIED that this case is scheduled

DATE:	TIME:	HEARING TYPE:	LOCATION:
7/24/2019	10:30 AM	HRNG - Hearing	2E (Main Branch) MB, 205 N. Dixie Highway West Palm Beach FL 33401

BE PREPARED TO PAY COURT COSTS AND FINES ASSESSED BY THE COURT AT THIS HEARING
"IF YOU INTEND TO REQUEST THE SERVICES OF THE PUBLIC DEFENDER, YOU MUST FILE AN APPLICATION AT THE CLERK &
COMPTROLLER'S OFFICE AND BE APPOINTED THE PUBLIC DEFENDER BEFORE YOUR COURT DATE. THE APPLICATION FEE IS $50.00."
Civil Traffic Charges are not eligible for a Public Defender.

SHARON R. BOCK,
CLERK & COMPTROLLER
BY: SH

Deft/Atty: DEFENDANT IN CUSTODY

Deputy Clerk

cc: RYAN MYERS
       BURNS, RAYMON A

Page 1 of 2

IN THE CIRCUIT/COUNTY COURT OF THE FIFTEENTH JUDICIAL CIRCUIT
IN AND FOR PALM BEACH COUNTY, FLORIDA

"If you are a person with a disability who needs any accommodation in order to participate in this proceeding, you are entitled, at no cost to you, to the provision of certain assistance. Please contact Tammy Anton, Americans with Disabilities Act Coordinator, Palm Beach County Courthouse, 205 North Dixie Hwy, West Palm Beach, FL 33401; telephone number (561) 355-4380 at least 7 days before your scheduled court appearance, or immediately upon receiving this notification if the time before the scheduled appearance is less than 7 days; if you are hearing or voice impaired, call 711."

"Si usted es una persona minusválida que necesita algún acomodamiento para poder participar en este procedimiento, usted tiene derecho, sin tener gastos propios, a que se le provea cierta ayuda. Tenga la amabilidad de ponerse en contacto con Tammy Anton, 205 N. Dixie Highway, West Palm Beach, Florida 33401; teléfono número (561) 355-4380, por lo menos 7 días antes de la cita fijada para su comparecencia en los tribunales, o inmediatamente después de recibir esta notificación si el tiempo antes de la comparecencia que se ha programado es menos de 7 días; si usted tiene discapacitación del oído o de la voz, llame al 711."

"Si ou se yon moun ki enfim ki bezwen akomodasyon pou w ka patisipe nan pwosedi sa, ou kalifye san ou pa gen okenn lajan pou w peye, gen pwovizyon pou jwen kèk èd. Tanpri kontakte Tammy Anton, kòòdonatè pwogram Lwa pou ameriken ki Enfim yo nan Tribinal Konte Palm Beach la ki nan 205 North Dixie Highway, West Palm Beach, Florida 33401; telefòn li se (561) 355-4380 nan 7 jou anvan dat ou gen randevou pou parèt nan tribinal la, oubyen imedyatman apre ou fin resevwa konvokasyon an si lè ou gen pou w parèt nan tribinal la mwens ke 7 jou; si ou gen pwoblèm pou w tande oubyen pale, rele 711."

On the date of 7/24/2019, in the Palm Beach County Court House, downtown West Palm Beach, Florida. While in custody of the Palm Beach County Sheriff's Department & requesting new representation. Recording what was taking place, by using a pencil & documentation. Being the first, **"Nelson Hearing"** ever presented by Judge Hanser. The time in this case was increasing continuously, for unnecessary reasons on the account of the Public Defense. The next semester at Palm Beach State College was about to start. While being inside the block Mr. Bailey was bothered by the fact that, he now had government loans for college & was having a high GPA, smothered by a delayed timeline & the government was using the court system to create a future with financial difficulties. Only leaving one more citizen in debt & lost opportunities to scholarships.

Reading HB + Law Writing (Money Bag) P9 800 Exercise Squats	Reading HB Conference Call (Public Defender) Working on case	Visitor — PD + Doctor Lisa Faraldo Working on case Reading HB/Church
23 Reading HB + 300 Law Writing squat (Money bag) Exercise Reading HB + Law	24 (CANCELED Court) (Meeting w/ case) NO VEGAN Nelson (TRIAL) Hearing 74 Days	25 (Church) Reading HB + Law Exercise (Money Bag)
30 (No Vegan) Tray at Breakfast Tray Exercise Reading HB Meeting w/ Sergeant Bryan	31 (No Vegan) Tray at Breakfast (No Indigent) (Package Arrived)	1 August Reading HB + Law Volume 11 P9 142 (church) Exercise
6 Video call Mr. Burns TRANSPORTED	7	8

7/24/2019

Researching Public Defenders & Qualifications

The Fifteenth Judicial Circuit

Criminal Division

Documents, Paperwork

Case# 50-2019-MM-005685-AXXX-MB

Topic: **Public Defender Title**

Listed: **Public Defender**

Mr. Brian Bailey was researching this case while it was open, when reviewing documentation passed by The Fifteenth Judicial Circuit Court. He found something that caught his attention. The title name for **Public Defender** was listed as **Public Defender**. When researching in West's Florida legal law book, he came across **Statute 27.50**. In this Statue definition he found that the **Public Defender** must be in **good standing** of the **Florida Bar** for **5 years**. Where this became **misleading** is on **documentation** passed from The Fifteenth Judicial Circuit Court is the title showing **Public Defender**, had listed **Mr. Raymon Burns. APD Raymon A. Burns** only being in **good standing of the Florida Bar for 9 months.**

APD Raymon A. Burns professional business title is, *"Assistant Public Defender."*

Nowhere on any of **The Fifteenth Judicial Circuit Court documentation does it show** a title position for **Assistant Public Defender.** When researching **Assistant Public Defender** in West's Florida legal **Law book.** He was unable to locate any of their requirements needed as an **Assistant Attorney.** Leaving some of the **Public Defender** with little to know experience & under qualified, when comparing with Statute **27.50.** Five years' experience verses months is a big difference when someone's life is on the line.

Chapter 27 Section 50 - 2012 Florida Statutes - The Florida Senate

The Florida Senate
2012 Florida Statutes

Title V	Chapter 27	SECTION 50
JUDICIAL BRANCH	STATE ATTORNEYS; PUBLIC DEFENDERS; RELATED OFFICES	Public defender; qualifications; election.
	Entire Chapter	

27.50 **Public defender; qualifications; election.** — For each judicial circuit, there shall be a public defender who shall be, and shall have been for the preceding 5 years, a member in good standing of The Florida Bar. The public defender shall be elected at the general election, for a term of 4 years, by the qualified electors of the judicial circuit. The public defender shall be an elector of the state and shall reside within the territorial jurisdiction of the judicial circuit in which he or she serves.

History.—s. 1, ch. 63-409; s. 15, ch. 73-333; s. 1, ch. 80-376; s. 137, ch. 95-147.

Staff Referral Form

Palm Beach County Sheriff's Office, Fl.
Palm Beach West Detention
38811 James Wheeler Way
Belle Glade , FL 33430

Staff Referral Form
Mental Health

Patient Name	Patient Number	Booking Number	Birth Date	Date Of Service
BRIAN DALE BAILEY	04403731	20190613060	2/24/1979	7/24/2019

Type: ○ Emergent ○ Urgent ⦿ Routine

Mental Health: ☐ Psychiatric Provider ☑ MH Professional ☐ MH Nurse ☐ Other

Other:

Reason for Referral:
PHD SW JULY 30, 2019

Additional Information (including interim actions taken):
AT REQUEST OF PUBLIC DEFENDER, POSSIBLE MH ISSUES

Improper Documentation - Title is Assistant Public Defender

Public Defender requesting a Psychologist or Mental Health

Does, "NOT" Help the Defense of the Case.

E-Signed by Ruth Osborne, Mental Health Supervisor on 07/24/2019 09:25 AM EST
E-Signed by Amie Nicole Clark, Administrative Assistant on 07/25/2019 10:48 AM EST

Page 1 of 1

7/26/2019
Expert for Examination

IN THE COUNTY COURT OF THE FIFTEENTH JUDICIAL CIRCUIT,
IN AND FOR PALM BEACH COUNTY, FLORIDA
CRIMINAL DIVISION "B"

STATE OF FLORIDA
CASE NO. 19MM005685AMB

vs.

Brian Dale Bailey,
Defendant.

_____

ORDER REAPPOINTING EXPERT FOR EXAMINATION
OF DEFENDANT'S COMPETENCY

THIS CAUSE having come before the Court on July 24, 2019 for a Status Check regarding Defendant's competency to proceed. Based on the proceedings before the Court, and the Court being otherwise fully advised, it is

ORDERED AND ADJUDGED

1. **Dr. Lisa Faraldo is reappointed to examine the Defendant whose address is 140 JFK Drive, Suite 146, Atlantis, FL 33462 and whose telephone number is (954) 812-0900**

3. If the defendant is in custody, the Sheriff of Palm Beach County shall permit the above-named expert(s) to enter the Palm Beach County Jail to conduct the foregoing evaluation of the defendant upon presentment of this Order. If the defendant is not in custody, the expert is to contact defense counsel, or pro se defendant, for scheduling.

4. The expert is to give timely notice to the parties of the date and place of the examination.

5. A copy of the order serves as authorization for the expert to inspect and copy any discoverable information relating to the Defendant maintained by the defense counsel, Clerk of this Court, State Attorney's Office, any hospital, doctor, or any health care provider, therapist, psychiatrist, psychologist, counselor, or any mental health provider, or other social or human services agency without the necessity of written consent by Defendant.

6. This cause is scheduled for a hearing on the issue of the defendant's competency to proceed on, **Friday, August 2, 2019 at 8:30 AM.**

7. The expert shall submit a written evaluation of the defendant's mental condition to this Court with copies to the Assistant State Attorney and the Attorney for the Defendant on or before the 1st day of August, 2019, which shall include but is not limited to:

a. **Competence to Proceed** (See Fla.R.Crim.P. 3.211(a), F.S. §§916.115, 916.301). Whether the defendant has sufficient present ability to consult with counsel with a reasonable degree of rational understanding and whether the defendant has a rational, as well as factual, understanding of the pending proceedings. In considering the issue of competence to proceed, the examining expert shall consider and include in their report, the following

FILED

SCANNED

JUL 2 6 2019

JUL 2 6 2019

SHARON R. BOCK, CLERK
PALM BEACH COUNTY, FL
COUNTY CRIMINAL

State v. Brian Dale Bailey
Case No. 19MM005685AMB
Order Granting Examination of
Defendant's Competency
Page 2

factors, and any other factors deemed relevant by the experts, as they pertain to the defendant's capacity and/or ability to:

1. Appreciate the charges or allegations against him;
2. Appreciate the range and nature of possible penalties which may be imposed against him;
3. Understand the adversary nature of the legal process;
4. Disclose to his attorney facts pertinent to the proceedings at issue;
5. Manifest appropriate courtroom behavior;
6. Testify relevantly;

b. **Recommend Treatment** (See Fla.R.Crim. P. 3.211(b)). Should the appointed expert find that the defendant is incompetent to proceed, then the expert shall determine whether the defendant meets the criteria for involuntary hospitalization and report on any recommended treatment for the defendant to attain competence to proceed. The expert's report and recommendations shall include consideration of the following:

1. The mental illness or intellectual disability causing the incompetence;
2. The treatment or treatments appropriate for the mental illness or intellectual disability of the defendant and an explanation of each of the possible treatment alternative in order of choices;
3. The availability of acceptable treatment, including whether the treatment is available in the community and whether the treatment involves community or residential facilities or inpatient or outpatient settings;
4. The likelihood of the defendant attaining competence under the recommended treatment, an assessment of the probable duration of the treatment required to restore competence, and the probability that the defendant will attain competence to proceed in the foreseeable future;

8. All written reports submitted by the expert shall contain the following:

a. A list of the specific matters referred for evaluation;
b. A description of the evaluation procedure, techniques and tests used in the examination and purpose for each;
c. The expert's clinical observations, findings, and opinions on each issue referred for evaluation by the Court, and specific identification of those issues which the expert could not give an opinion;
d. An identification of the sources of information used by the expert and a presentation of the factual basis for the expert's clinical findings and opinions.

All information contained in the motion to determine competency of the defendant or in any report submitted under this order, insofar as the information relates solely to the issues of competency to proceed or to commitment, shall be used only in determining the mental competency to proceed or the commitment or other treatment of the defendant.

State v. Brian Dale Bailey
Case No. 19MM005685AMB
Order Granting Examination of
Defendant's Competency
Page 3

9. If an order is entered for the determination of competence, the appointed expert shall be paid in accordance with his or her current contract with the responsible party, or in the absence of a contract, the current Administrative Order regarding payment of appointed experts. Evaluations that include both competency and sanity will be proportionally paid for by the responsible parties.

10. Payment for competency evaluations to determine competence to proceed or to determine recommended treatment for competence to proceed shall be made by the Court in accordance with the contract between the Court and the expert, or if no contract exists, then in accordance with the current Administrative Order regarding payment of appointed experts. The expert shall submit the bill and appropriate invoice with an attached copy of this Order Directing Examination of the Defendant's Competency to the Court at:

> Court Administration
> Administrative Office of the Courts
> 205 North Dixie Highway, 5th Floor
> West Palm Beach, FL 33401

When a request is made for an evaluation of the defendant to determine the defendant's sanity or as an aid for sentencing, the requesting party shall pay. Payment shall be made in accordance with the contract between the responsible party and the expert, or if no contract exists, then in accordance with the current Administrative Order regarding payment of appointed experts.

DONE AND ORDERED in Chambers at West Palm Beach, Palm Beach County, Florida this 26 day of July, 2019.

LEONARD HANSER
County Court Judge

Copies furnished:
Expert, Lisa Faraldo 140 JFK Drive, Suite 146, Atlantis, FL 33462, (954) 812-0900 lwretzel@gmail.com
Palm Beach County Sheriff's Office 3228 Gun Club Road West Palm Beach, FL 33406 Email:
IMDCourtOrders@pbso.org
Ryan Myers, Assistant State Attorney, Division B
401 N Dixie Hwy, West Palm Beach, FL 33401, Email: rmyers@sa15.org
Raymon Burns, Assistant Public Defender, Division B
421 3rd Street west Palm Beach, FL 33401, Email: rburns@pd15.org; jmechetti@pd15.org
Paulina Pasquarelli, Court Administration, 205 N. Dixie Highway, 5th Floor, West Palm Beach, FL. 33401 email
PPasquarelli@pbcgov.org

7/26/2019

Expert for Examination

IN THE COUNTY COURT OF THE FIFTEENTH JUDICIAL CIRCUIT,
IN AND FOR PALM BEACH COUNTY, FLORIDA
CRIMINAL DIVISION "B"

STATE OF FLORIDA   CASE NO. 19MM005685AMB

vs.

Brian Dale Bailey,
    Defendant.

ORDER REAPPOINTING EXPERT FOR EXAMINATION
OF DEFENDANT'S COMPETENCY

THIS CAUSE having come before the Court on July 24, 2019 for a Status Check regarding Defendant's competency to proceed. Based on the proceedings before the Court, and the Court being otherwise fully advised, it is

ORDERED AND ADJUDGED

1. **Dr. Lisa Faraldo is reappointed to examine the Defendant whose address is 140 JFK Drive, Suite 146, Atlantis, FL 33462 and whose telephone number is (954) 812-0900**

3. If the defendant is in custody, the Sheriff of Palm Beach County shall permit the above-named expert(s) to enter the Palm Beach County Jail to conduct the foregoing evaluation of the defendant upon presentment of this Order. If the defendant is not in custody, the expert is to contact defense counsel, or pro se defendant, for scheduling.

4. The expert is to give timely notice to the parties of the date and place of the examination.

5. A copy of the order serves as authorization for the expert to inspect and copy any discoverable information relating to the Defendant maintained by the defense counsel, Clerk of this Court, State Attorney's Office, any hospital, doctor, or any health care provider, therapist, psychiatrist, psychologist, counselor, or any mental health provider, or other social or human services agency without the necessity of written consent by Defendant.

6. This cause is scheduled for a hearing on the issue of the defendant's competency to proceed on, **Friday, August 2, 2019 at 8:30 AM.**

7. The expert shall submit a written evaluation of the defendant's mental condition to this Court with copies to the Assistant State Attorney and the Attorney for the Defendant on or before the 1st day of August, 2019, which shall include but is not limited to:

    a. **Competence to Proceed** (See Fla.R.Crim.P. 3.211(a), F.S. §§916.115, 916.301). Whether the defendant has sufficient present ability to consult with counsel with a reasonable degree of rational understanding and whether the defendant has a rational, as well as factual, understanding of the pending proceedings. In considering the issue of competence to proceed, the examining expert shall consider and include in their report, the following factors, and any other factors deemed relevant by the experts, as they pertain to the defendant's capacity and/or ability to:

1. Appreciate the charges or allegations against him;
2. Appreciate the range and nature of possible penalties which may be imposed against him;
3. Understand the adversary nature of the legal process;
4. Disclose to his attorney facts pertinent to the proceedings at issue;
5. Manifest appropriate courtroom behavior;
6. Testify relevantly;

b. **Recommend Treatment** (See Fla.R.Crim. P. 3.211(b)). Should the appointed expert find that the defendant is incompetent to proceed, then the expert shall determine whether the defendant meets the criteria for involuntary hospitalization and report on any recommended treatment for the defendant to attain competence to proceed. The expert's report and recommendations shall include consideration of the following:

1. The mental illness or intellectual disability causing the incompetence;
2. The treatment or treatments appropriate for the mental illness or intellectual disability of the defendant and an explanation of each of the possible treatment alternative in order of choices;
3. The availability of acceptable treatment, including whether the treatment is available in the community and whether the treatment involves community or residential facilities or inpatient or outpatient settings;
4. The likelihood of the defendant attaining competence under the recommended treatment, an assessment of the probable duration of the treatment required to restore competence, and the probability that the defendant will attain competence to proceed in the foreseeable future;

8. All written reports submitted by the expert shall contain the following:

a. A list of the specific matters referred for evaluation;
b. A description of the evaluation procedure, techniques and tests used in the examination and purpose for each;
c. The expert's clinical observations, findings, and opinions on each issue referred for evaluation by the Court, and specific identification of those issues which the expert could not give an opinion;
d. An identification of the sources of information used by the expert and a presentation of the factual basis for the expert's clinical findings and opinions.

All information contained in the motion to determine competency of the defendant or in any report submitted under this order, insofar as the information relates solely to the issues of competency to proceed or to commitment, shall be used only in determining the mental competency to proceed or the commitment or other treatment of the defendant.

On the date of 7/26/2019, Mr. Bailey had a visit
with the clinic inside the jail. Requesting to add a
bag of peanut butter to the meal he was receiving
due to unhealthy weight loss. The doctor on staff
granted the peanut butter bag, after having nurses
document his current weight by scale. Once
receiving the following meal, the tray didn't show
any bag with peanut butter inside. He brought this
to the attention of the Sheriff's Department & the
end result was no addition to any current meals,
in assistance to weight gain. In return, the Sheriff's
Department was, "not" complying with the
medical staff, creating a block in proper nutrition.
Mr. Bailey continued writing a book called,
"Money Bag" just to keep his mind in the
imagination.

18 No Bread	19 No Bread	20 No Bread
Visitor — PD+ Doctor Lisa Farildo working on case reading HB/Church	Reading HB + Law Exercise P9810 (working on case) (Boat Names 110)	Reading HB+ Law (Designing Plant moon) Exercise
25 (Church) Law Reading HB + Law Exercise money Bag)	26 (Visit Doctor) (Bag lunch) Reading (writing Money Bag) (Paid doctor. Exercise Visit)	27 Reading HB working on case Exercise (Money Bag) (500 sqin)
1 August Reading HB + Law Volume 11 Pg 142 (church) Exercise	2 Main Court House status check No Vegel in my Nome (working) from a case	3 writing reading HB working on case civil + criminal Defense) Law

218

X-Ray Request Form

Palm Beach County Sheriff's Office, FL Palm Beach West Detention 38811 James Wheeler Way Belle Glade , FL 33430		X-Ray Request Form		 wellpath

Patient Name	Patient Number	Booking Number	Birth Date	Date Of Service
BRIAN DALE BAILEY	0403731	20190512050	2/24/1979	7/26/2019

Exam Requested:

X RAY of Left SHOULDER

Reason for Request:

LEFT SHOULDER PAIN Pain Since Incarceration on 5/12/2019

Requested by (Name and Title): *LOUIDOR ALLIANCE, MD*

Page 1 of 1

7/26/2019

Provider Progress Notes

Dr. Louider Alliance

Palm Beach County Sheriff's Office, FL
Palm Beach West Detention
38811 James Wheeler Way
Belle Glade , FL 33430

Provider Progress Notes

wellpath

Patient Name	Patient Number	Booking Number	Birth Date	Date Of Service
BRIAN DALE BAILEY	0403731	20190512060	3/24/1979	7/26/2019

Orders:

No Applicable Data Found For Patient

Patient Problems:

Observed Date	Category	Type	Problem		Confirmed By
06-08-2019	Acute	Symptoms	Abnormal weight loss		

Patient Allergies:

Observed Date	Type	Allergy		Reaction
06-06-2019	Allergy Items	No Known Drug Allergies		

☑ **Vital Signs Taken**

Patient Vitals:

Observed Date	BP	Pulse	Resp	Temp	Pulse Ox	Weight	BMI	PF#1	PF#2	PF#3	Waist
07-26-2019 12:11 PM EST	97/63	69	16	98.40	100	138	18.7	-	-	-	-

Weight 138

☐ **Current Med List Reviewed** ☐ **Psychiatrists Notes Reviewed** ☐ **Caseworker Notes Reviewed**

Notes / History:	○ Free Text ⦿ SOAPE

S:

> Added 07/26/2019 05:25 PM EST by LAlliance Provider
>
> Pain in the left shoulder moderate to severe with numbness of the arm. Has pain for the few months and has received physical therapy while he was outside. He would like to have some help. He refused to take analgesics for the pain. Due to side affects while grouped with inmates.

(No Pain Relief in Safe Quarters)

O:

> Added 07/26/2019 05:25 PM EST by LAlliance Provider
>
> AOx2 NAD

Palm Beach County Sheriff's Office, FL
Palm Beach West Detention
38811 James Wheeler Way
Belle Glade, FL 33430

Provider Progress Notes

 wellpath

Patient Name	Patient Number	Booking Number	Birth Date	Date Of Service
BRIAN DALE BAILEY	0403731	20190512060	2/24/1979	7/26/2019

Orders:

AOx3 NAD

HEENT: PERRLA EOMI

HEART: S1S2 NL

LUNG: CTA BIL

EXT: no EDEMA LEFT SHOULDER: Limited ROM

ABD: WNL

A:

Added 07/26/2019 05:25 PM EST by LAlliance Provider

LEFT SHOULDER PAIN Extreme Pain Since date of Incarceration on 5/12/2019.

P:

Added 07/26/2019 05:25 PM EST by LAlliance Provider

X-Ray of Left Shoulder.

E:

221

Filing # 93313810 E-Filed 07/29/2019 02:43:15 PM

IN THE CIRCUIT COURT OF THE FIFTEENTH JUDICIAL CIRCUIT
IN AND FOR PALM BEACH COUNTY, FLORIDA
CRIMINAL DIVISION "B"

CASE NO. 2019MM005685AMB

STATE OF FLORIDA,

vs.

BRIAN DALE BAILEY.

_____/

ORDER DIRECTING PAYMENT OF EXPERT

THIS MATTER, having come before the Court, *sua sponte*, and the Court being otherwise fully advised in the premises, it is hereby

ORDERED AND ADJUDGED that Court Administration is to pay $250.00 to Dr. Lisa Faraldo, the expert appointed to evaluate Defendant's Competency to Proceed, in accordance with this Court's order of July 26, 2019. This amount is in accordance with Administrative Order 2.601 and covers payment for the attempted evaluation and travel fee to Belle Glade, FL.

DONE AND ORDERED in Chambers, West Palm Beach, Palm Beach County, Florida this 29 day of July, 2019.

LEONARD HANSER
County Court Judge

Copies furnished to:
Dr. Lisa Faraldo, lwretzel@gmail.com
Ryan Myers, Assistant State Attorney
Raymon Burns, Assistant Public Defender
Court Administration- Court Finance
Paulina Pasquarelli, Mental Health Case Manager

222

7/29/2019

Questions for APD Raymon A. Burns

Case# 50-2019-MM-005685-AXXX-MB

1) Why has this case not been brought to trial?
   Answer:

Statute violation: 960.0015 – Victim's right to a speedy trial;
speedy trial demand by the State Attorney
(B) If a **misdemeanor case**, it is not resolved **within 45 days** after
the date that formal charges are filed, and the defendant is
arrested or the date that notice to appear in lieu of arrest
is served upon the defendant.

1) What does this Statute mean?
   Answer:
2) Does the same rule apply for a defendant?
   Answer:
3) Has the Prayer Card been received as discovery?
   Answer:
4) Can I pass a letter through the court's officials, to be
   received by Pastor Oscar Soto?
   Answer:
5) Can we request Pastor Oscar Soto's licensing, revolving
   around behavior analyst and mental health?
   Answer:

Question 6 reflects on the conversation that took place on 5/5/2019.

6) The police report is showing incorrect information, can we
   have the case dismissed on those grounds?
   Answer:
7) Can the case be dismissed due to the Statute definition
   showing through the courts?
   Answer:
8) Would you please compare the Statute definition for 810.09
   (2A) with the book and online?
   Answer:

Brian Bailey   Mr. RAYMOND BURNS
                (CASE questions)

CASE # 50-2019-MM-005685-AXXX-MB

1) Why has this case not been brought to trial?
ANSWER:

s. 960.0015 - Victim's right to a speedy trial; speedy
                trial demand by the state attorney

        (3) If a misdemeanor case, it is not resolved within **45**
            days after the date that formal charges are filed
            And the defendant is Arrested on the date that
            notice to appear in lieu of arrest is served
            upon the defendant.

2) What does this statue mean?
   ANSWER:

3) Does the same rule apply for a defendant?
   ANSWER:

4) Has the prayer card been recieved as discovery?
   ANSWER:

5) Can I pass a letter through the courts officals, to be recieved by Pastor
   Oscar?
   ANSWER:

6) Can we request Pastor Oscar's licensing, revolving, around
   behaviour analyst and mental health?
   ANSWER:

   Question (6) reflects on the conversation that took place on 5/5/2019

7) The police report is showing incorrect information, can we have the
   case dismissed on those grounds?
   ANSWER:

8) Can the case be dismissed due to the statue definition
   showing through the courts?
   ANSWER:
   Would you please compare the statue definition for 810.09 (2A) with
                                                               Book
                                                               outline

7/29/2019

Filing # 93313810 E-Filed 07/29/2019 02:43:15 PM

IN THE CIRCUIT COURT OF THE FIFTEENTH JUDICIAL CIRCUIT
IN AND FOR PALM BEACH COUNTY, FLORIDA
CRIMINAL DIVISION "B"

CASE NO. 2019MM005685AMB

STATE OF FLORIDA,

vs.

BRIAN DALE BAILEY.

_____/

ORDER DIRECTING PAYMENT OF EXPERT

THIS MATTER, having come before the Court, *sua sponte,* and the Court being otherwise fully advised in the premises, it is hereby

ORDERED AND ADJUDGED that Court Administration is to pay $250.00 to Dr. Lisa Faraldo, the expert appointed to evaluate Defendant's Competency to Proceed, in accordance with this Court's order of July 26, 2019. This amount is in accordance with Administrative Order 2.601 and covers payment for the attempted evaluation and travel fee to Belle Glade, FL.

DONE AND ORDERED in Chambers, West Palm Beach, Palm Beach County, Florida this 29 day of July, 2019.

LEONARD HANSER
County Court Judge

Copies furnished to:
Dr. Lisa Faraldo, lwretzel@gmail.com
Ryan Myers, Assistant State Attorney
Raymon Burns, Assistant Public Defender
Court Administration- Court Finance
Paulina Pasquarelli, Mental Health Case Manager

7/30/2019

No Vegan Tray

On the morning of 7/30/2019, the, "Vegan / Rad" tray Mr. Bailey had been receiving, did not show up. The officer on duty was Officer Ferguson, when diet trays were being handed out, Mr. Bailey stood in line & waited to hear his name. It was never called; He was now standing last in the diet line next to Officer Ferguson. He explained to Officer Ferguson, that he should be receiving Vegan / Rad, she then reviewed her list of names & informed him that he was listed as a regular tray. Mr. Bailey looked on the tray to see if there was anything that matched up with Vegan / Rad. On the tray was syrup.

Grits, bread, slice of cheese & a piece of meat. He accepted the tray & ate the matching items like, the grits, bread and syrup. Officer Ferguson assisted in this situation by advising him to fill out a medical request form. He let her know, that he had met with the doctor on 7/26/2019, & that the doctor approved a peanut butter bag to increase his weight. The doctor called this, "Enhanced" continuing his, "Vegan / Rad" & adding a peanut butter bag, which never showed up. Even after being approve by a doctor & completing the request form the night before.

Officer Ferguson explained, if Mr. Bailey gives her the request that she would turn it over to medical. He already had a medical request complete; he walked over to the bunk area & grabbed the filled-out request form. Then walking back to the area Officer Ferguson was standing. He passed her the request form & return to his bunk area. A few minutes passed & Officer Ferguson came over to the bunk area, & informed him to add, "Vegan / Rad" to the details on his medical request form. Officer Ferguson then return to the desk area. After making the corrections to the request, he walked back over to Officer Ferguson & passed her the request form. When it was time for lunch, he stood in line with the diets.

Officer Harris was the on-duty officer, working the line, handling the list of names. Once all the diet trays had been passed out, Mr. Bailey said to Officer Harris, "I'm Vegan / Rad". Officer Harris explained his breakfast tray also had not shown up Vegan / Rad. Officer Harris called the kitchen & let him know that he was listed as, "Enhanced". After being informed from Officer Harris of what the kitchen said. He asked Officer Harris if he could contact medical & have them reach out to the kitchen, making the correction. Officer Harris being so kind to work with him in this situation, did just that. Mr. Bailey didn't eat anything off the lunch tray & now lunch had ended.

Mr. Bailey returned to his bunk area & after doing so, an inmate known as, "*Houseman Patrick*" came over to where Mr. Bailey was sitting & informed him the Sergeant was on her way to speak with him. Patrick was referring to Sergeant Bryant, before she showed up Officer Cooper came in the block. Making her way over to where he was sitting. Then asking him what was taking place? Mr. Bailey replied, "Are you referring to the food"? She smiled & said, "Yes" Mr. Bailey explained what was taking place, & she shared that **Sergeant Bryant** was on her way & just stepped in the block.

Officer Cooper walked over to Sergeant Bryant & explained the situation. After this Sergeant Bryant, Officer Cooper & Mr. Bailey met in the vest. Where Sergeant Bryant explained the details of what was taking place with his meals. Asking him to make a decision between the religious tray called, "Vegan / Rad" or the "Enhanced" tray called regular. He explained what the doctor had told him. That the doctor said Mr. Bailey you've been assigned Vegan / Rad & he would add a **peanut butter bag**.

He never mentioned that it would cancel the current **Vegan / Rad.** Mr. Bailey made the decision to stick with religion & continue Vegan / Rad. Sergeant Bryant said let me go down to the kitchen & see what's going on. Sometime went by & a Vegan / Rad tray showed up in block E-1. Officer Harris called Bailey to the desk, he made his way up there & received a Vegan / Rad tray. Then sitting down at a table, having a prayer before eating his food.

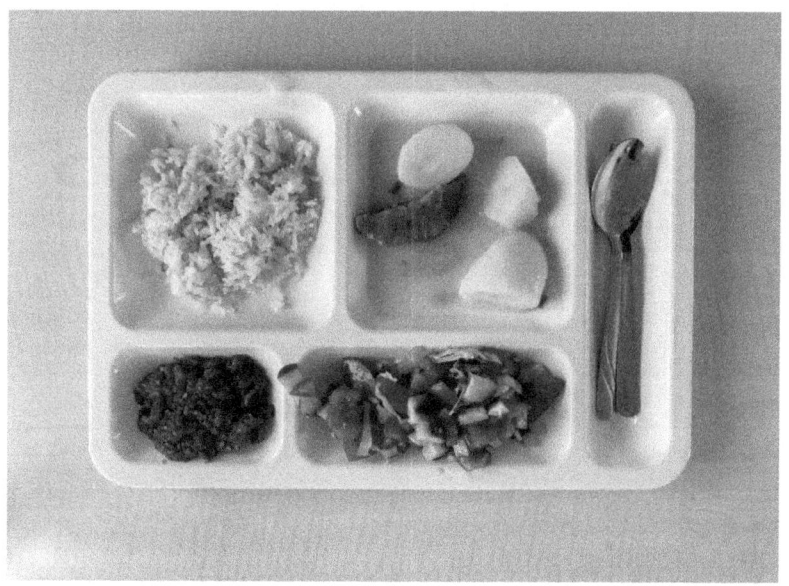

Brian Bailey   7/30/2019

No Vegan Trays

On the morning of 7/30/2019 the "Vegan/Rad" tray I had been receiving, did not show up. The Officer on duty was Officer Ferguson, when diet trays were being handed out, I stood inline and waited to hear my name. It was never called, I was now standing last in the diet line next to Officer Ferguson. I explained to Officer Ferguson, that I should be receiving Vegan/Rad, she then reviewed her list of names and informed me that I was listed as a regular tray. I looked on the tray to see if there was anything that matched up with Vegan/Rad. On the tray was syrup, grits, bread, slice of cheese and a piece of meat. I Accepted the tray and ate the matching items like, the grits, bread, and syrup.

Officer Ferguson assisted in this situation by advising me to fill out a medical request form. I let her know, that I had met with the doctor on 7/26/2019, and that the doctor approved a peanut butter bag to increase my weight. The doctor called this "Enhanced", continuing my Vegan/Rad and adding a peanut butter bag. Also explaining that my peanut butter bag had never shown up and that had turned in a request from the night before. Officer Ferguson explained if I give her the request that she would turn it over to medical. I already had a medical request complete, I walked over to the bunk area and grab the filled out request form.

Then walking back to the area Officer Ferguson was standing, I passed her the request form and return to my bunk area. A few minutes passed and Officer Ferguson came over to the bunk area, and informed me to add "Vegan/Rad" to the details on my medical request form. Officer Ferguson then return to the desk area. After making the corrections to the request, I walked back over to Officer Ferguson and passed her the request form.

When it was time for lunch, I stood inline with the diets. Officer Harris was the on duty Officer working the line, handling the list of names. Once all the diet trays had been passed out, I said to Officer Harris, "I'm Vegan/Rad". Officer Harris explained the kitchen has me down as a regular tray. I explained my breakfast tray also had not shown up Vegan/Rad. Officer Harris called the kitchen and let me know that I was listed as "Enhanced".

230

After being informed from Officer Harris of what the kitchen said, I asked Officer Harris if he could contact medical and have medical reach out to the kitchen, making the correction. Officer Harris being so kind to work with me in this situation, did just that. I didn't eat anything off the lunch tray and now lunch had ended. I returned to my bunk area and after doing so, an inmate known as "Houseman Patrick" came over to where I was sitting and informed me the Sergent was on her way to speak with me.

Patrick was reffing to Sergent Bryant, before she showed up, Officer Cooper came in the block. Making her way over to where I was sitting. Then asking me what was taking place? I replied "Are you reffering to the food"? She smiled and said "yes" I explained what was taking place, and she shared that Sergent Bryant was on her way and just stepped in the block. Officer Cooper walked over to Sergent Bryant and explained the situation. After this Sergent Bryant, Officer Cooper and myself met in the vest.

Where Sergent Bryant explained the details of what was taken place with my meals. Asking me to make a decession between the religious tray called "Vegan/Rad" or the "Enhanced" tray called regular. I explained what the doctor had told me. That he saw I was on Vegan/Rad and would add a peanut butter bag. He never metioned that it would cancel my current Vegan/Rad. I made the decession to stick to my religious and continue Vegan/Rad Sergent Bryant said let me go down to the kitchen and see what's going on.

Sometime went by and a Vegan/Rad tray showed up in block E-1. Officer Harris called Barclay to the desk. I made my way up there and received a Vegan/Rad tray. Then sitting down at a table, having a prayer before eating my food.

7/30/2019

APD Raymon A. Burns, "Video Call"

referring to Dr. Watson

Case# 50-2019-MM-005685-AXXX-MB

On the afternoon of 7/30/2019, Mr. Bailey was called to the desk by Sheriff's Department. When he arrived, Mr. Bailey was informed his attorney was ready for him, by video call. When he walked into the room, he could see APD Raymon A. Burns on the video screen. He picked up the telephone & greeted APD Raymon A. Burns. He starts explaining, "I understand you didn't meet with the doctor earlier." Mr. Bailey explained, the Sheriff's Department informed him that there was a Ms. Watson here to see him, & he informed Officer Harris, that without his representation, he wouldn't be seen.

Mr. Bailey continued by asking Mr. Burns why was he not able to show up? APD Raymon A. Burns explaining that another Assistant Public Defender by the name, "APD Marshall" was going to meet with us, but was unable to attend. Violating the Statutes listed below:

Statute violations:

27.0065 (1) (2) – **Witness coordination.** – Each state attorney and public defender shall be responsible for:

> 1) Coordinating court appearances, including **pretrial conferences** & depositions, for all witnesses who are subpoenaed in criminal cases, including law enforcement personnel.

> 2) **Contacting witnesses & securing information necessary** to place a witness on an on-call status with regard to his or her court appearance.

27.51 (1) **Duties of Public of Defender.**

> 1) The Public Defender shall **represent**, without additional compensation, any person determined to be **indigent** under s. 27.52.

27.40 *(1) (9)* **Court-appointed counsel; circuit registries; minimum requirements; appointment by court.**

1) *Counsel shall be appointed to represent any individual in a criminal or civil proceeding entitled to court-appointed counsel under the Federal or State Constitution or as authorized by general law. The court shall appoint a* **public defender** *to* **represent** *indigent persons as authorized in s.* <u>27.51</u>*. The office of criminal conflict & civil regional counsel shall be appointed to represent persons in those cases in which provision is made for court-appointed counsel, but only after the public defender has certified to the court in writing that the public defender is unable to provide representation due to a conflict of interest or is not authorized to provide representation. The public defender shall report, in the aggregate, the specific basis of all conflicts of interest certified to the court. On a quarterly basis, the public defender shall submit this information to the Justice Administrative Commission.*

9) *Any interested person may advise the court of* **any circumstance affecting the quality of representation,** *including,* **but not limited to,** *false or fraudulent billing, misconduct, failure to meet continuing legal education requirements, solicitation to receive compensation from the client the attorney is appointed to represent, or failure to file appropriate motions in a timely manner.*

Mr. Bailey asked, "why did you not call the doctor & cancel the appointment? Before hearing him answer Mr. Bailey said, "this is the third time you have not represented me, once in the courtroom & now twice at the block. This is what I was explaining to the Judge."APD Raymon A. Burns explains, "I did show up out there, but you refuse to have the meeting". APD Raymon A. Burns is referring to is a time just prior, after being dismissed as representation by the defendant, until the judge scheduled the "Nelson hearing". Mr. Bailey replied, "The day before I informed you to cancel the doctor". Due to seeking new representation & needing to see the Judge. APD Raymon A. Burns shares that he didn't have the telephone number, nor did he setup the appointment.

Mr. Bailey asked, "are all the Assistant Public Defender in the same building"? APD Raymon A. Burns replies, "Yes" Mr. Bailey replied, "Then why couldn't you reach out & get the telephone number & cancel the appointment. I'm very disappointed in your team, you're failing by wasting people's time".

(Violating statute 27.0065)

Assistant Public Defender Raymon A. Burns replies by being apologetic, Mr. Bailey replied, "I don't wanna hear an apology, I wanna hear solutions". Explaining, I'm on the inside, told what to do by Sheriff's Department, unable to change what is taking place outside the block. Again, Assistant Public Defender Raymon A. Burns & his team have dropped the ball, while Mr. Bailey is incarcerated only creating more time between now & trial.

*Assistant Public Defender Raymon A. Burns ask, "Do you have any questions for me"? Mr. Bailey replied, "No" APD Raymon A. Burns explains, I wanted to talk with you first, & let you know what was going on. **Again, my representation has not been there to represent me.** APD Raymon A. Burns continues by explaining, he's gonna go upstairs & speak with the others, we then ended the conversation.*

Brian Bailey **Assistant Public Defender** 7/30/2019
(Mr. Benjamin Burns "Video call" referring to Dr. Watson)

Case # 50-2019-MM-005685-AXXX-MB

On the afternoon of 7/30/2019, I (Brian Bailey) was called to the desk by Sheriff's Department. When I arrived, I was informed my attorney was ready for me, by video call. When I walked into the room, I could see Mr. Burns on the video screen. I picked up the telephone and greeted Mr. Burns. He starts explaining, I understand you didn't meet with the doctors emails. I explained, the Sheriff's Department informed me that there was a Ms. Watson here to see me, and I informed Officer Harris, that without my representation, I wouldn't be seen. I continued by asking Mr. Burns why was he not able to show up? Mr. Burns explaining that another assistant public defender by the name "Ms. Marshall" was going to meet with me, but was unable to attend. (Violating Statue 27.0065 (1)(2) 27.51 (1) 27.40(1)(9))

I asked, why did you not call the doctor and cancel the appointment? Before hearing him answer I said, this is the third time you have not represented me, once in the courtroom and now twice at the block. This is what I was explaining to the judge, Mr. Burns explains, I did show up out there but you refuse to have the meeting. I replied, The day before I informed you to cancel the doctor. Due to me seeking new representation, and needing to see the judge. Mr. Burns shares that he didn't have the doctor's telephone number, nor did he set up the appointment. I asked, are all the assistant public defenders in the same building? Mr. Burns replies "Yes." I replied "Then why couldn't you reachout and get the telephone number, and cancel the appointment. I'm very disappointed in your team, your failing by wasting people's time. (Violating Statue 27.0065 Line 5) read it →

Mr. Burns replies by being apologetic, I replied "I don't wanna here an apology, I wanna hear solutions. Explaining Him on the inside, told what to do by Sheriff's Department, unable to change what is taking place, outside the block. Again Mr. Burns and his team have dropped the ball, while I'm incarcerated, only creating more time between now and trial. Mr. Burns ask "Do you have any questions from me? I replied "No" Mr. Burns explains, I wanted to talk with you first, and let you know what was going on. Again my representation has not been there to represent me. Mr. Burns continues by explaining, he's gonna go upstairs and speak with the others, we then ended the conversation.

Statue Violation:

S. 27.0065 - Witness Coordination

Each state attorney and public defender shall be responsible for:

* (1) Coordinating court appearances, including pretrial conferences and depositions, for all witnesses who are subpoenaed in criminal cases, including law enforcement personnel.

* (2) Contacting witnesses and securing information necessary to place a witness on on-call status with regard to his or her court appearance.

(3) Contacting witnesses to advise them not to report to court in the event the case for which they have been subpoenaed has been continued or has had a plea entered, or in the event there is any other reason why their attendance is not required on the dates they have been ordered to report.

(4) Contacting the employer of a witness, when necessary, to confirm that the employee has been subpoenaed to appear in court as a witness.

* In addition, the state attorney or public defender may provide additional services to reduce time and wage losses to a minimum for all witnesses.

S. 27.51 - Duties of public defender

* (1) The public defender shall represent, without additional compensation, any person determined to be indigent under s. 27.52 and:

(B) Under arrest for, or charged with:

1. A misdemeanor authorized for prosecution by the state attorney;

S. 27.40 - Court-appointed counsel; circuit registries; minimum requirements; appointment by court

* (1) Counsel shall be appointed to represent any individual in a criminal or civil proceeding entitled to court-appointed counsel under the Federal or State Constitution or as authorized by general law. The court shall appoint a public defender to represent indigent person as authorized in s. 27.51. The office of criminal conflict and civil regional counsel shall be appointed to represent persons in those cases in which provision is made for court-appointed counsel but the public defender is unable to provide representation due to a conflict of interest or is not authorized to provide representation.

* (7) Any interested person may advise the court of any circumstances affecting the quality of representation, including, but not limited to, false or fraudulent billing, misconduct, failure to meet continuing legal education requirements, solicitation to receive compensation from the client the attorney is appointed to represent, or failure to file appropriate motions in a timely manner.

7/31/2019
No Vegan / Rad Diet

Case# 50-2019-MM-005685-AXXX-MB

While being incarcerated in **West Detention Center, Belle Glade**. A few days after arriving, Mr. Bailey received a **NIV Holy Bible**. While in repent for his sins he was reading the NIV Holy Bible. After going **18 Days without eating**, starting on the day he arrived in the jail. Mr. Bailey was dropped by a **Higher Power,** going from a standing position to then being on the floor. When opening his eyes medical staff & officers were coming into block E-1, placing him on a stretcher, & rolling it to a medical center within the West Detention Center. Separating him from the items in my bunk area, one item being the **NIV Holy Bible**.

Leaving off on page 860, the date was **5/28/2019**, he's locked in a confined cell with glass windows facing medical staff. **Requesting the NIV Holy Bible** from the officers on duty, but he was unable to succeed in retrieving one. On **5/29/2019** after learning more about the details of what's inside the Holy Bible, Mr. Bailey started a vegan diet while in solitaire confinement. On **5/30/2019** he continued exercising in solitaire confinement. On the date of **6/2/2019**, one of the commanding officers from the Sheriff's Department, advised him that he was not authorized to exercise.

(No Vegan Meal)
Statute violation: **950.04**

Then reading the D.O.C. Department of Corrections Inmate Rules & Regulations. During his time in solitaire confinement, he created a few new recipes for the restaurant Planet Moon, to go with a lifestyle of eating a vegetarian style diet. After 8 Days in a cell & being watched by medical staff, while eating a vegan diet, he was returned back to block E-1. The date was **6/4/2019**, his new NIV Holy Bible had arrived, & he was able to return the borrowed one another inmate had allowed him to use. Mr. Bailey started reading right where he left off on page 860, it took him four more days to complete the NIV Holy Bible.

On the date of **6/8/2019**, he had completed reading the **NIV Holy Bible**, this was the largest book he had ever read. Now he was practicing the Christian Religion, allowing the hair on his face & head to grow into a beard, looking like a cave man. Following, The Nazirite, after growing the beard & hair long, from the date of **5/12/2019** to **7/7/2019**, he trimmed both the beard & hair out of respect for the judge. The very next day he was transported to the main courthouse to stand before the judge, while the defense attorney required that Mr. Bailey see a doctor in reference to competence.

Mr. Bailey now started reviewing the Holy Bible, when he re-read **Numbers:6:5** Mr. Bailey realized that he crossed a religious rule, by putting a razor to his head.

Below is a list of days, that an assigned meal did "**NOT**" show up

(No Vegan meal arrived)

Dates	Mealtime	Location
6/11/2019	Lunch	Main Court House
No Vegan bag		
7/2/2019	Lunch	Main Court House
No Vegan bag		
7/24/2019	Lunch	Main Court House
No Vegan bag		
7/30/2019	Breakfast/Lunch	Block E-1
No tray		
7/31/2019	Breakfast	Block E-1
No tray		
8/2/2019	Lunch	Main Court House
No Vegan bag, with my name		
8/4/2019	Unknown	Block E-1
No peanut butter bag / Officer Folkwood		
(Working case)		

Sheriff's Department has been advised by Medical since 5/29/2019, that Mr. Bailey received a vegan meal on schedule at least three times a day.

Violating Statutes: **950.04 Penalty for Neglect of the Duty in Keeping Prisoners in the United States.**

Brian Bailey

No Vegan/Rad Diet   7/31/2019

Case # - 50-2019-MM-005685-AXXX-MB

While being incarcerated in West Detension Center, Belle Glade.
A few days after arriving, I received a Holy Bible. While in repent for my sins I read
this Holy Bible. After going 18 days without eating, I was dropped by a higher power.
Medical staff and officers came into block E-1, placed me on to a stretcher, rolling it
to a medical center within the West Detention Center. Separating me from the items in
my bunk area, one item being the Holy Bible. Leaving off on page 860, the date
was 5/28/2019. I am locked in a confined cell with glass windows facing medical staff.
Requesting the NIV Holy Bible from the officers on duty, but I was unable to succeed
in retrieving one. On 5/29/2019 After learning more about the holy Bible, I started a
vegan diet while in solitary confinement. On 5/30/2019 I continued screening in
solitary confinement. On 6/2/2019 one of the Sheriff's Department Officers advised
me that I was not authorized to exercise. Then reading the D.O.C. Inmate Rules and regulations. After 3 days of
confinement, and eating vegan, I was returned back to block "E-1". The date was
6/4/2019, my new NIV Holy Bible had arrived. I started reading right where I left off
on page 860, it took me four more days to complete the NIV Holy Bible. The date
now was 6/8/2019, this was the largest book I had ever read. Now I was practicing
my christian religion, letting my beard grow, as well as the hair on top of my
head. Following The Nazirite, After growing my beard And hair long, from 5/12/2019 to
7/7/2019 I trimmed both my beard and hair out of respect for not judging. The very next
day I was transported to the main courthouse to stand before the judge, while the defense attorney
required that I have this by a dozen references to commentaries. I now started reviewing
the Holy Bible. When I re-read Numbers : 6:5 I realized that I broke a religious rule, by putting
a razor to my head.

No Vegan Meals Arrived

Dates	Meal			Location	Notes
6-11-2019	B	(L)	D	Main Court House	No Vegan bag
7-2-2019	B	(L)	D	Main Court House	No Vegan bag
7-24-2019	B	(L)	D	Main Court House	No Vegan bag
7-30-2019	(B)	(L)	D	Block E-1	No Tray
7-31-2019	(B)	L	D	Block E-1	No Tray
8-2-2019	B	(L)	D	Main Court house	No Vegan bag, with my Name
8-4-2019	B	L	D	Block E-1	No vegan butter bag / Officer Falk mood (watching case)
	B	L	D		
	B	L	D		
	B	L	D		
	B	L	D		
	B	L	D		
	B	L	D		
	B	L	D		
	B	L	D		

△CCS
CORRECT CARE
SOLUTIONS

HEALTHCARE REQUEST

SOLICITUD DE SERVICIO DE SALUD

RECEIVED
Date: 7/31/19
Initials:
Time: 1432

Name (Nombre): Brian Bailey   ID # (Nº de identificación): 0403731

Living Unit / Dorm (Unidad): E-1   Bed # (cama/cuarto): _____

☑ Medical (Medico)   ☐ Behavioral Health (Salud Mental)   ☐ Dental (Dental)   ☐ Other_____
☐ Medication Refills (Suplemento / recarga de Medicamento)   ☐ Eye Clinic (Clinica para la vision)

Nature of problem or Request (be specific)   Naturaleza del problema o solicitud (sea específico)

After visiting with the doctor and being told I would receive an
enhanced meal. It has not happened. I'm currently
Approved by Chaplin & Medical for Rad Vegan

I consent to be treated by Health Care Staff for the condition described. I understand that the facility may charge me for some of these services and may deduct it from my account during this current or future stays in the facility. I understand that I will receive health care regardless of my ability to pay.

Doy mi consentimiento para ser tratado por el personal de atención de salud para las condiciones descritas. Entiendo que la instalación me puede cobrar por algunos de estos servicios y pueden descontarlo de mi cuenta durante esta o futuras estancias. Entiendo que voy a recibir atención médica, independientemente de mi capacidad de pago.

Patient Signature (Firma del Paciente): B. Bailey   Date (Fecha): 7/29/2019

If you are deaf or hard-of-hearing, do you need any communication assistance for this healthcare visit? (Si es usted sordo/a o padece de alguna disminución del oído (sordera parcial, por ejemplo), ¿necesita ayuda para comunicar sus voluntades cuando tiene una visita médica?)

☐ No   ☐ Yes: Video Remote Interpreter (VRI) (via "purple" laptop)   (Intérprete a distancia a través de un link de video (IRV) (a través del portátil morado)

☐ Yes: In-person qualified interpreter.   Please explain why you need an in-person interpreter rather than VRI (Intérprete calificado en persona (de carne y hueso). Por favor, explica por qué se necesita un intérprete presente en persona en vez del sistema IRV)_____

☐ Yes: Other (Please Specify) (Otro medio (favor de explicar a continuación) _____

This is a confidential document and should only be placed in a designated area, medical box or given directly to medical staff.
Este es un documento confidencial y sólo debe ser colocado en un área designada, caja médica o entregada directamente al personal médico.

DO NOT WRITE BELOW THIS LINE

(TO BE COMPLETED BY TRIAGING STAFF)

| TRIAGE: | ☐ Emergent | ☐ Urgent | ☒ Routine | Triage Date: 7/31/19 | Initials: | Time: 1432 |

INITIAL: ☐ Sick Call   ☐ Nurse   ☒ HCP   ☐ Dentist   ☐ Behavioral Health   ☐ Eye Clinic   ☐ Other_____

RESPONSE TO PATIENT / COMMENTS: _____

☒ Patient seen (if applicable)
☐ Response sent to patient (if applicable)   ☐ Patient refused, Refusal Form completed
☐ Patient released from custody
☐ Does Patient require auxiliary aides?   Yes   No

Co-pay Charges: ☒ No   ☐ Yes   ☐ $3.00 non-formulary medication - # of prescriptions_____ Total Cost $_____
☐ $3.00 Sick Call   ☐ $5.00 for glasses   ☐ $10.00 for appliances   ☐ Other charges $_____

NOTE: Treatment information should not be noted above but should be documented on the appropriate treatment form(s)

Staff Signature _____   Date 7/31/19   (Print Patient Name) Brian Bailey   Number 2019051205O   Date 7/13/19

Patient Signature B. Bailey

Form Number: SC001UNKYDOCACCBI120117 (KYDOC)   2-Part Form   Page 1 of 1

Brian Bailey   The General   8/1/2019

I.D. PT 295 K 01 02

The item I'm holding is a gift.
This gift is a tool for the world.
It CAN be used for many things.
By the touch it is hard.
It carries no scent by the smell.
Rubber is a part of this item.
The color by sight is yellow.
It's a key to many puzzles.
With shiney metal at one end.
It can be used to hold a line.
Made long and thin from hardwood.
Holding a circular shape at one end.
Filled with a soft metal.
Coded with it's own identification.
Helping educate is one of it's strengths.
It's known for creating art.
When combined with tree material.
Can bring the power of knowledge to life.

Do you know the name of this item?

Introducing the number two pencil!

I'm used to trace, draw and write.
I live in the family of education.
I help people communicate and learn.
My name is the number two pencil.

BB

Brian Bailey   The Lion   8/1/2019

I start off as a man,
eating the blood of animals.
Gaining power and strength,
while mutating into a bull.
On Gods green earth,
with heaven and light.
In the deepblue there comes darkness,
weightless without the feeling of gravity,
having no sense of smell.
Rescued by those we call Lords.
To only be devoured by the king,
creating food and energy,
for the recirculation of Life.

IN THE COUNTY COURT OF THE FIFTEENTH JUDICIAL CIRCUIT
IN AND FOR PALM BEACH COUNTY, FLORIDA - CRIMINAL DIVISION
CIRCUIT/COUNTY COURT
Court Event Form

DEFENDANT: BRIAN DALE BAILEY
CASE NO: 50-2019-MM-005685-AXXX-MB

STATE OF FLORIDA   DATE: 8/2/2019
vs.
DEFENDANT: BRIAN DALE BAILEY   JACKET #:   0403731
CASE NO: 50-2019-MM-005685-AXXX-MB   BOOKING #:   2019015844
DIVISION: B: Cnty Crim - B (County)

PRESIDING JUDGE: HANSER, JUDGELEONARD   START TIME: 9:12 AM
ASA: MYERS, RYAN   END TIME: 9:27 AM
ATTORNEY:
PUBLIC DEFENDER: BURNS, RAYMON
CO-COUNSEL: COURT REPORTER
DEPUTY CLERK: ME   COURT TYPE: STCK - STATUS
                                                                  CHECK

COURT ROOM: 2E (Main Branch)

Reset For
Court Date Scheduled - STCK - STATUS CHECK - 8/13/2019 8:30 AM - 2E (Main Branch) MB, 205 N. Dixie
Highway West Palm Beach FL 33401 - RE: COMPETENCY

Motion to Withdraw - Denied   - PD - DEFENDANT
Other: DEFENDANT PRESENT AND IN CUSTODY
Other: NELSON HEARING TAKES PLACE AT THE REQUEST OF THE DEFENDANT
Other: DEFENDANT PRESENT, SWORN AND TESTIFIED, AND ADVISED OF RIGHTS

Count 1 - MF TRESPASS AFTER WARNING 810.09(2A)

FILED: PALM BEACH COUNTY, FL SHARON R BOCK, CLERK 08/02/2019 09:27:25 AM

8/2/2019

IN THE CIRCUIT/COUNTY COURT OF THE FIFTEENTH JUDICIAL CIRCUIT
IN AND FOR PALM BEACH COUNTY, FLORIDA

STATE OF FLORIDA

-Vs-

BRIAN DALE BAILEY
GENERAL DELIVERY
WEST PALM BEACH, FL 32200

Date: 08/02/2019

Case No: 50-2019-MM-005685-AXXX-MB

Division: B: Cnty Crim - B (County)

NOTICE OF HEARING

THE DEFENDANT MUST BE PRESENT AT THIS HEARING

For Criminal Charges: Failure to Appear will result in a Bond Forfeiture or
revocation of own recognizance (O.R.) and a Capias/Warrant being issued for your arrest.
For Civil Traffic Charges: Failure to appear may result in the suspension of your driver's license.
IF YOUR CASE IS ON-CALL, CONTACT YOUR ATTORNEY FOR THE TIME TO APPEAR
YOU ARE HEREBY NOTIFIED that this case is scheduled

DATE:	TIME:	HEARING TYPE:	LOCATION:
8/13/2019	8:30 AM	STCK - STATUS CHECK	2E (Main Branch) MB, 205 N. Dixie Highway West Palm Beach FL 33401

BE PREPARED TO PAY COURT COSTS AND FINES ASSESSED BY THE COURT AT THIS HEARING
"IF YOU INTEND TO REQUEST THE SERVICES OF THE PUBLIC DEFENDER, YOU MUST FILE AN APPLICATION AT THE CLERK &
COMPTROLLER'S OFFICE AND BE APPOINTED THE PUBLIC DEFENDER BEFORE YOUR COURT DATE. THE APPLICATION FEE IS $50.00."
Civil Traffic Charges are not eligible for a Public Defender.

SHARON R. BOCK,
CLERK & COMPTROLLER
BY: _ME_

Deft/Atty: DEFENDANT IN CUSTODY

Deputy Clerk

cc: RYAN MYERS
       BURNS, RAYMON A

Page 1 of 2

IN THE CIRCUIT/COUNTY COURT OF THE FIFTEENTH JUDICIAL CIRCUIT
IN AND FOR PALM BEACH COUNTY, FLORIDA

"If you are a person with a disability who needs any accommodation in order to participate in this proceeding, you are entitled, at no cost to you, to the provision of certain assistance. Please contact Tammy Anton, Americans with Disabilities Act Coordinator, Palm Beach County Courthouse, 205 North Dixie Hwy, West Palm Beach, FL 33401; telephone number (561) 355-4380 at least 7 days before your scheduled court appearance, or immediately upon receiving this notification if the time before the scheduled appearance is less than 7 days; if you are hearing or voice impaired, call 711."

"Si usted es una persona minusválida que necesita algún acomodamiento para poder participar en este procedimiento, usted tiene derecho, sin tener gastos propios, a que se le provea cierta ayuda. Tenga la amabilidad de ponerse en contacto con Tammy Anton, 205 N. Dixie Highway, West Palm Beach, Florida 33401; teléfono número (561) 355-4380, por lo menos 7 días antes de la cita fijada para su comparecencia en los tribunales, o inmediatamente después de recibir esta notificación si el tiempo antes de la comparecencia que se ha programado es menos de 7 días; si usted tiene discapacitación del oído o de la voz, llame al 711."

"Si ou se yon moun ki enfim ki bezwen akomodasyon pou w ka patisipe nan pwosedi sa, ou kalifye san ou pa gen okenn lajan pou w peye, gen pwovizyon pou jwen kèk èd. Tanpri kontakte Tammy Anton, kòòdonatè pwogram Lwa pou ameriken ki Enfim yo nan Tribinal Konte Palm Beach la ki nan 205 North Dixie Highway, West Palm Beach, Florida 33401; telefòn li se (561) 355-4380 nan 7 jou anvan dat ou gen randevou pou parèt nan tribinal la, oubyen imedyatman apre ou fin resevwa konvokasyon an si lè ou gen pou w parèt nan tribinal la mwens ke 7 jou; si ou gen pwoblèm pou w tande oubyen pale, rele 711."

248

IN THE COUNTY COURT OF THE FIFTEENTH JUDICIAL CIRCUIT,
IN AND FOR PALM BEACH COUNTY, FLORIDA
CRIMINAL DIVISION "B"

STATE OF FLORIDA

CASE NO. 19MM005685AMB

vs.

Brian Dale Bailey,
Defendant.

FILED

AUG 02 2019

SHARON R. BOCK, CLERK
PALM BEACH COUNTY, FL
COUNTY CRIMINAL

ORDER GRANTING EXAMINATION
OF DEFENDANT'S COMPETENCY

THIS CAUSE came before the Court for a Status Check regarding the defendant's competency. Based on the proceedings before the Court, and the Court being otherwise fully advised, it is

ORDERED AND ADJUDGED

1. That another doctor shall be appointed to evaluate Defendant's competency to proceed.

2. **One of the following doctors from Court Psychology whose business address is 205 N. Dixie Highway, #5.1130, West Palm Beach, FL 33401 and whose telephone number is (561) 355-2108, is appointed to examine the Defendant: Dr. Lynn Hargrove, Dr. Michaelanne Marie, Dr. Gretchen Moy, Dr. Stephen McGraw, or Dr. Jeff Dalia.**

3. If the defendant is in custody, the Sheriff of Palm Beach County shall permit the above-named expert(s) to enter the Palm Beach County Jail to conduct the foregoing evaluation of the defendant upon presentment of this Order. If the defendant is not in custody, the expert is to contact defense counsel, or pro se defendant, for scheduling.

4. The expert is to give timely notice to the parties of the date and place of the examination.

5. A copy of the order serves as authorization for the expert to inspect and copy any discoverable information relating to the Defendant maintained by the defense counsel, Clerk of this Court, State Attorney's Office, any hospital, doctor, or any health care provider, therapist, psychiatrist, psychologist, counselor, or any mental health provider, or other social or human services agency without the necessity of written consent by Defendant.

6. This cause is scheduled for a hearing on the issue of the defendant's competency to proceed on **Tuesday, August 13, 2019 at 8:30 AM**.

7. The expert shall submit a written evaluation of the defendant's mental condition to this Court with copies to the Assistant State Attorney and the Attorney for the Defendant on or before the 12th day of August, 2019, which shall include but is not limited to:

a. **Competence to Proceed** (See Fla.R.Crim.P. 3.211(a), F.S. §§916.115, 916.301). Whether the defendant has sufficient present ability to consult with counsel with a reasonable degree of rational understanding and whether the defendant has a rational, as well as factual,

SCANNED
AUG 02 2019

SCANNED
AUG 02 2019

understanding of the pending proceedings. In considering the issue of competence to proceed, the examining expert shall consider and include in their report, the following factors, and any other factors deemed relevant by the experts, as they pertain to the defendant's capacity and/or ability to:

1. Appreciate the charges or allegations against him;
2. Appreciate the range and nature of possible penalties which may be imposed against him;
3. Understand the adversary nature of the legal process;
4. Disclose to his attorney facts pertinent to the proceedings at issue;
5. Manifest appropriate courtroom behavior;
6. Testify relevantly;

b. **Recommend Treatment** (See Fla.R.Crim. P. 3.211(b)). Should the appointed expert find that the defendant is incompetent to proceed, then the expert shall determine whether the defendant meets the criteria for involuntary hospitalization and report on any recommended treatment for the defendant to attain competence to proceed. The expert's report and recommendations shall include consideration of the following:

1. The mental illness or intellectual disability causing the incompetence;
2. The treatment or treatments appropriate for the mental illness or intellectual disability of the defendant and an explanation of each of the possible treatment alternative in order of choices;
3. The availability of acceptable treatment, including whether the treatment is available in the community and whether the treatment involves community or residential facilities or inpatient or outpatient settings;
4. The likelihood of the defendant attaining competence under the recommended treatment, an assessment of the probable duration of the treatment required to restore competence, and the probability that the defendant will attain competence to proceed in the foreseeable future;

8. All written reports submitted by the expert shall contain the following:

a. A list of the specific matters referred for evaluation;
b. A description of the evaluation procedure, techniques and tests used in the examination and purpose for each;
c. The expert's clinical observations, findings, and opinions on each issue referred for evaluation by the Court, and specific identification of those issues which the expert could not give an opinion;
d. An identification of the sources of information used by the expert and a presentation of the factual basis for the expert's clinical findings and opinions.

All information contained in the motion to determine competency of the defendant or in any report submitted under this order, insofar as the information relates solely to the issues of competency to proceed or to commitment, shall be used only in determining the mental competency to proceed or the commitment or other treatment of the defendant.

State v. Brian Dale Bailey
Case No. 19MM005685AMB
Order Granting Examination of
Defendant's Competency
Page 3

9. If an order is entered for the determination of competence, the appointed expert shall be paid in accordance with his or her current contract with the responsible party, or in the absence of a contract, the current Administrative Order regarding payment of appointed experts. Evaluations that include both competency and sanity will be proportionately paid for by the responsible parties.

10. Payment for competency evaluations to determine competence to proceed or to determine recommended treatment for competence to proceed shall be made by the Court in accordance with the contract between the Court and the expert, or if no contract exists, then in accordance with the current Administrative Order regarding payment of appointed experts. The expert shall submit the bill and appropriate invoice with an attached copy of this Order Directing Examination of the Defendant's Competency to the Court at:

> Court Administration
> Administrative Office of the Courts
> 205 North Dixie Highway, 5th Floor
> West Palm Beach, FL 33401

When a request is made for an evaluation of the defendant to determine the defendant's sanity or as an aid for sentencing, the requesting party shall pay. Payment shall be made in accordance with the contract between the responsible party and the expert, or if no contract exists, then in accordance with the current Administrative Order regarding payment of appointed experts.

DONE AND ORDERED in Chambers at West Palm Beach, Palm Beach County, Florida this 2 day of August, 2019.

LEONARD HANSER
County Court Judge

Copies furnished:
Expert, Court Psychology 205 N. Dixie Highway, Suite. 5.1130, West Palm Beach, FL 33401, (561) 355-2108 psd-courtpsychology@pbcgov.org; mrsmith@pbcgov.org
Palm Beach County Sheriff's Office 3228 Gun Club Road West Palm Beach, FL 33406 Email: IMDCourtOrders@pbso.org
Ryan Myers, Assistant State Attorney, Division B
401 N Dixie Hwy, West Palm Beach, FL 33401, Email: rmyers@sa15.org
Burns, Raymon, Assistant Public Defender, Division B
421 3rd Street west Palm Beach, FL 44401, Email: rburns@pd15.org;jmecbetti@pd15.org
Paulina Pasquarelli, Court Administration, 205 N. Dixie Highway, 5th Floor, West Palm Beach, FL 33401 email PPasquarelli@pbcgov.org

On the date of 8/2/2019, while visiting the main courthouse & being held in the basement. Looking to receive a vegan/rad diet with no meat or dairy, while reading the NIV Holy Bible. Once again, there was, "**no vegan**" meal in his name. While 70% of our country is obese & inmates are in standing & sitting positions regularly, being escorted & ordered what to do by authority.

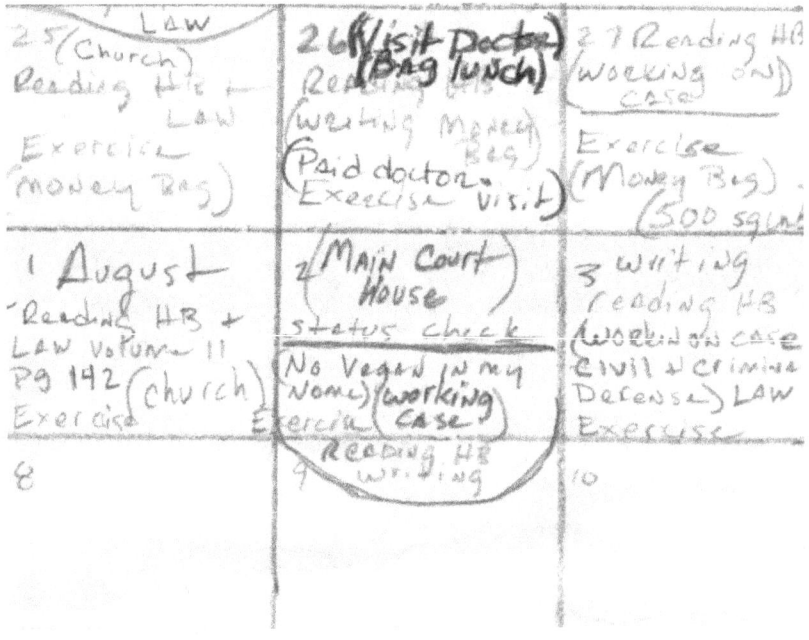

8/2/2019

In the courtroom

Case# 50-2019-MM-005685-AXXX-MB

While in custody on **8/2/2019**, Mr. Bailey was walked into the courtroom by Sheriff's Department, with the courtroom quiet & no cases in session. His handcuffs were removed, & he was then seated. Mr. Bailey was approached by APD Raymon A. Burns, they then greeted each other, APD Raymon A. Burns explained what was about to take place. Sharing that he was going to let the Judge know, that the visit with a competence doctor hadn't taken place.

Due to unattendance from appointed representation, neither APD Raymon A. Burns nor APD Marsh were able to make it out to the West Detention Center, Belle Glade, Department of Corrections. Mr. Bailey respond to APD Raymon A. Burns explaining, "Due to unattendance of his team, there have been three **Statute violations.** He shared the letter with details, of the three Statute violations that had occurred. APD Raymon A. Burns reviewed the handwritten letter & while doing so Mr. Bailey explained, "I would like to tell the Judge about the Statute violations & want you to request for a **Nelson hearing**".

APD Raymon A. Burns handed him back the letter & explained, "I don't know if the judge will do that, but I'll try". APD Raymon A. Burns walks away & calls the case out to the Judge. Both the State & APD Raymon A. Burns discussed that the date for competence had not been met. Then moving forward with a future date of **8/13/2019**, for hearing in reference to competence. Mr. Bailey then waived APD Raymon A. Burns over to where he was sitting & said, "What about the **Nelson hearing**"? APD Raymon A. Burns replied, "We have to do this part first & then I can ask the Judge for a **Nelson hearing**". Mr. Bailey replied, "Ok".

APD Raymon A. Burns returned to his position at the stand, & then requested the **Nelson hearing**. Mr. Bailey was asked to stand by Sheriff's Department as the Judge was listening to APD Raymon A. Burns. Once he finished Judge Leonard Hanser allowed the **Nelson hearing**, then swearing Mr. Bailey in under oath & explaining anything he says can be used against him in the court of law. He replied, "Yes your honor" with his letter in hand, he started reading the details of why he would like new representation. When doing so, Mr. Bailey also shared the three Statute violations.

Judge Leonard Hanser denied his request, sharing his take & voicing the reason for his decision. Mr. Bailey sat back down & shortly thereafter APD Raymon A. Burns came back over to where he was seated. APD Raymon A. Burns shared that before the date of **8/13/2019** they were going to setup another meeting with a new doctor. Mr. Bailey asked for the company or business name of Ms. Watson. APD Raymon A. Burns said, "From what I understand it was Dr. Lisa Faraldo that was out there". He replied, "The Sheriff's Department told me the name was Ms. Watson".

Again, APD Raymon A. Burns replied, "It was Dr. Faraldo & she said she would not return again, So, I will have to get someone new". Our conversation came to an end. Now APD Raymon A. Burns started speaking aloud with Judge Leonard Hanser. Judge Leonard Hanser shared why don't you have Mr. Bailey transported to Gun Club if that makes things easier. They both went back & forth on the topic, not ending with a conclusion. Mr. Bailey was then asked by Sheriff's Department to stand, then being handcuff & walked out of the courtroom.

When arriving downstairs at the holding cells, he gave his name to receive a lunch bag. There was no Vegan / Rad with his name on it, he was given one with the **Dunn C Quinn, L.** In the bag was a tablespoon size of peanut butter & two slices of white bread, the officer also handed him an apple & fruit juice. During transportation from the courthouse to West Detention Center, Belle Glade **my right hand went completely numb**, Mr. Bailey tried adjusting the cuffs, but it wasn't helping!

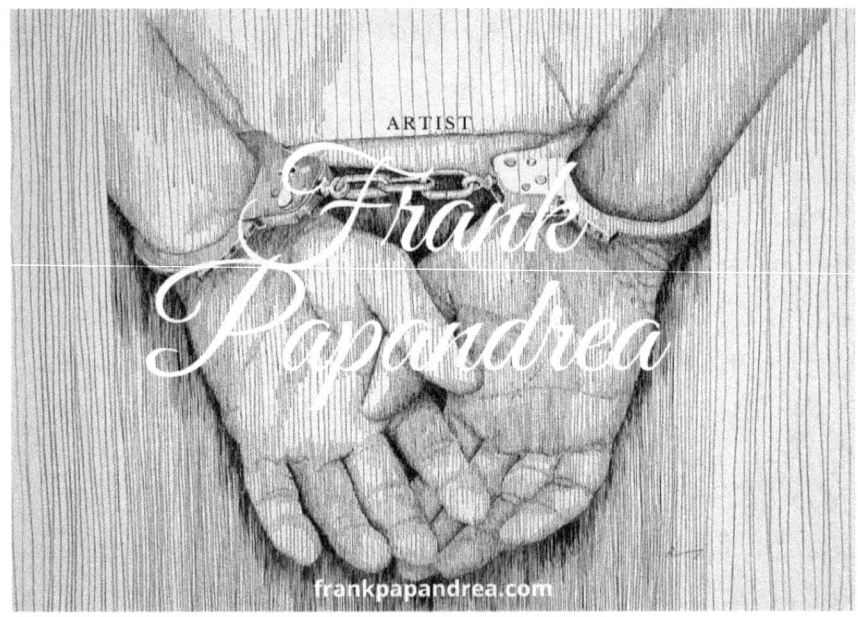

CASE # 50-2019-MM-005635-AXXX-MB

While in custody on 8/2/2019, I was walked into the courtroom by Sheriff's Department, with the courtroom quiet and no cases in session. My handcuffs were removed and I was then seated. I was approached by Mr. Raymond Burns, we then greeted each other. Mr. Burns explained what was about to take place. Showing that he was going to let the judge know, that the visit with a competency doctor hadn't taken place. Due to unattendance from appointed representation. Neither Mr. Burns or Ms. Mensh were able to make it out to the West Detention Center, Belle Glade, Department of Corrections. I respond to Mr. Burns explaining "Due to the unattendance of his team, there have been three Statue Violations.

I shared the letter, with details, of the three Statue Violations that had occurred. Mr. Burns reviewed the hand written letter, and while doing so I explained "I would like to tell the judge about the Statue Violations, ans want you to request for a Nelson hearing. Mr. Burns handed me back the letter and explained "I don't know if the judge will do that, but I'll try". Mr. Burns walks away and calls the case out to the judge. Both the state and Mr. Burns discussed that the date for competence had not been met. Then moving forward with a future date of 8/13/2019 for hearing in reference to competence. I then waived Mr. Burns over to where I was sitting and said "What about the nelson hearing? Mr. Burns replied "We have to do this part first and then I can ask the judge for a nelson hearing". I replied "Ok"

Mr. Burns returned to his position at the stand, and then requested the nelson hearing. I was ask to stand by Sheriff's Department as the judge was listening to Mr. Burns. Once he finished Judge Hanson allowed the nelson hearing, then swearing me in under oath that explaining anything I say can be used against me in the court of law. I replied "Yes your honor. With my letter in hand I started to read the details of why I would like new representation. When doing so I also shared the three statue violations. Judge Hanson denied my request, shaking his head. And voiding the reason for his decession. I sat back down and shortly there after Mr. Burns came back over to where I was seated.

Mr. Burns shared that before the date of 8/13/2019 they were going to setup another meeting with a new doctor. I asked for the company or business name of Mrs. Watson. Mr. Burns said "From what I understand it was Liza Faraldo that was out there". I replied "The Sheriff's Department told me the name was Mrs. Watson". Again Mr. Burns replied "It was Dr. Faraldo and she said she would not return again, so I will have to get someone new". Our conversation came to an end. Now Mr. Burns started speaking aloud with judge Hanson. Judge Hanson shared why don't you have Mr. Bailey transported to Gun Club if that makes things easier. They both went back and forth on the topic, not ending with a conclusion. I was then asked by Sheriff's Department to stand, then being recuffed and walked out of the courtroom.

When arriving downstairs at the holding cells, I gave my name to receive a lunch bag. There no vegan/food with my name on it. I was given one with the name DONN C. QUINN, L. In the bag was a table spoon sole of peanut button and two slices of white bread, the officer also handed me an apple and fruit juice. During transportation from the courthouse to west detention center, Belle Glade, my right hand went completely numb, I tried adjusting the cuffs, but it wasn't helping!

On the date of 8/2/2019, while in the main courthouse basement. After requesting for a vegan/rad meal & the officer explaining that one didn't show up with Mr. Bailey's name. The officer then handed him a bag meal with another name on it called, "**Dunn C Quinn, L**" he accepted the bag, but was concerned as to why one wasn't showing up with his name. Below is the evidence collected while in the Palm Beach County Courthouse & being transported by Sheriff's Department:

John Rivera
Assistant Public Defender

Jennifer Marshall
Assistant Public Defender
— assigned to the Mental Health Division

DUNN C (QUINN, L)
1 W-FI Rad Neg.

WORDS

In this place, it's a game of words.
There is more than one team.
Attire is ceremonial clean.
With a King who oversees.
The power of God standing in.
An American flag is in plain view.
Collecting data every step of the way.
Understanding each rule is key.
Timing and thought play a role.
Creating challenges to overcome.
The best woman has an advantage.
Spelling better, but will not win.
Organization will gain their confidence.
Come with Truth, Honor, and Dignity.
Be prepared to battle.
Time in will be long-term.
A coach will not be needed.
Voting takes place in the crowd.
There's no bell among the discuss.
Covering land by the square miles.
In the end it's a game of NUMBERS.

What am I?

I am the Judicial Court System of the United States of America.

Brian Bailey # Defense: Court Violations 8/3/2019

Case # 50-2019-MM-005685-AKXX-MB

On the date of 5/12/2019 I (Brian Bailey) was charged with (1) count of Mf Trespass After warning, statue 810.09 section (2) after being in custody while incarcerated the court has violated 9 statues, they are:

(sections)
1) 27.40 (1),(B)1.,(9) Court-Appointed counsel; circuit registries; minimum requirements; appointment by court

2) 27.405 (1) Court-Appointed counsel; Justice Administrative Commission tracking and Reporting

3) 27.50 Public defender; qualifications; election

4) 27.51 (1) Duties of public defender

5) 27.0065 (1),(2) Witness Coordination

6) 393.17 (1) Behavioral programs; certification of behavior analysts

7) 393.18 Comprehensive transitional education program

8) 490.005 Licensure by examination

9) 960.0015 (B) Victim's Right to a speedy trial; speedy trial demand by the State attorney

While being held in custody by the Sheriff's Department, statue 950.04 has been violated 6 times, this statue reads.

10) 950.04 Penalty for neglect of duty in keeping prisoners of the United States

This means while being in custody of the Sheriff's Department since 5/12/2019, that there have been a total of 16 statue violations. While I have been in need of two surgicial procedures, one is a reconstructive surgery of the left Shoulder, and the second is my right weist, which is fractured. But I will not forget the Holy Bible the Sheriff's Department, has gifted me with.

Brian Bailey

In Time

8/3/2019

What would you do?
If you knew when

What would you do?
If you knew how

What would you do?
If you only had the time

What would you do?
If you did not know

What would you do?
If you had the money

What would you do?
If it was given to you

What would you do?
If you heard a voice

What would you do?
If you met the Lord

What would you do?
If the Lord called on you

Ask yourself, what would I do?
I would pray to God.

Now it is your turn!

Brian Bailey

PLAYER

8/3/2019

Topic) The Number is 52

The Player) By Age it puts you just over the hill

Knowledge) Wisdom is the name of the game

(Deck) 52 is how many cards are in the deck

Numbers Are the game

(Ace) The power is in the Ace — Higher

(4 Aces) In this chance you have 25%

(King) Kings Need A mate ⎫

(Queen) Security is in your Queen ⎬ Face cards

(Jack) The Jack is in your family ⎭

Numbers Are the game

(matching/Groups of 4) They come in groups — Matches

(2-10) But sequence will grow large

(Game) Signs Are brought to the table

(Hearts) Love is in the air ⎫

(Spades) Darkness is in your deck ⎬ Deck

(Diamonds) A jewel must be delt ⎬

(Clubs) Equipment for golf is not needed ⎭

A dealer starts with 396

Never play with one

Numbers Are the game

BB

```
Aces   = 15 × 4 = 60
Kings  = 10 × 4 = 40
Queen  = 10 × 4 = 40
Jack     10 × 4 = 40
10     = 10 × 4 = 40
9      =  9 × 4 = 36
8      =  8 × 4 = 32
7      =  7 × 4 = 28
6      =  6 × 4 = 24
5      =  5 × 4 = 20
4      =  4 × 4 = 16
3      =  3 × 4 = 12
2      =  2 × 4 = 8
Jokers =  0 × 2 = 0

Total  =      396
```

Report: BAILEY, BRIAN - MRN-ID: 0403731 - Portable Medical Diagnostics FL - EXAM DATE: 2019-06-08 - CLINICIAN: MORCOS

Portable Medical Diagnostics, Inc.
8080 Belvedere Rd. Ste. 6 West Palm Beach, FL 33411
Phone: 888.387.XRAY Fax: 888.493.1890
pmdxu.com

Radiology Interpretation

PATIENT NAME: BRIAN BAILEY
DATE OF BIRTH: 02/24/1979
ID/MRN: 0403731
PHYSICIAN: MORCOS
FACILITY: West County Detention
DATE OF EXAM: 08/06/2019 ✓
HISTORY: PAIN

Pain

SIGNIFICANT FINDINGS   (Left) Shoulder X-Ray

Portable LEFT SHOULDER X-Ray Complete 2 or more views:
Osteoporosis and changes of chronic osteoarthrosis are noted. No fracture or dislocation can be seen. No acute findings noted. Is significantly thinned articular cartilage at the glenohumeral joint.

IMPRESSION:
Osteoporosis and changes of chronic osteoarthrosis.

Electronically Signed By: Dr. Robin Connolly M.D. 08/06/2019 13:02:19 EDT

Connolly notified Ncide NMXR of significant findings. Ncide NMXR notified VERIFIED W/KRISTY at Portable Medical Diagnostics FL of significant findings at 2019-08-06 13:24:20.

8-6-19

Normal _____
Abnormal;
No Follow Up Needed ____
Abnormal;
Pull Chart ____
Signature/stamp:

8/7/19

- 1 -   6 Aug 2019 13:51

On the date of 8/6/2019, while being held at West Belle Glade – Detention Center. There was a **Ms. Foss** who visited the Block E-1, requesting information from Mr. Bailey without contacting the Public Defender's Office first or having the APD Raymon A. Burns at the jail for the attempted interview. This woman had Mr. Bailey placed in a suicide cell, after he requested for her professional title & making a decision not to move forward with a face-to-face meeting without representation. Officer Mondragon was on duty & kindly wrote her name on the evidence below:

Written by officer:
Mondragon ⇒   Mary Foss.

8/6/2019
West Detention Center,
Belle Glade Block E-1
Ms. Mary Foss with Mental Illness
(Belle Glade Detention Center)

Case# 50-2019-MM-005685-AXXX-MB

On the morning of **8/6/2019**, around 10:00am Mr. Bailey was called to the desk, by Sheriff's Department. Officer Mondragon advised him that he needed to go with Officer Sneed. Officer Sneed & Mr. Bailey made their way outside the E-1 block, then Officer Sneed guided him in the direction of medical staff, where there was a portable X-ray machine. Mr. Bailey greeted staff & was then advised to have a seat, where X-rays of his left shoulder were taken. The gentleman from medical staff snapped a few X-rays.

Then dismissing him from the room, & into the custody of Officer Cooper, who walked him back to the E-1 block. Mr. Bailey made his way back to the bunk area, not long after he was called by Sheriff's Department again. Officer Mondragon was the one who announce the call, Mr. Bailey made his way to the desk area & saw Officer Mondragon standing at the exit door, holding it open. He said, "You have someone here you need to meet with". He looked into the vest & saw a woman standing alone, then he made his way in the vest where she was standing.

She introduced herself as, "Mary Foss from mental health" at West Detention Center. Now together they both walked into the room for meetings & sat down. Mr. Bailey asked her if she had spoken with the Public Defender? Ms. Mary Foss replied, **"No I have not"**. After hearing this Mr. Bailey went through his case files & pulled out a page with five questions, starting with. What is your professional business title & name? He placed the paper with questions on the table, & slid it in her direction, asking, "Would you please write down your professional business title & name"? Ms. Foss replied, "I gave you my name!" Mr. Bailey replied, "Would you please write down?"

Ms. Foss replies, **"No I will not"** then stating, "I work with mental illness within the jail." Mr. Bailey replied, "Without representation I would not like to move forward with the meeting." Ms. Foss closed her folder that was open on table. Then saying, "So your refusing" Mr. Bailey replied, "I would like my representation to be present." Ms. Foss replied, **"Ok, then I'll just put you down as suicide."** She then exited the room, knocking on the entrance door to E-1, Officer Mondragon unlocking the door & allowing her in, they shared a conversation, that Mr. Bailey was unable to hear.

Ms. Foss then exited block E-1, & shortly after, Officer Mondragon came into the meeting room where he was sitting, packing his paperwork. Below are the statutes violated by Ms. Mary Foss.

Statute violation:

1) **490.009 (i) Discipline**
   - (i) I) Willfully making or filing a **false report** or **record**; failing to file a report or record required by state or federal law; willfully impeding or obstructing the filing of a report or record; or inducing another person to make or file a false report or record or to impede or obstruct the filing of a report or record. Such report or record includes only a report or record which requires the signature of a person licensed under this chapter.
   - (ii) L) Making misleading, deceptive, **untrue**, or **fraudulent representations** in the practice of any profession licensed under this chapter.

Officer Mondragon placed him in handcuffs with his hands behind his back. Mr. Bailey waited there while Officer Mondragon went over to his bunk area, & packed his personal property. When he returned, he placed Mr. Bailey in custody of Officer Smith, she walked him down to medical. Mr. Bailey was then stripped of everything he was wearing, then handed a tissue paper gown to place over his skin & asked to step inside the suicide cell. Mr. Bailey asked staff to please call the commanding officer down so, he could explain this unprofessional situation. All this taking place for simply requesting his representation be present.

He stood in this cell from 11:00am to 1:00pm, until the transport crew arrived. At 1:00pm Officer Lopez opens the door & hands him the blue lines he was asked to remove. Mr. Bailey put on the clothes & asked to speak with someone in charge for the second time. Right then a Sergeant shows up at the medical desk. His name unknown, but he was kind enough to allow Mr. Bailey to share what was taken place. After doing so, he explained he was unable to change any decision made by medical staff. Officer Lopez & a second Officer then moving him to a transport bus, taking him to the Main Detention Center, located on Gun Club rd.

Below is a handcrafted calendar showing the date of 8/6/2019, while being transported to the **Main Detention Center.**

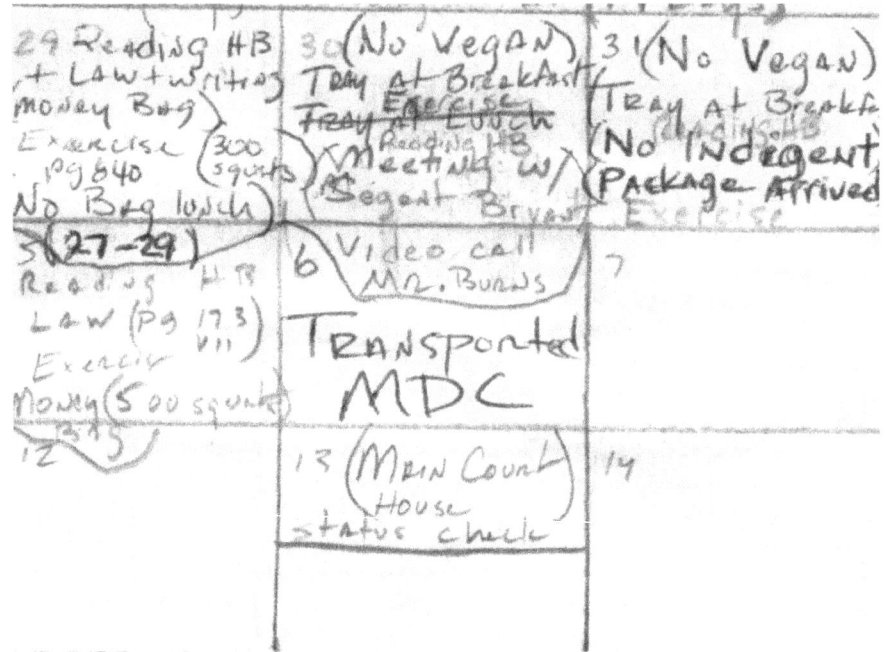

Brian Bailey (West Detention Center, Block E-1)
(Ms. Mary Foss with mental illness)   8/7/2019

Case #

On the morning of 8/6/2019, around 10:00 a.m. I (Brian Bailey) was called to the desk, by sheriff's department. Officer Mondragon advised me that I needed to go with officer Sneed. Officer Sneed and myself made our way outside the E-1 block, then officer Sneed guided me in the direction of medical staff, where there was a portable X-ray machine. I greeted staff and was then advised to have a seat, where X-rays of my left shoulder were taken. The gentleman from medical staff snapped a few X-rays. Then dismissing me from the room, and into the custody of officer Cooper, who walked me back to the E-1 block.

I made my way back to the bunk area, not long after I was called by sheriff's department again. Officer Mondragon was the one who answered the call, I made my way to the desk area and saw officer Mondragon standing at the exit door, holding it open. He said "You have someone here you need to meet with." I looked into the vest and saw a woman standing alone, then made my way into the vest where she was standing. She introduced as "Mary Foss from mental health" at West Detention Center. Now together we both walked into the room for meetings and sat down. I asked her if she had spoke with the public defender. Ms. Foss replied "No I have not!"

After hearing this I went through my case files and pulled out a page with five questions. Starting with, what is your professional business title and name? I placed the with questions on the table, and slid it in her direction, asking "Would you please write down your professional business title and name"? Ms. Foss replied "I gave you my name" I replied "Would you please write it down"? Ms. Foss replied "No I will not" then stating "I work with mental illness within the jail." I replied "Without representation I would not like to move forward with the meeting". Ms. Foss closed her folder that was open on the table. Then saying "So your refusing" I replied "I would like my representation to be present."

Pg 1

Ms. Foss replied "Ok, then I'll just put you down as suicide". She then exited the room, knocking on the entrance door to E-1, officer Mondragon unlocking the door and allowing her in, they shared a conversation, that I was unable to hear. Ms. Foss then exited block E-1, and shortly there after, officer Mondragon came into the meeting room where I was sitting, packing my paperwork. Officer Mondragon placed me in handcuffs with my hands behind my back.

I waited there while he went over to my bunk area, packing my personal belongings. When he returned he placed me in the custody of officer Smith, she walked me down to medical. I was then stripped of everything I was wearing, then handed a tissue paper gown to place over my skin, and asked to step inside the suicide cell. I asked staff to please call the commanding officer down so I could explain this unprofessional situation. All this taking place for simply requesting my representation be present. I stood in this cell from 11:00 a.m. to 1:00 p.m. until the transport crew arrived.

At 1:00 p.m. officer Lopez opens the door and hands me the blue lines I was asked to remove. I put on the clothes and asked to speak with someone in charge for the second time. Right then a sergeant shows up at the medical desk. His name unknown, but he was kind enough to allow me to share what was taken place. After doing so, he explained he unable to change any decision my medical staff had made. Officer Lopez and a second officer then moving me to a transport bus, taking me to the Main Detention Center, located on Gun Club rd.

<u>Statue Violation:</u>

490.009(i) Discipline

(i) Willfully making or filing a <u>false report</u>; failing to file a report or

(L) record required by state or federal law; willfully impeding or obstructing the filing of a report or record; or inducing another person to make or file a false report or record or to impede or obstruct the filing of a report

Pg 2

Mental Health Progress

Palm Beach County Sheriff's Office, FL
Palm Beach Main Detention
3228 Gun Club Road
West Palm Beach, FL 33406

Mental Health Progress Notes

✚ wellpath

Patient Name	Patient Number	Booking Number	Birth Date	Date Of Service
BRIAN DALE BAILEY	0403731	20190512050	2/24/1979	8/6/2019

Patient Problems:

Observed Date	Category	Type	Problem	Confirmed By
06-08-2019	Acute	Symptoms	Abnormal weight loss	

Patient Allergies:

Observed Date	Type	Allergy	Reaction
06-06-2019	Allergy Items	No Known Drug Allergies	

Enter Date/Time for every Progress Note. ● Free Text ○ SOAPE

Ms. Mary Foss Statute Violation 490.009 Discipline

Added 08/06/2019 11:09 AM EST by MFoss Mental Health Professional

Mental Health Incidental Note: Writer attempted to assess pt. in interview room on E1 dorm. Pt. advised of purpose of assessment, did not agree to cooperative. Pt. asked whether writer was there regarding "the competency exam". Writer stated she was not, but was there at the request of pt's APD, to provide any assistance pt. might need regarding mental health issues. Pt. stated "until I have representation present, this interview is terminated". When asked whether pt. had any suicidal or homicidal thoughts, intentions or plans, pt. refused to respond. Writer advised D/S to transfer pt. to Medical on Q15 suicide watch. Transfer documentation given to nurse to advise Classification of need for transfer to MDC S3A. False Reporting by Ms. Mary Foss

1-Signed by Mary Foss, Mental Health Professional on 08/06/2019 11:09 AM EST
1-Signed by Ruth Osborne, Mental Health Supervisor on 08/28/2019 09:24 AM EST

Page 1 of 1

Progress Notes

Palm Beach County Sheriff's Office, FL
Out Of Facility
3228 Gun Club Road
West Palm Beach , FL 33406

Progress Notes

wellpath

Patient Name	Patient Number	Booking Number	Birth Date	Date Of Service
BRIAR DALE BAILEY	0403731	20190512060	2/24/1979	8/6/2019

Orders:

No Applicable Data Found For Patient

Patient Problems:

Observed Date	Category	Type	Problem	Confirmed By
06-08-2019	Acute	Symptoms	Abnormal weight loss	

Patient Allergies:

Observed Date	Type	Allergy	Reaction
06-06-2019	Allergy Items	No Known Drug Allergies	

☐ **Vital Signs Taken**

Patient Vitals:

Observed Date	BP	Pulse	Resp	Temp	Pulse Ox	Weight	BMI	PF#1	PF#2	PF#3	Waist

Notes / History: ◉ Free Text ○ SOAPE

Added 08/06/2019 01:33 PM EST by ML Phillips RN

1311 Pt picked for to S3A MDC. No distress noted. - No Distress Noted

E-Signed by Marcia L Phillips, RN on 08/06/2019 01:33 PM EST

8/7/2019
Main Detention Center
Suicide Cell

Case# 50-2019-MM-005685-AXXX-MB

Once getting in the jail Mr. Bailey was walked into a, **"Suicide Cell"** & asked to strip off all his clothes for the second time. This time he was separated from his personal property, with over 60 hours logged of writing paperwork & details, two civil cases, all Judicial Circuit Courts legal paperwork, including a gift from WDC, which was the **NIV Holy Bible** version, a book he's writing, articles of clothing, etc. Mr. Bailey was given another tissue paper gown to place over his skin & asked to get in this suicide cell with two other men, wearing only tissue paper.

The time now was 3:00pm, Mr. Bailey stood in this cell with no seating for 12 hours, at 3:00am his legs were powered down, he was colder than usual & sat down on the floor. At some point, in the early a.m. hours a staff member not wearing a Sheriff's Department uniform, spoke through the door while holding a clipboard. Saying, "Are you suicidal"? Mr. Bailey replied, "No" He then asked, "Do you wanna hurt yourself"? Mr. Bailey replied, "No" Then the man walked away from the door & over to the desk area. Now sometime between 8-9:00am a psychologist shows up, & has an officer open the meal slot in the door.

He was sitting just outside the door in a plastic chair. He calls over another inmate by name, to sit down on the floor close to the door. The two of then started sharing a conversation, it made him even more uncomfortable that he was placed in a locked cell with two men, that within the last 24 hours were having some type of mental illness. When they were done speaking, the psychologist called Mr. Bailey over to the door & directed him to have a seat on the floor. Not knowing this man's name or professional business title, he started asking Mr. Bailey questions in reference to suicide. Then asking, "Why are you here"? Mr. Bailey explained, "While being in custody at WDC a Ms. Foss was attempting to have a meeting with me, & I was requesting my representation to be present".

Ms. Foss said I was refusing & had me taken into custody as being suicidal, & that's how I ended up here. The psychologist then replied, "Ok I'm gonna take you off suicide watch" I replied, "Thank you". Sometimes between 10:30 and 11:00am, an officer opens the meal slot, passing blue linens to another inmate & Mr. Bailey. Once we were dressed the officer allowed us to step outside the suicide cell. When outside he requested a few items, like the sweatshirt he was wearing when he came in, long black socks & crocks. The officer was unable to find any of his personal property items that came with him from WDC.

Mr. Bailey now had, "No" legal paperwork or case defense in his possession. Now he was shipped to another level of the jail. Holding two-man cells, he then put in a request for the personal property items missing.

Case #

Once getting in the jail I was walked into a suicide cell and asked to strip off all my clothes for the second time. This time I was seperated from my personal belongings, in the bag was things like my case defense, with over 60 hour logged, of writing paperwork and details, two civil cases, all Judicial Circuit Courts legal paperwork, including a gift from WDC, which was the Holy Bible NIV version, a book I'm writing, articles of clothing, etc. I was given another tissue paper gown to place over my skin and asked to get in this suicide cell with two other men, wearing only tissue paper.

The time now was 3:00 p.m., I stood in this cell with no seating for 12 hours, at 3:00 a.m. my legs were tired, I was colder than usual and sat down on the floor. At some point in the early a.m. hours a staff member not wearing a sheriff's department uniform, spoke through the door while holding a clipboard. Are you suicidal? I replied "No" He then asked "Do you wanna hurt yourself"? I replied "No" Then the man walked away from the door and over to the desk area.

Now sometime between 8-9:00 a.m. a psycologist shows up, and has an officer open the meal slot in the door. He was sitting just outside the door in a plastic chair. He calls over another inmate by name, to sit down on the floor close to the door. The two of them starting sharing a conversation, it made me even more uncomfortable that I was placed in a locked cell with two men, that within the last 24 hours were having some type of mental illness.

Pg 3

280

When they were done speaking, the psycologist called me over to the door and directed me to have a seat on the floor. Not knowing this man's name or professional business title, He started asking me questions in reference to suicide. Then asking "why are you here"? I explained "While being in custody at WDC a Ms. Foss was attempting to have a meeting with me and I was requesting my representation to be present". Ms. Foss said I was refussing and had me taken into custody as beinging suicidal, and that's how I ended up here.

The psycologist then replied "Ok, I'm gonna take you off suicide watch" I replied "Thank you". Sometime between 10:30 and 11:00 a.m. An officer opened the meal slot, passing blue linens the other inmate and myself. Once we were dressed the officer allowed us to step outside the suicided cell. When outside I requested a few items, like the sweat shirt I was wearing when I came in, black long socks and crocks. The officer was unable to find any of my personal items that came with me from WDC.

I now had no legal paperwork on case defense in my possesen. Now I was shipped to another level of the jail. Holding two man cells, I then put in a request for the personal Items missing.

Suicide Watch Initial Assessment

Palm Beach County Sheriff's Office, FL
Palm Beach Main Detention
3228 Gun Club Road
West Palm Beach , FL 33406

Suicide Watch Initial Assessment

Patient Name	Patient Number	Booking Number	Birth Date	Date Of Service
BRIAN DALE BAILEY	0403731	20190512060	2/24/1979	8/7/2019

☐ **Check if patient refuses to answer**

SUICIDE IDEATION DEFINITIONS AND PROMPTS
Ask Questions that are bolded and CAPITALIZED.

Ask Questions 1 and 2

1. Wish to be Dead: Past Month

Person endorses thoughts about a wish to be dead or not alive anymore, or wish to fall asleep and not wake up.

Past Month

HAVE YOU WISHED YOU WERE DEAD OR WISHED YOU COULD GO TO SLEEP AND NOT WAKE UP?   ○ Yes ⦿ No

2. Suicidal Thoughts: Past Month

General non-specific thoughts of wanting to end one's life/commit suicide, "I've thought about killing myself" without general thoughts of ways to kill oneself/associated methods, intent, or plan.

Past Month

HAVE YOU ACTUALLY HAD ANY THOUGHTS OF KILLING YOURSELF?   ○ Yes ⦿ No

If YES to 2, ask questions 3, 4, 5, and 6. If NO to 2, go directly to question 6.

3. Suicidal Thoughts with Method (without Specific Plan or Intent to Act):

Person endorses thoughts of suicide and has thought of a least one method during the assessment period. This is different than a specific plan with time, place or method details worked out. "I thought about taking an overdose but I never made a specific plan as to when where or how I would actually do it....and I would never go through with it."

Past Month

HAVE YOU BEEN THINKING ABOUT HOW YOU MIGHT KILL YOURSELF?   ○ Yes ⦿ No

4. Suicidal Intent (without Specific Plan):

Active suicidal thoughts of killing oneself and patient reports having some intent to act on such thoughts, as opposed to "I have the thoughts but I definitely will not do anything about them."

Past Month

HAVE YOU HAD THESE THOUGHTS AND HAD SOME INTENTION OF ACTING ON THEM?   ○ Yes ⦿ No

282

Palm Beach County Sheriff's Office, FL
Palm Beach Main Detention
3228 Gun Club Road
West Palm Beach , FL33406

Suicide Watch Initial Assessment

 wellpath

Patient Name	Patient Number	Booking Number	Birth Date	Date Of Service
BRIAN DALE BAILEY	0403731	20190512060	2/24/1979	8/7/2019

ACTING ON THEM? ○ Yes ⦿ No

> **5. Suicide Intent with Specific Plan:**

Thoughts of killing oneself with details of plan fully or partially worked out and person has some intent to carry it out

	Past Month
HAVE YOU STARTED TO WORK OUT OR WORKED OUT THE DETAILS OF HOW TO KILL YOURSELF?	○ Yes ⦿ No
DO YOU INTEND TO CARRY OUT THIS PLAN?	○ Yes ⦿ No

> **6. Suicide Behavior Question:**

HAVE YOU EVER DONE ANYTHING, STARTED TO DO ANYTHING, OR PREPARED TO DO ANYTHING TO END YOUR LIFE?   ○ Yes ⦿ No

Examples: Collected pills, obtained a gun, gave away valuables, wrote a will or suicide note, took out pills but didn't swallow any, held a gun but changed your mind or it was grabbed from your hand, went to the roof but didn't jump; or actually took pills, tried to shoot yourself, cut yourself, tried to hang yourself, etc.

Type of Watch and Frequency:

○ Constant ⦿ Staggered 15 minutes ○ Other, indicate watch frequency

Date placed on Watch   8/6/2019

Number of Days on Watch   1

Time placed on Watch   13:50

Reason for Watch:

⦿ Ideation/Threat ○ Plan ○ Act ○ Other

Placed on Watch by:

⦿ Behavioral Health ○ Nursing ○ Medical Provider ○ Security ○ Psychiatric Provider ○ Other
Other

Events Leading to Suicide/Self-Harm Watch (include patient's report as well as the official records of the event):

283

Patient Name	Patient Number	Booking Number	Birth Date	Date Of Service
BRIAN DALE BAILEY	0403731	201905/13060	2/24/1979	8/7/2019

of the event):

Pt. transferred to S3A from WDC on Q15 status after presenting as uncooperative and unwilling to respond to questioning regarding his mental status (suicidal ideation). Evaluation originally requested from PD to assess for mental health concerns (currently involved in competency proceedings).

Mental Status Examination

Appearance:

☑ Appropriate ☐ Meticulous ☐ Unclean ☐ Disheveled ☐ Bizarre ☐ Other

Speech:

☐ Appropriate ☑ Expressive ☐ Loud ☐ Slowed ☐ Pressured ☐ Slurred ☐ Other

Mood:

☐ Appropriate ☐ Depressed ☐ Euphoric ☑ Anxious ☑ Angry ☐ Irritable ☐ Other

Affect:

☑ Appropriate ☐ Tearful ☐ Blunted ☐ Flat ☐ Labile ☐ Hostile ☐ Other

Thought Form:

☑ Coherent ☐ Circumstantial ☐ Tangential ☐ Loose Assoc.

☐ Poverty of Thought ☐ Flight of Ideas ☐ Other

Thought Content:

☑ Appropriate ☐ Hallucinations ☐ Comp/Obsess. ☐ Thought Insertion

☐ Broadcasting ☐ Delusional ☐ Suicidal ☐ Homicidal ☑ Other

Paranoid

Orientation to:

☑ Person ☑ Place ☑ Time ☑ Situation

Intelligence:

☐ Above Average ☑ Average ☐ Below Average ☐ Well Below Average

Memory:

☑ Intact ☐ Immediate Impaired ☐ Recent Impaired ☐ Remote Impaired

Insight:

☐ Intact ☐ Good ☑ Fair ☐ Poor

Judgment:

☐ Intact ☐ Good ☑ Fair ☐ Poor

Behavior:

☑ Appropriate ☐ Belligerent ☐ Agitated ☐ Impulsive ☐ Withdrawn ☐ Other

284

Suicide Watch Initial Assessment

 **wellpath**

Patient Name	Patient Number	Booking Number	Birth Date	Date Of Service
BRIAN DALE BAILEY	0403731	20190512060	2/24/1979	8/7/2019

~~Behavior:~~

☑ Appropriate ☐ Belligerent ☐ Agitated ☐ Impulsive ☐ Withdrawn ☐ Other

Current Status

Orders:

No Applicable Data Found For Patient

Medication Compliant?	◉ N/A ○ Yes ○ No
Current Suicidal Ideations?	○ Yes ◉ No ○ Refuses to Answer
Current Homicidal Ideations?	○ Yes ◉ No ○ Refuses to Answer
Estimated current self-harm/suicide risk level	○ High ○ Medium ◉ Low
Date of last self-harm incident:	NA

Behaviors of Concern:
 Bizarre affect, grandiosity, some mild paranoia.

Treatment Goals (check all that apply)

☐ Decrease/eliminate self-injurious behaviors
☐ Decrease risk level as evidenced by
☑ Eliminate self-harm / self-harm statements
☐ Improve medication compliance
☐ Other

Risk Factors

☐ Hopelessness, feelings of guilt or worthlessness
☑ Impulsive
☐ Major Depressive/Manic episode
☐ 1st incarceration/arrest
☐ Family history of suicide attempts
☐ Prior suicide attempts or suicide note found
☐ Prior suicide watch placement in jail
☐ New legal issues (new charges, newly sentenced, lengthy sentence, denied parole)

Page 4 of 5

285

Palm Beach County Sheriff's Office, FL
Palm Beach Main Detention
3228 Gun Club Road
West Palm Beach , FL 33406

Suicide Watch Initial Assessment

 wellpath

Patient Name	Patient Number	Booking Number	Birth Date	Date Of Service
BRIAN DALE BAILEY	0403731	20190512050	2/24/1979	8/7/2019

☐ New legal issues (new charges, newly sentenced, lengthy sentence, denied parole)

☐ Bad news (loss of loved one, visit cancelled or no show, privileges revoked, serious illness, recent rejection or loss)

☐ Humiliating events/rejection (sexual assault)

☐ High profile crime (media attention)

☐ Intoxicated or detoxing from alcohol/ other drugs

☐ Placement in segregation/isolation

☐ Reports of giving items away

☐ Recent release from psychiatric hospital

☐ Anniversary of important loss

☐ Other (describe)

Protective Factors

☑ Identifies reason for living

☐ Fear of death or dying due to pain and suffering

☑ Supportive social network of family - Incorrect Information on Report

☑ Responsibility to family or others; living with family - Incorrect

☑ Engaged in work or school

☐ Belief that suicide is immoral; high spirituality

☐ Other (describe)

Plan: (check all that apply)

☑ Discharge from watch, follow up in accordance with policy or sooner as clinically indicated

☐ Continue current suicide watch and follow up daily

☐ Property Allowed

Consultation   ☑ Not indicated

Consultation with

☐ Refer to   ☐ Psychiatry ☐ Medical ☐ Special Needs ☐ Other

286

Behavioral Health Initial Evaluation

Palm Beach County Sheriff's Office, FL Palm Beach Main Detention 3228 Gun Club Road West Palm Beach , FL 33406		Behavioral Health Initial Evaluation		✚ wellpath
Patient Name BRIAN DALE BAILEY	Patient Number 0403731	Booking Number 20190512060	Birth Date 2/24/1979	Date Of Service 8/7/2019

Status   ◉ Adult ○ Juvenile

Reason for Referral

Referral is based on   Other

Reviewed Receiving Screening   ○ Yes ○ No

Reviewed Initial Health Assessment   ○ Yes ○ No

Other   Social Worker

Pt. transferred to S3A from WDC on Q15 status after presenting as uncooperative and unwilling to respond to questioning regarding his mental status (suicidal ideation). Evaluation originally requested from PD to assess for mental health concerns (currently involved in competency proceedings).

Patient Problems:

Observed Date	Category	Type	Problem	Confirmed By
06-08-2019	Acute	Symptoms	Abnormal weight loss	

Patient Allergies:

Observed Date	Type	Allergy	Reaction
06-06-2019	Allergy Items	No Known Drug Allergies	

Mental Health Treatment

Mental Health Outpatient Treatment?	○ Yes ◉ No
Psychiatric Hospitalizations?	○ Yes ◉ No
Current psychotropic medications:	○ Yes ◉ No
Prior Psychotropic Medications?	○ Yes ◉ No
Prior Diagnosis	○ Yes ◉ No ○ Unknown
Prior Mental Health Court Services	◉ Yes ○ No
Active competency hearing on current case (Trespassing).	
Prior SSDI	○ Yes ◉ No
Prior Guardianship	○ Yes ◉ No
Past Self-Harm/Suicide Attempts	○ Yes ◉ No ○ Refuses to Answer
Current Self-Harm Thoughts?	○ Yes ◉ No ○ Refuses to Answer
Concerns about ability to cope while incarcerated	○ Yes ◉ No ○ Refuses to Answer

Palm Beach County Sheriff's Office, FL
Palm Beach Main Detention
3228 Gun Club Road
West Palm Beach, FL 33406

Behavioral Health Initial
Evaluation

 wellpath

Patient Name BRIAN DALE BAILEY	Patient Number 0403731	Booking Number 2019051206	Birth Date 2/24/1979	Date Of Service 8/7/2019

Concerns about ability to cope while incarcerated   ○ Yes ⊛ No ○ Refuses to Answer

Substance Use History

Substance Use   ⊛ Yes ○ No

Type   Unclear

Last Used   Pt. reports "experimenting" with illicit substances although was evasive about
identifying such.

☐ check for add'l entry

History of Inpatient Treatment?   ○ Yes ⊛ No

History of Outpatient Treatment?   ○ Yes ⊛ No

History

Educational History (including special education):
Diploma, reports being currently enrolled in EMS training program.
Employment History:
Video Producer.
Military History:
None.
Legal History:
Pt. reports a history of one other arrest in Palm Beach County in 2010.   Mr. Bailey was Never Arrested in 2010
Housing Status prior to arrest:
Homeless.
Family/Social Support:
Brother in Tennessee.

History of Violent Behavior   ○ Yes ⊛ No

History of Sexual Offense (perpetrating)   ○ Yes ⊛ No

History of Victimization   ○ Yes ⊛ No

History of Head Injury   ○ Yes ⊛ No

Patient strengths
Cooperative, able to verbalize needs.

Current Status

Page 2 of 3

288

Palm Beach County Sheriff's Office, FL
Palm Beach Main Detention
3228 Gun Club Road
West Palm Beach , FL33406

Behavioral Health Initial
Evaluation

Patient Name	Patient Number	Booking Number	Birth Date	Date Of Service
BRIAN DALE BAILEY	0403731	20190512060	2/24/1979	8/7/2019

Current Status

Medication Compliant?	◉ N/A ○ Yes ○ No
Suicidal Ideations noted?	○ Yes ◉ No ○ Refuses to Answer
Homicidal Ideations noted?	○ Yes ◉ No ○ Refuses to Answer

Risk Level

Pt. denies any current suicidal or homicidal ideation, plan, or intent; and does not appear to be in any acute psychiatric distress.

☐ Hopelessness, feelings of guilt or worthlessness

☐ Impulsive

☐ Major Depressive/manic episode

☐ 1st incarceration or arrest

☐ Prior suicide attempts or suicide note found

☐ New legal issues (new charges, newly sentenced, lengthy sentence, denied parole)

☐ Bad news (loss of loved one, visit cancelled or no show, privileges revoked, serious illness, recent rejection or loss)

☐ Placement in segregation / isolation

☐ Family history of suicide attempts

☐ Intoxicated or detoxing from alcohol / other drugs

☐ Humiliating events / rejection (sexual assault)

☐ High profile crime (media attention)

☐ Anniversary of important loss

☐ Prior suicide watch placement in jail

☐ Recent release from psychiatric hospital

☐ Reports of giving items away

☐ Other (describe)

List Protective Factors

☑ Identifies reason for living

☐ Fear of death or dying due to pain and suffering

☑ Responsibility to family or others; living with family

☐ Belief that suicide is immoral, high spirituality

☑ Supportive social network of family

289

☑ Supportive social network of family — Incorrect Information on Report

☐ Engaged in work or school

☐ Other (describe)

Additional Information

Mental Status Exam

Appearance:

☑ Appropriate ☐ Meticulous ☐ Unclean ☐ Disheveled ☐ Bizarre ☐ Other

Speech:

☐ Appropriate ☑ Expressive ☐ Loud ☐ Slowed ☐ Pressured ☐ Slurred ☐ Other

Mood:

☐ Appropriate ☐ Depressed ☐ Euphoric ☑ Anxious ☐ Angry ☑ Irritable ☐ Other

Affect:

☐ Appropriate ☐ Tearful ☑ Blunted ☐ Flat ☐ Labile ☐ Hostile ☐ Other

Thought Form:

☑ Coherent ☐ Circumstantial ☐ Tangential ☐ Loose Assoc.

☐ Poverty of Thought ☐ Flight of Ideas ☐ Other

Thought Content:

☑ Appropriate ☐ Hallucinations ☐ Comp/obsess. ☐ Thought insertion

☐ Broadcasting ☐ Delusional ☐ Suicidal ☐ Homicidal ☑ Other

Paranoid at times.

Orientation:

☑ Person ☑ Place ☑ Purpose ☑ Time

Intelligence:

☐ Above Average ☑ Average ☐ Below Average ☐ Developmentally Disabled

Memory:

☑ Intact ☐ Immediate Impaired ☐ Recent Impaired ☐ Remote Impaired

Insight:

☐ Intact ☐ Good ☑ Fair ☐ Poor

Judgment:

☐ Intact ☐ Good ☑ Fair ☐ Poor

Palm Beach County Sheriff's Office, FL
Palm Beach Main Detention
3228 Gun Club Road
West Palm Beach , FL 33406

Behavioral Health Initial
Evaluation

 wellpath

Patient Name	Patient Number	Booking Number	Birth Date	Date Of Service
BRIAN DALE BAILEY	0403731	20190513050	2/24/1979	8/7/2019

Judgment:

☐ Intact ☐ Good ☑ Fair ☐ Poor

Behavior:

☑ Appropriate ☐ Belligerent ☐ Agitated ☐ Withdrawn

Comments

Plan (Please check all that apply)

☐ Treatment not indicated at this time, educated on how to further access services. Behavioral Health to follow up PRN

☐ Complete Suicide Watch Initial Assessment and start suicide precautions

☑ Behavioral Health will follow up within _____ days/date:
Three and Five day mental health follow-up to be scheduled.

☐ Consult with:

☐ Homework given on:

☑ Other
Treatment Team: DC Q15 and transfer to S2D for continued monitoring and observation. Pt. DOES NOT meet Baker Act criteria at this time.

☐ Refer to:

    ☐ Psychiatric Provider ☐ Medical ☐ Special Needs ☐ Discharge Planner ☐ Other

BH220UN0000ACCEN081516

8/8/2019

Meeting for Competence

Case# 50-2019-MM005685-AXXX-MB

Professional Business title & names

Psychology: Doctor Gretchen Moy

Assistant Public Defender: Jennifer Marshall

Inmate: Brian Dale Bailey

(This meeting is held while Mr. Bailey has no legal
documentation or written questions
for these two individuals)

**(Sheriff's Department still holding
his personal property)**

On the morning of **8/8/2019**, Mr. Bailey was in
custody at the Main Detention Center by Sheriff's
Department. He was called out of his cell by Officer
Chiquito. He advised him there was somebody here
to visit with him. Mr. Bailey made his way into a
room held for meetings as he approached, he could
sees a woman sitting at the table through the glass
window. When he entered the room & introduced
himself by saying, "Hi I'm Brian Bailey" she then
greeted me.

Her name is Psychologist Doctor Gretchen Moy, she was visiting with him regarding competence for the court. **(This meeting happening just after being released from a suicide cell, with other men inside).** After our greeting he asked, "Have you spoken with the Public Defender"? Dr. Moy replied, "Yes & she should be here shortly, "he replied, "Ok". Dr. Moy & Mr. Bailey had some short conversation, revolving around small talk. Another woman approached the room for meetings. When she entered, Mr. Bailey stood up from his seat & introduced himself as Brian Bailey, she greeted him as well & they shook hands. Her name is Assistant Public Defender Jennifer Marie Marshall, there to be Mr. Bailey's representation.

She made her way around the table, & sat down, then setting up her computer. With all the introductions now made; we officially started the meeting. Dr. Moy asking permission from Ms. Marshall if she could lead the conversation, by asking Mr. Bailey some questions. APD Jennifer M. Marshall giving her permission to go ahead. Dr. Gretchen Moy went ahead & started asking questions, about things like, positions held in the Judicial Circuit Court System & what they mean? What was my education history? Was Mr. Bailey able to focus while attending High School?

Had he ever been diagnosed with mental illness or mental disability? They talked about his weight loss, Mr. Bailey answered her questions about the court & explained some history about his youth. He also, shared that he had never been examined for either mental illness or mental disability. Dr. Gretchen Moy then asking about suicide & any history he may have with it. During their meeting he mentioned that since being transferred to the Main Detention Center by Sheriff's Department, he had been separated from his personal property, holding his case defense including all legal paperwork.

Sometime after this we heard from APD Jennifer M. Marshall asking some questions guided in Mr. Bailey's direction, like why are you jail? Mr. Bailey replied, "I don't know" APD Jennifer M. Marshall replied, I'm going to look into that & try & get you out of here. Then asking, "Would you be ok with them dropping the charges & getting out of jail? Mr. Bailey explained, "There is now a financial loss due to incarceration, then asking how does that get replaced"? APD Jennifer M. Marshall offered to assist in housing by looking into a grant. Mr. Bailey was more than pleased to hear any positive news. He answered APD Jennifer M. Marshall questions to the best of his ability.

Now Dr. Gretchen Moy picked up right where she left off, continuing in Mr. Bailey's direction. This went on for several minutes of Q & A. Towards the end of their meeting he asked APD Jennifer M. Marshall if she could speak with anyone within the jail, in reference to his personal property. She explained she was headed to speak with mental health & would see what she would do, but made it clear the chance was slim to none. In the end Mr. Bailey greeted both ladies with a thanks & God Bless you. Then making my way back to the cell.

Meeting for Competence

8/8/2019

CASE #

Professional Business title 3 names
Psychology : Doctor Gretchen May
Assistant Public Defender : Ms. Jennifer Marshall
Inmate : Mr. Brian Bailey

On the morning of 8/8/2019, I (Brian Bailey) was in custody at the Main Detention Center, by Sheriff's Department. I was called out of my cell by officer Chiquito. He advised me there was somebody here to visit with me. I made my way into a room held for meetings. As I approached I could see a woman sitting at the table through the glass window. When I entered the room and introduced myself by saying "Hi I'm Brian Bailey" she then greeted me. Her name is psychologist Dr. Gretchen May, she was visiting with me regarding competence for the court. After our greeting I asked "Have you spoken with the public defender"? Dr. May replied "Yes and she should be here shortly" I replied "Ok".

Dr. May and I had some short conversation, revolving around small talk. Another woman approach the room for meetings. When she entered, I stood up from my seat and introduced myself as Brian Bailey, she greeted me as well and we shook hands. Her name is Assistant Public Defender, Jennifer Marshall, there to be my representation. She made her way around the table, and sat down, then setting up her computer. With all the introductions now made, we offically started the meeting. Dr. May asking permission from Ms. Marshall if she could lead the conversation, by asking myself some questions. APD Ms. Marshall giving her permission to go ahead. Dr. May went ahead and started asking questions, about things like, positions held in the Judical Circuit Court System and what they mean? What was my education history? Was I able to focus in High School?

Had I ever been diagnoised with mental illness or mental disability? We talked about my weight loss, I answered her questions about the court and explained the history on my youth. I also shared that I had never been examined for either mental illness or mental disability. Dr. May then asking about suicide and any history, I may have had with it. During our meeting, I mentioned that since being transfered to the Main Detention Center by Sheriff's Department, I had been seperated from my personal belongings, holding my case defense. Including all legal paperwork. Sometime after this we heard from APD Ms. Marshall asking some questions guided in my direction, like "why are you in jail"? I replied "I don't know" APD Ms. Marshall replied "I'm going to look into that and try and get you out of here."

Then asking "would I be ok with them dropping the charges and getting out of jail? I explained "There is now a financial lose due to incarseration, then asking how does that get replaced"? APD Ms. Marshall offered to assist in housing by looking into a grant. I was more than pleased to hear any positive news. I answered Ms. Marshall questions to the best of my ability. Now Dr. May picked up right where she left off, continuing in my direction. This went on for sereral minutes of Q and A. Towards the end of our meeting I asked APD Ms. Marshall if she could speak with anyone with in the jail, in reference to my personal belongings. She explained she was headed to speak with mental health and would see what she could do, but made it clear the chance was slim to none. In the end I greeted both ladies with a thanks and God Bless you. Then making my way back to my cell.

Below are the scrap pieces of paper that Mr. Bailey used to request the names of both agents in the meeting held on 8/8/2019.

gretchen Moy Ph.D.
Psychology

(Time in)
12:00 P.m
3:00 P.m

Jennifer Marshall
Assistant Public Defender

10 - 11:00 Am

Write Down
Financial Loss
Due to Incarceration

(Competence Meeting)

Chi. Calendar

Needs	Wants
college degree	Kite board
	Surfboard
Housing	boPro Camera
	Editing Computer
	Body laser
Transportation	weight gain
	Cya micro shy
Surgery	Pen (L)
	Wrist (R)
	Healthy
	Food

Date   Time in   Time out   Hour   Total
(Loss)   Body upgrades (whole or costs)   After   loading the A.S.

Brinn Bailey

INNER Strength

8/8/2019

Loss of flesh creates pain
With depression comes thought
There's no easy way around it
Your on two journeys
Loss or gain
No one wants to lose
You have to earn gain
Your mental strength controls decession
Power moves your body
Creating ache with in
Feeling signals the brain
Your decession has to be made
Give up on yourself
Find drive and overcome
Challenge your heart
Push every limit
Reach for what you cannot see
Build what has not been done
Piece together muscle and technology
Through sight looks crippled
By mind conquers the world
Only come to win
When it hurts
Your Alive!

B.B

Brian Bailey

International Connection

2/8/2019

What do you have time for?
Or what do you want to spend money on?
If you had the time
You don't usually have the money
If you had the money
You don't usually have the time
Create your plan with a timeline
Set annual financial goals
Value your time
Save your money
Put time on your side
Have money work for you
The clock never stops
Currency continues moving
You count by the minute
Spending by the day
Dead by the hour
Living to create income
Counting on the fiscal
Loans for a promise
Contract on precious time
Percent for a sum
Calendar for a moment
Weight for a price
Trade by a gear
Crypto counts the dollar
Powered by electronics
Funds printed on paper
Now you have the time
Go blow the money!

BB

Brian Bailey

Life's Obvious

Life comes with hard hands
Building strong backs
Absorbing information growing mental strength
Comes with pain churned by challenge
The eyes see two sides
A hard laborer who moves there body
And a thinker who strains there mind
Working smart and planning long
Thinking by the minute and working hard
Professionals appreicate the creators
Artist appreicate design
Together is relationship
That foundation is business
The working people
Creating communities among us
Developing families of more than one
Powered by group
Restart the circulation
Brain's and hands

BB

Brian Bailey

Planet Moon

8/8/2019

There's A 3 B with meat in the middle
And we don't eat meat
We just want solutions
Go green or stay soft
Charge with alkalinity
Fitness is key
Blood flow is a must
Feed the brain
With energy comes muscle
Diet is a lifestyle
Decesions change health
Knowledge when feeding the body
Saves your health
Grow with profits
Discipline defines you
With integrity and shape
Leaders provide answers
Pleasure is through taste
Enjoyment is satisfaction
Green saves the skin
Families do matter
Flavor your style
Choose wrong
Pay the price on a doctor
Choose Right
Grow with benefits and life
It's your time!

BB

Brian Bailey   "The Box"   8/8/2019

When the flesh shows
And the feet are cold
With souls among you
No words to dispore
6 dementian. All made of concrete
The floor colder than ice
No protection on your feet
Voice speak out frustration
Thoughts ring with your problems
Bodies filled with ache
Shaking like a flag in the wind
Having out of body experiences
Only to ease the pain
The uniform of power is in charge
Time is not on your side
Thinking of the things you do not have
Missing what you once loved
Walls showing signs of hate
History of blood shed
Silence takes over the room
The power of the Lord setting in
Understanding what we don't know about God
Learning the power of human strength
To who holds the key of the locked door

Brian Bailey

The Shower

8/8/2019

Remeber having dirt on your skin
Remeber when you were in the mud
Remeber being stuck out in the snow
Remeber the boat leaving you in the deep blue ocean
Remeber camping with no running water
Remeber walking the road
Remeber living outside
Remeber standing in the rain
Appreciate those days you can remeber
Bubbles on your head
Flesh covered in suds
Washing off sweat from heat
Having a fresh smell among you
Warm water rolling down your body
Dirt is now on the floor
Cleanliness changed how you felt
Remeber God created heaven and earth
Remeber Jesus Christ as your Lord and savior
Remeber all of these days
Now being ceremonial clean
You walk with Lord
Welcome Home!
    Amen.

Brian Bailey   "Walk the road"   8/8/2019

When your gonna walk the road
Humbling yourself with God
Losing any understanding
You once had
Your feet in forward motion
Mind in think mode
Listening to a voice of reason
The earth still spinning
While for you time is standing still
Weight loss is in your future
Jesus shows your bones
With the Lord creating your plan
Color in black & white
Thinking your not seen
Law closing in with statues
Blue and red flashes in your eyes
The door now closes
An American flag on the other side
Blind to those around you
Learn the words of God
faith lies in your future
Goals pave the yellow road
God Bless us all

Brian Bailey

History Report MDC   8/8/2019

Date	Exercise	Reading	Holy Bible	Law	Misc.
8-6-2019	1001 Squats ✓	writing	✓		Writing money bag
8-7-2019		writing	still w. bible	✓	Writing Poems / Working on case defense
8-8-2019	300 Squats ✓	writing	still w. bible		Writing Poems / Working on case defense
8-8-2019	Sheriff's Department		Meeting	No paperwork →	Still No possessed property (Request)
8-8-2019	Inmate Request	Form	was returned	(No Property	
8-8-2019	Squats ✓	writing	still w. bible	(Personal Property)	Writing Poem / Writing a second request
8-9-2019	700 Squats ✓	writing	still w. bible		Writing Poem Motion
8-9-2019	Inmate Request	Requesting	to be	Moved to (WDC)	
8-10-2019	500 Squats ✓	writing	still w. bible		Cleaning B.i.
8-10-2019	Inmate Request form for			(Personal Property)	
8-10-2019	Inmate Request form for			legal Definition	45%
8-11-2019	legal request form				
8-11-2019	Inmate Request form			(Personal Property)	
8-11-2019	Inmate Request form			(Med)	
8-11-2019	✓	✓	still w. bible		Working case defense
8-11-2019	legal request form	for legal Definitions			950.04 / 490.009
8-11-2019	legal request form	for legal Definition			393.17(1) / 392.10
8-11-2019	legal request form for	legal Definitions			27.40 / 27.51(5)(B)1.
8-11-2019	legal request form for	legal Definitions			27.80 / 27.41(2)(A)
8-11-2019	legal request form for	legal Definition			27.006(d) / 27.405(d)
8-12-2019	50 squats ✓	—	still w. bible	—	Legal Paper work / showed up (No Definition
8-13-2019	100 Squats ✓	—	still w. bible	No Law codes	(No writing utensil)
8-14-2019	600 Squats ✓	writing Poem	Bible Shared Up	No Law Books	No writing paper Available
8-14-2019	Personal Property		Arrived	(with no cracks)	
8-14-2019	legal request form	for legal Definitions			950.04
8-15-2019	Inmate Request Form	transfer	to WDC		
8-15-2019	Inmate Request form				(Request Church)
8-15-2019	Request to sheriff's department		for Blank Paper		No Blank paper Available
8-15-2019	Viseo call (video)		Grant housing	Working on housing	Social Worker / Jessica Tower
8-15-2019	Visit with Medical staff & Doctor				(No paperwork) Regards (L) Shower (R) wrist
8-16-2019	legal Request form	for	legal Definitions		
8-16-2019	Squats / Abs ✓	✓	✓		creating New food recipe
8-16-2019	legal Request forms	recieved	8/14/2019 8/15/2019		950.04 / 90.612
8-16-2019			✓		working on meeting defense
8-17-2019	legal Request form		Definitions		490.005 / Lack of knowledge
8-17-2019	Squats & abs ✓	writing Poem	Using the Bible		Designing New Food Fruit / Cooking
8-18-2019	Squats	writing (Planet Moon)		✓	Working on Definition CH
8-18-2019	legal Request forms	for legal Definitions			393.17 / 393.18
8-19-2019	legal Request forms	for legal Definitions			27.40 / 27.401 Requesting wristband I.D

306

8/9/2019

Main Detention Center
(Cell Transfer)

Case# 50-2019-MM-005685-AXXX-MB

On the afternoon of **8/9/2019**, Mr. Bailey was alerted by Sheriff's Department that he needed to pack his belongings & go with two Officers. They left the cell he was in called 2D-02 & ended at East 4A where there were no bottom bunks open. Mr. Bailey walked into the 408 cell & made his bed on the top bunk. With a right fractured wrist & a left shoulder needing reconstruction surgery, Mr. Bailey worked his way up there. This was an extremely difficult situation that caused him pain every time he moved his left arm or right wrist. He finished making his bed & made his way off the top bunk.

Also, there is no ladder to get up & down. He sat down at the desk & started working on the defense for his case. Now, he was transferred to a dorm with no law books, in order to reference Statutes to his case. After having 60 hours logged on a timesheet & a strong defense in this case, now moved to a dorm with no law books or bottom bunks while being injured. Medical already advised the Sheriff's Department on more than one document, that Mr. Bailey needs a "**Low Bunk**". This is completely **NEGLECT**, which violated **statute 950.04.**

Statute violation:

1) 950.04 – **Penalty for neglect of duty in keeping prisoners of the United States.**—*The keeper of each jail shall be subject to the same penalties for* **any neglect** *or* **failure of duty in keeping prisoners** *who are committed to his or her charge* **under the authority of the United States** *as he or she would be subject to under the laws of this state for the like* **neglect** *or failure in the case of prisoners committed under the authority of the said laws; provided, the United States pays or causes to be paid to the jailer such fees as the jailer would be entitled to for like service rendered by virtue of the existing laws of this state during the time such prisoners shall be therein confined; & moreover, supports such of the prisoners as shall be committed for offenses.*

The **Sheriff's Department** still unable to find any of his legal paperwork, after separating him from his personal property. So, they could have him stand in a cell for approximately 18 hours **serving no purpose, for improving mental illness**, while being extremely cold to the point of shaking continuously. Now after requesting for trial & spending the last 90 days preparing his case. His left in a cell with no legal documentation to review. No law book for statute studies & missing his calendar, showing each day the Sheriff's Department didn't have a Vegan / Rad meal for Mr. Bailey, which was a total of 6 times.

Violating Statute: **950.04 Penalty for neglect of duty in keeping prisoners of the United States.**

The **Sheriff's Department** passes out one book for free, with opportunity an to keep, so inmates learn the **Word of God.**

The Holy Bible reads:

Deuteronomy: Do not pervert Justice to the indigent & poor or favor the righteous.

(How about the Sheriff's Department & the Judicial Circuit Court System, honor what they Hand out!!!!)

Mr. Bailey continuously being moved around, while filling out inmate request forms & by the time the Sheriff's Department has time to review his request & get back to him with the forms, he's already been moved again. Created a gap in the request & time loss to move forward with learning laws to defend his case. There is also no clock in the cell East 4A, allowing for a time log. Which means he's unable to log his hours working on the case.

PALM BEACH COUNTY
SHERIFF'S OFFICE
RIC L. BRADSHAW, SHERIFF
DEPARTMENT OF CORRECTIONS

INMATE REQUEST

☑ MAIN DETENTION CENTER   ☐ WEST DETENTION CENTER

*Only one request allowed per form.   *Solamente se permite una solicitud por formulario.   *Li entèdi pou fè plis pase yon demann sou chak fòmilè.

☐ Commanding Officer	☐ Program	☐ Chaplain
Oficial de Mando / Ofisye siperyè	Programas / Pwogram	Capelán / Chaplen
☐ Public Defender	☐ Reading Library	☐ Bible Study
Defensor público/ Avoka defans piblik	Biblioteca para lectura / Bibliyotèk pou lekti	Estudio Bíblico / Li labib
☐ Notary Service	☐ Educational Program	☐ Spanish Church Service
Servicio de Notario / Sèvis notè	Programas Educacionales / Pwogram	Servicio en Español / Legliz panyòl
☐ Classification	edikasyonèl	☐ Catholic Church Service
Clasificación/ Klasifikasyon	☐ AA/NA Meetings	Servicio Católico / Legliz katolik
☐ Property	Reuniones de AA/NA / Reyinyon AA/NA	☐ Jewish Service
Propiedad / Pwopriyete	☐ Another Way Drug Education Dorm	Servicio Judío / Sèvis jwif
☐ Canteen	Dormitorio para la Educación sobre drogas	☐ Jehovah's Witness
Cantina / Kantin	"Another Way" / Dòmitwa Another Way pou	Testigo de Jehováh / Temwen
☐ Inmate Records / Court	edikasyon sou dwòg	jewova
Information	☐ Re-Entry	☐ Muslim Prayer
Registro de Reclusos/Información de Corte/	Reingreso / Retou	Oración Musulman / Priyè
Dosye prizonye/enfòmasyon sou jijman	☐ Alternative Custody / IHA	mizilman
☐ Visitation	Detención Alterna/Arresto Domiciliario /	☐ Non-Denominational Church
Visitas / Vizit	Gad altènatif / kouvrefe adomisil	Servicio No-Denominación /
☑ Other Wristband I.D.	☐ Work Release	Legliz san denominasyon
Otro / Lòt	Salida para Trabajar / Sòti pou ka travay	☐ Request for Bible
		Pedido de Biblia / Demann pou Bib

Name (Print): Brian Bailey
Nombre (Letra de molde / Non (akri ak gwo lèt)

Date of Birth: 2/24/1979
Fecha de Nacimiento / Dat nesans

Date: 8/19/2019 Jacket #: ~~~~~~ Pouch #: _____ Housing Unit: East 4A
Fecha / Dat   Número de "Jacket" / Nimewo "Jaket"   Numero de "Pouch" / Nimewo "Pouch"   Unidad de Vivienda / Inite lojman

State the reason for submitting this request:
Explique la razón porque presenta esta solicitud: / Eksplike rezon pou demann sa a:

Request for wristband identification and size 9 crocks. ~~~~~~~~~~~~~~~~~~~~~~~~ The Crock shoes were in my personal property After being B15 from Belle Glade. When I received the personal property back on 8/14/2019, there were no crocks. I've been without a wristband, here a the Main Detention Center since 8/6/2019

Request received by (Print)	ID #	Signature	Date

Official Response:
Respuesta Oficial: / Repons ofisyèl:

Official's Name (Print)	ID #	Official's Signature	Date

PBSO CF #0019 REV. 05/12

Brian Bailey

MAIN DETENTION CENTER
(Cell Transfer)

8/9/2019

On the afternoon of 8/9/2019 I (Brian Bailey) was alerted by Sheriff's department that I needing to pack my belongings and go with two officers. We left the cell I was in called 2D-02 and ended at East 4A where there were no bottom bunks open. I walked into the 408 cell and made my bed on the top bunk. With a right fractured neck and a left shoulder needing reconstructive surgery, I worked my way up there. This extremely difficult situation causes me pain everytime I move my left arm or right wrist. I finished making my bed and made my way off the top bunk. Also there is no ladder to get up or down.

I set down at the desk and started working on the defense for my case. Now I was transferred to a dorm with no law books, in order to refine statues to my case. After having 60 hours logged on a time sheet and a strong defense in this case, now moved to a dorm with no law books on bottom bunk while being injured. This is completely ~~neglect~~, violated statue 950.04 stating.

950.04 Penalty for neglect of duty in keeping prisoners of the United States

The Sheriff's Department still unable to find any of my legal paperwork, after separating myself from my belongings. So they could have me stand in a cell for approximately 18 hours serving no purpose, for improving mental illness, while being extremely cold to the point of shaking continuously.

Now after requesting for trial and spending the last 90 days preparing my case. I'm left in a cell with no legal documentation to review. No law book for statue studies and ~~at a dead end and~~ now missing my calendar, showing each day the Sheriff's department didn't ~~get~~ have a Vegan/Bad Meal for me, which was a total of 6 times. Also, Violating statue: 950.04 - Penalty for neglect of duty in keeping prisoners of the ~~United~~ United States   ①→

I'm continuously being moved and everytime I put in paperwork called/inmate request forms and by the time the Sheriff Department has time to review my request and get back to me I've been moved again. There is also no clerk in the ~~cell~~ cell I'm staying in now. Which means I am unable log my hours working on my

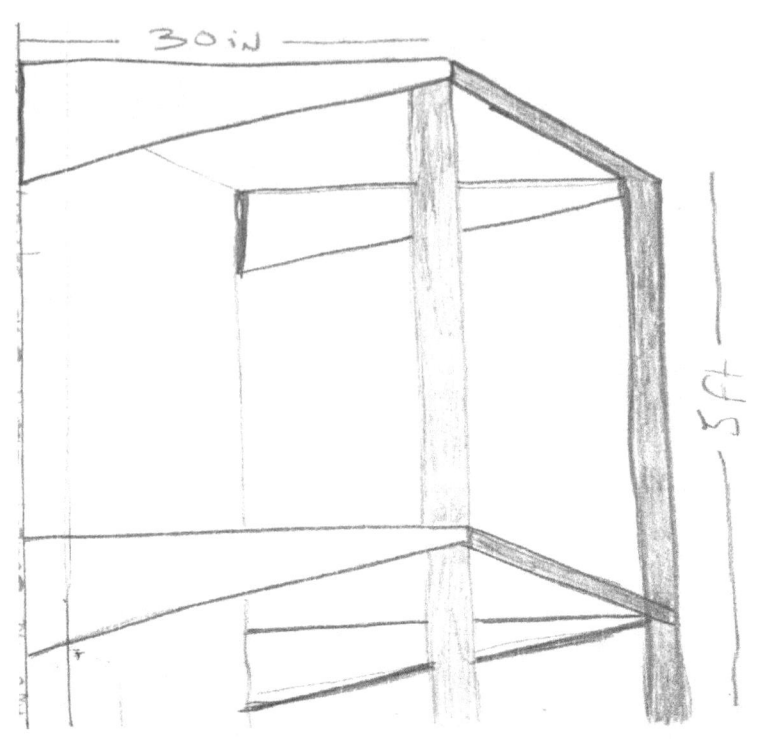

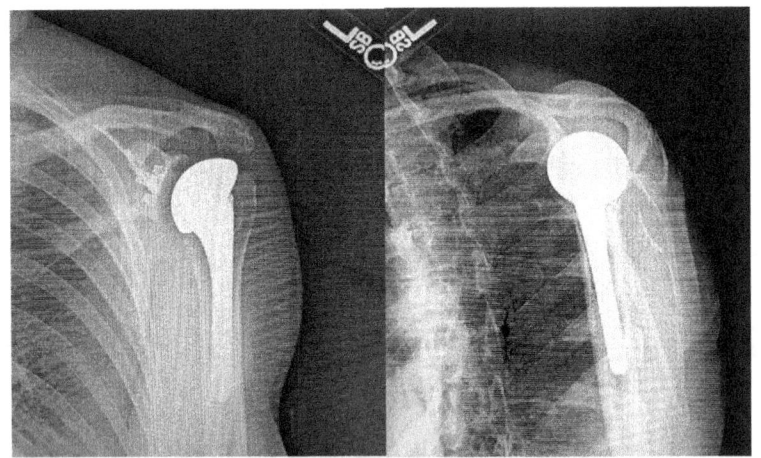

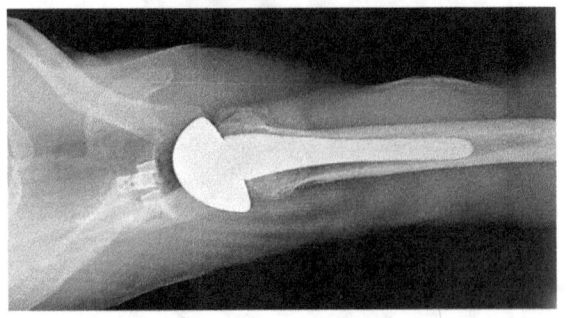

8/9/2019
Case Defense
(Religious Reasons)
Case# 50-2019-MM-005685-AXXX-MB

On the afternoon of **8/6/2019**, Mr. Bailey was transported from West Detention Center, Belle Glade to the Main Detention Center, West Palm Beach, Florida. When arriving at this location, he stepped off the transport bus & was handed a bag holding his personal property. This bag contained items like: The Holy Bible with markings on verses throughout the book, legal paperwork including case defense, two civil cases, one pair of crocks, a book he was writing, with 74 pages complete, two sweatshirts, a pair of long black socks, a pair of white short socks, dental floss, deodorant.

Still having no bracelet for tracking & identification purposes after having it removed by staff at the West Detention Center, once being falsely Q15 by Ms. Mary Foss. This blocked Mr. Bailey from being able to participate in any outside or religious activities. Creating a barrier for the religious practices the Sheriff's Department opens for inmates, while decreasing his stamina for exercise.

Then placed in a cell & he was asked by **Sheriff's Department** *to* **remove all articles of clothing***.*
Statute violation:

1) *800.03 –* **Exposure of sexual organs***. - It is* **unlawful** *to* **expose or exhibit one's sexual organs** *in public or on the* **private premises** *of another, or so near thereto as to be seen from such private premises, in a vulgar or indecent manner, or to be naked in public except in any place provided or set apart for that purpose. Violation of this section is a misdemeanor of the first degree, punishable as provided in s. 775.082 or s. 775.083. A mother's breastfeeding of her baby does not under any circumstance violate this section.*

This violates his religion practice. Then an Officer handed him a tissue paper gown to place over his skin. While in a cell with two other men, also part naked. Now completely separated from the NIV Holy Bible version, which he read completely the first month of being incarcerated. This is the book Sheriff's Department passes, into the hands of inmates free of charge. While learning the **Word of God** *& marking verses for future reference. He had well over 100 hours invested into that one* **NIV Holy Bible***.*

While incarcerated he was also sharing the word of God with other inmates. At the same time his ears were being burned by sin constantly, hearing hate, crime, dealers & offenders speaking out about what they have done, creating an extremely hostile environment. Putting him in various different dangerous situations. Before being incarcerated, he was a man of prayer, worship, serving, tithing & helping brothers & sisters. After being incarcerated he was never angry with anyone among the Christ Fellowship Church, who might have been responsible for having Mr. Bailey arrested while being a member of the church. He continued with prayer, & worship within the jail, but it wasn't the same. It was a much colder atmosphere, & he didn't hear one brother actually speaking the **Word of God** that was an inmate, without sin on the tongue.

Brian Bailey

CASE DEFENSE
(Religious Reasons)

8/9/2019

Case #

On the afternoon of 8/6/2019, I (Brian Bailey) was transported from West Detention Center, Belle Glade to Main Detention Center, West Palm Beach. When arriving at this location, I stepped off the transport bus and was handed a bag holding my personal property. This bag contained items like: The Holy Bible with markings on verses throughout the book, legal paperwork including case defense, two civil cases, one pair of crocks, a book I was writing, with 74 pages complete, two sweat shirts, a pair of black long socks, a pair of white short socks, dental floss, deoderant.

Once placed in a cell I was asked by sheriff's department to remove all articles of clothing. This violates my religion practice. Then an officer handed me a tissue paper gown to place over my skin. While in a cell with two other men, also part naked. Now completely seperated from the Holy Bible NIV version, which I read completely the first month of being incarcerated. This is the book sheriff's department passes on free of charge. While learning the word of God and marking verses for future reference. I had well over 100 hours invested into that one NIV Holy Bible.

While incarcerated I was also sharing the word of God with other inmates. At the same time my ears were being bruised by sin constantly, hearing hate, crime, dealers and offenders speaking out about what they have done, creating an extremely hostal invironment. Putting me in various different dangerous situations. Before being incarcerated, I was a man of prayer, worship, serving, tithing and helping brothers and sisters. After being incarcerated I never was angry with anyone among the Christ Fellowship Church, who might have been responsable for having me arrested while being a member of the church.

I continued with prayer, and worship with in the Jail, but it wasn't the same. It was a much colder atmosphere, and I didn't hear one brother actually speaking the word of God that was an inmate.

I'm now uncomfortable with commiting to any voluntering service or serving for the community, if being incarcerated is how I'm being repaid in the end. Not only do I tithe my 10% worship, serve and pray, I'm also a Palm Beach State College Student in the Emergency Medical Services Program. Health means everything to me, and after being incarcerated by the sheriff's department, I now have severe muscle loss, lower cardiovascular energy, and loss of strength. This has taken a toll on my body and mental mind.

I've now lost the financial gains that I had coming to me. Especially knowing while I'm in the community, I do anything asked of me within the law. Before incarcerated my life consisted of two things, my education in college and serving for Christ Fellowship Church. I will no longer be attending the Christ Fellowship Church. Having me arrested has not helped our community in anyway shape or form. I will continue to pray and worship as I see fit for my needs from this day forward.

I will also mention that while being incarcerated I was exercising the lower half of my body, Also cleaning block E-1, by scrubbing toilets, showers, and floor. While having a fractured right wrist and a left shoulder needing reconstruction surgery, that is in pain when it moves. I'm very uncomfortable with the unprofessionalism of "Mary Foss" working in mental health. I would only hope and pray that she doesn't abuse ~~the~~ her power, like she has done with me.

Thank you and God Bless!

To repent for religious reasons, when first being incarcerated I didn't eat only fasting for 12 ~~days~~ to 18 days. After being taken to medical I started a vegan/raw diet while continuing to read the Holy Bible, learning the word of God and continuing ~~to~~ with passover on every 14th of the month. I am now in the ~~state~~ ~~process~~ of The Nazirite, showing my respect for Go

Brian Bailey

Motion

8/9/2019

In this lifetime
Have a key to success
There is do And don't
And we do
Motion is the key
Your count starts at one
Repatition builds class
Series gains muscle
Cardio trims fat
In the long run
Altering your attire
To burn means you sweat
Healing brings pleasure
Quiters do not Achive
Team members break records   (break or set)
To push allows you to feel
Trying makes you human
Elevated heart rate
Gets the blood flowing
Pumping iron comes Natural
Creating intensity for the body
Move the souls' position
Feeling on charge
Pace is speeding up
Adapting to a movement
Breathing is harder
Exuast your energy
Wear at a level of Achievement
Forward motion is your Answer
Only you can!

BB

8/13/2019

IN THE COUNTY COURT OF THE FIFTEENTH JUDICIAL CIRCUIT
IN AND FOR PALM BEACH COUNTY, FLORIDA - CRIMINAL DIVISION
CIRCUIT/COUNTY COURT
Court Event Form

DEFENDANT: BRIAN DALE BAILEY
CASE NO: 50-2019-MM-005685-AXXX-MB

STATE OF FLORIDA
vs.
DEFENDANT: BRIAN DALE BAILEY
CASE NO: 50-2019-MM-005685-AXXX-MB
DIVISION: B: Cnty Crim - B (County)

DATE: 8/13/2019

JACKET #: 0403731
BOOKING #: 2019015844

PRESIDING JUDGE: HANSER, JUDGELEONARD
ASA: MYERS, RYAN
ATTORNEY:
PUBLIC DEFENDER: BURNS, RAYMON
CO-COUNSEL:
DEPUTY CLERK: ME

COURT ROOM: 2E (Main Branch)

START TIME: 10:42 AM
END TIME: 10:46 AM

COURT REPORTER
COURT TYPE: STCK - STATUS
CHECK

Reset For
Court Date Scheduled - CC - CALENDAR CALL - 8/27/2019 8:30 AM - 2E (Main Branch) MB, 205 N. Dixie
Highway West Palm Beach FL 33401

Other: DEFENDANT PRESENT AND IN CUSTODY

Count 1 - MF TRESPASS AFTER WARNING 810.09(2A)

FILED: PALM BEACH COUNTY, FL SHARON R BOCK, CLERK 08/13/2019 10:46:06 AM

319

8/13/2019

IN THE CIRCUIT/COUNTY COURT OF THE FIFTEENTH JUDICIAL CIRCUIT
IN AND FOR PALM BEACH COUNTY, FLORIDA

STATE OF FLORIDA

-Vs-

Date: 08/13/2019

Case No: 50-2019-MM-005685-AXXX-MB

Division: B: Cnty Crim - B (County)

BRIAN DALE BAILEY
GENERAL DELIVERY
WEST PALM BEACH, FL 32200

NOTICE OF HEARING

THE DEFENDANT MUST BE PRESENT AT THIS HEARING

For Criminal Charges: Failure to Appear will result in a Bond Forfeiture or
revocation of own recognizance (O.R.) and a Capias/Warrant being issued for your arrest.
For Civil Traffic Charges: Failure to appear may result in the suspension of your driver's license.
IF YOUR CASE IS ON-CALL, CONTACT YOUR ATTORNEY FOR THE TIME TO APPEAR

YOU ARE HEREBY NOTIFIED that this case is scheduled

DATE:	TIME:	HEARING TYPE:	LOCATION:
8/27/2019	8:30 AM	CC - CALENDAR CALL	2E (Main Branch) MB, 205 N. Dixie Highway West Palm Beach FL 33401

BE PREPARED TO PAY COURT COSTS AND FINES ASSESSED BY THE COURT AT THIS HEARING
"IF YOU INTEND TO REQUEST THE SERVICES OF THE PUBLIC DEFENDER, YOU MUST FILE AN APPLICATION AT THE CLERK &
COMPTROLLER'S OFFICE AND BE APPOINTED THE PUBLIC DEFENDER BEFORE YOUR COURT DATE. THE APPLICATION FEE IS $50.00."
Civil Traffic Charges are not eligible for a Public Defender.

SHARON R. BOCK,
CLERK & COMPTROLLER
BY: ME

Deft/Atty: DEFENDANT IN CUSTODY

Deputy Clerk

cc: RYAN MYERS
      BURNS, RAYMON A

320

"If you are a <u>person with a disability</u> who needs any accommodation in order to participate in this proceeding, you are entitled, at no cost to you, to the provision of certain assistance. Please contact Tammy Anton, Americans with Disabilities Act Coordinator, Palm Beach County Courthouse, 205 North Dixie Hwy, West Palm Beach, FL 33401; telephone number (561) 355-4380 at least 7 days before your scheduled court appearance, or immediately upon receiving this notification if the time before the scheduled appearance is less than 7 days; if you are hearing or voice impaired, call 711."

"Si usted es una <u>persona minusválida</u> que necesita algún acomodamiento para poder participar en este procedimiento, usted tiene derecho, sin tener gastos propios, a que se le provea cierta ayuda. Tenga la amabilidad de ponerse en contacto con Tammy Anton, 205 N. Dixie Highway, West Palm Beach, Florida 33401; teléfono número (561) 355-4380, por lo menos 7 días antes de la cita fijada para su comparecencia en los tribunales, o inmediatamente después de recibir esta notificación si el tiempo antes de la comparecencia que se ha programado es menos de 7 días; si usted tiene discapacitación del oído o de la voz, llame al 711."

"Si ou se yon <u>moun ki enfim</u> ki bezwen akomodasyon pou w ka patisipe nan pwosedi sa, ou kalifye san ou pa gen okenn lajan pou w peye, gen pwovizyon pou jwen kèk èd. Tanpri kontakte Tammy Anton, kòòdonatè pwogram Lwa pou ameriken ki Enfim yo nan Tribinal Konte Palm Beach la ki nan 205 North Dixie Highway, West Palm Beach, Florida 33401; telefòn li se (561) 355-4380 nan 7 jou anvan dat ou gen randevou pou parèt nan tribinal la, oubyen imedyatman apre ou fin resevwa konvokasyon an si lè ou gen pou w parèt nan tribinal la mwens ke 7 jou; si ou gen pwoblèm pou w tande oubyen pale, rele 711."

321

IN THE COUNTY COURT OF THE FIFTEENTH
JUDICIAL CIRCUIT, CRIMINAL DIVISION
IN AND FOR PALM BEACH COUNTY, FLORIDA

TO: DON EDWARD HELVEY
9905 SOUTHERN BLVD.
ROYAL PALM BEACH, FL 33411
PALM BEACH

CASE NO. 2019MM005685AMB
DIVISION: "B"
Police Case No 06-19-070132
ME. No.

STATE OF FLORIDA
vs.
BRIAN DALE BAILEY

CALENDAR CALL
2 WEEK DOCKET - REMAIN ON CALL
COUNTY COURT - DIVISION B

You are commanded to appear at the Palm Beach County Courthouse, 205 North Dixie
Highway, West Palm Beach, FL 33401, COURTROOM 2E, beginning at 8:30 AM, on
08/27/2019. PLEASE DO NOT APPEAR BEFORE CALLING: (561) 355-7413 (or 1-(800)
353-3859 7413 if out of the area) to verify if you will be needed for the trial.

Failure to appear will subject you to contempt of Court. This subpoena is binding day to
day and week to week until the case is closed.

VICTORIA SUAREZ
Assistant State Attorney
Fla. Bar No.1010141

August 13, 2019
* *
I received this subpoena on the _____ day of _____, 2019, and executed the same on the _____ day
of _____, 2019, in Palm Beach County, Florida.

SHERIFF, PALM BEACH COUNTY

By: _____
Deputy Sheriff

If you are a person with a disability who needs any accommodation in order to participate
in this proceeding, you are entitled, at no cost to you, to the provision of certain assistance.
Please contact the ADA Coordinator in the Administrative Office of the Court, Palm
Beach County Courthouse, 205 North Dixie Highway, Room 5.2500, West Palm Beach,
Florida, 33401; telephone number (561) 355-4380 at least 7 days before your scheduled
court appearance, or immediately upon receiving this notification if the time before the
scheduled appearance is less than 7 days; if you are hearing or voice impaired, call 1-800-
955-8771.

8/19/19 not a church
must recent home address for is
784 SE Villandry WAY
Port St. Lucie FL 34984 N/F

SCANNED
AUG 2 2 2019
DT

FILED: SHARON R. BOCK CLERK 8/21/2019 2:51:00 PM

322

In the courtroom 8/13/2019

Case# 50-2019-MM-005685-AXXX-MB

While in custody on **8/13/2019**, Mr. Bailey was walked into the courtroom by Sheriff's Department, then seated while cases were in session. After just a few minutes he was approached by APD Raymon A. Burns. Mr. Bailey then asked APD Raymon A. Burns, what was going to take place today in court. APD Raymon A. Burns shared that they are moving forward with a trial date for docket. Once he was done speaking, Mr. Bailey explained that he had a few questions & concerns, in reference to what was taking place in the county jail. Known as the West Detention Center, Belle Glade & Main Detention Center, West Palm Beach.

The first concern he shared with APD Raymon A. Burns was that a, "Mary Foss" who was working in mental illness for WDC, Belle Glade, had not spoken to the Public Defender at all prior to their meeting. This came to his attention after asking, "Ms. Mary Foss" did she speak with the Public Defender? Ms. Foss replied, "No" Then sharing with Ms. Foss that he would like his representation to be present. Ms. Foss refusing to write down her professional business title & name.

Mr. Bailey asked her a second time, then in frustration she stood up from the table where they were sitting, "**still refusing**." Then having Sheriff's Department put Mr. Bailey on suicide watch, called Q15 & transferred to the main jail. Then placed in a cell with two other men, who were suicidal. Now sharing with APD Raymon A. Burns that he was not suicidal at all, & this was done in a very unprofessional manner. Mr. Bailey then brought up the possibility for a **Statute violation 26.0065 Witness Coordination**. Then requesting she be checked for her mental illness licensing by the Public Defender. The next thing he shared with APD Raymon A. Burns is that after that chain of events. He had been separated from his case defense, evidence & personal property from within the jail.

Just prior to the competence meeting with two officials, held on 8/8/2019, revolving around mental health for competence. APD Raymon A. Burns wrote down his concerns on a piece of paper he was holding while in the courtroom, used for defense attorneys. The case was called to the attention of Judge Leonard Hanser, & Mr. Bailey was asked to stand. During the hearing, the State Attorney, Public Defender & Judge agreed upon a calendar call on **8/27/2019**.

Case # 50-2019-MM-005685-AXXX-MB

While in custody on 8/13/2019, I was walked into the courtroom by Sheriff's Department, then seated while cases was in session. After just a few minutes I was approached by (APD) Mr. Burns. I then asked (APD) Mr. Burns, what was going to take place today in courts. (APD) Mr. Burns shared that we are moving forward with a trial date for docket. Once he was done speaking, I explained that I had a few questions and concerns, in reference to what was taking place in the county jail known as the West Detention Center, Belle Glade and Main Detention Center, West Palm Beach. The first concern I shared with (APD) Mr. Burns was that a "Mary Foss" who was working in mental illness for WDC, Belle Glade, had not spoken to the public defender at all prior to our meeting.

This came to my attention after asking "Ms. Mary Foss" did she speak with the public defender? Ms. Foss replied "No." Then sharing with Ms. Foss that I would like my representation to be present. Ms. Foss refusing to write down her professional business title and name. I asked her a second time, then in frustration she stood up from the table we were sitting, still refusing. Then having sheriff's department put me on suicide watch, called QIS and transferred to the main jail. Then placed in a cell with two other men, who were suicidal. Now sharing with (APD) Mr. Burns that I was not suicidal at all, and this was done in a very unprofessional manner. I then brought up the possibility for a status violation 26.0065 without constitution.

Then requesting she be checked for her mental illness licensing by the public defenders. The next thing I shared with (APD) Mr. Burns is that after that chain of events. I had been separated from my case, defense, evidence and personal property from within the jail just prior to the competence meeting with two officials, held on 8/8/2019, revolving around mental health for competence. (APD) Mr. Burns wrote down my concerns on a piece of paper he was holding, while in the courtroom. After that (APD) Mr. Burns returned to a desk in the courtroom, used for defense attorneys. The case was called to the attention of Judge Hanser, and I was asked to stand. During the hearing, the state attorney, public defender and judge agreed upon a calendar call on 8/27/2019.

On the date of 8/14/2019, Mr. Bailey received the personal property that he was missing. In this property, was the documents that he created with questions for the APD & Psychology Doctor. Due to receiving the documentations six days after their meeting, the questions were never asked, due to having the personal property removed, that creates evidence in the case. Mr. Bailey was looking forward to referencing to the handwritten documentation, when speaking to both APD Jennifer M. Marshall & Doctor Gretchen Moy. Unfortunately, the department held the much-needed documents, creating a lapse in the cases.

					22.401(2)(a)
-11-2019	legal request	form for legal Definition			22.0065 / 22.405(1)
-12-2019	50 squats ✓	—	still no table	—	Legal Paper work showed up (No Definition)
-13-2019	100 squats ✓	—	still no table	No Law codes	(No writing utensil)
-14-2019	500 Squats ✓	Writing Room	Table Showed up	No Law books	No writing paper Available
-14-2019	Personal Property			Approved (with no crocks)	
-14-2019	legal request	form for legal Definition			950.04
-15-2019	Inmate request	Room transfer	to WDC		
-15-2019	Inmate request form				(Request Church)
-15-2019	Request the sheriff department	(No Blank Paper)			No Blank paper

Mr. Bailey was continuing to fast by not eating throughout the day. Focusing on the issues at hand & how he could work to solve them from inside the walls. On the date of 8/14/2019. Continuing to exercise by completing 600 squats & writing a poem. The writing came to an end when he finished the poem & was unable to retrieve any more paper or Law books while being held in a maximum security cell. In this cell, Mr. Bailey was given the opportunity to request legal definitions, by processing a legal request form. This usually takes days before receiving a returned package, sharing legal definitions & statues.

Brian Bailey

Seventy Percent

8/14/2019

There is light by the moon
Creating movement in H_2O
With colors like blue and green
Touching the world's edges
Growing life within
A treasure map for history
Holding on to the bacteria
Providing food among the living
It's open door for hobbies and sports
A battle ground for our nation's military
Researchers developing from it's resources
Lives being saved by the discoveries
Fortune's found in the depths
Transportation in every direction
Natures brewing pot for environmental destruction
Endless tunnel for science
Technologies grave yard
Secrets held beneith the surface
Lifting rain for the spread
Conducting electricity wide
Enormous is behind the eye
Sunlight shows the beauty
Reflection from above
Below is an underworld

I am your ocean!

BB

Palm Beach County Sheriff's Office, FL
Palm Beach Main Detention
3228 Gun Club Road
West Palm Beach , FL 33406

Provider Progress Notes

Patient Name	Patient Number	Booking Number	Birth Date	Date Of Service
BRIAN DALE BAILEY	0403731	20190512060	2/24/1979	8/15/2019

Orders:

No Applicable Data Found For Patient

Patient Problems:

Observed Date	Category	Type	Problem	Confirmed By
06-08-2019	Acute	Symptoms	Abnormal weight loss	

Patient Allergies:

Observed Date	Type	Allergy	Reaction
06-06-2019	Allergy Items	No Known Drug Allergies	

☑ **Vital Signs Taken**

Patient Vitals:

Observed Date	BP	Pulse	Resp	Temp	Pulse Ox	Weight	BMI	PF#1	PF#2	PF#3	Waist
08-15-2019 09:09 AM EST	107/72	78	18	98.40	100	131	18.3	-	-	-	-

☑ **Current Med List Reviewed** ☐ **Psychiatrists Notes Reviewed** ☐ **Caseworker Notes Reviewed**

Notes / History:	⦿ Free Text ◯ SOAPE

Added 08/15/2019 02:15 PM EST by CLegros Provider

40 years old male seen in med clinic complaining of chronic body pain , status post polytraumatism and other surgical interventions. Also, patient is requesting low bunk and extra snacks.

R O S: unremarkable.

Active, alert,

HEENT: PERRLA

CHEST: LUNGS CLEAR S1 S2 WNL.

Page 1 of 2

329

Palm Beach County Sheriff's Office, FL
Palm Beach Main Detention
3228 Gun Club Road
West Palm Beach, FL 33406

Provider Progress Notes

 **wellpath**

Patient Name	Patient Number	Booking Number	Birth Date	Date Of Service
BRIAN DALE BAILEY	0403731	20190512060	2/24/1979	8/15/2019

Orders:

CHEST: LUNGS CLEAR S1 S2 WNL

ABDOMEN: SOFT NO MASS PALPABLE.

EXTREMITIES :F R O M , SCAR OF SURGICAL INCISION ON LEFT HIP ,RIGHT KNEE.

CNS: NO DEFICIT.

ASSESSMENT: CHRONIC PAIN SP POLYTRAUMATISM.

PLAN ;

SEE ORDER

RET TO CLINIC PRN.

330

8/15/2019
Police Report
(Improper Documentation)

Case# 50-2019-MM-005685-AXXX-MB

On the morning of **8/8/2019**, during a meeting with, Assistant Public Defender Jennifer M. Marshall, Doctor Gretchen Moy & Mr. Bailey. Then given the opportunity to **read, recite & review**, the police report taken on **5/12/2019**. After doing so, he noticed the report was incorrect with improper information, **violating Statute 90.604**.

Violating Statute – **90.604 Lack of Knowledge**

1) Except as otherwise provided in s. **90.702**, a witness may not testify to a matter unless **evidence** is introduced which is sufficient to **support a finding** that the witness has personal knowledge of the matter. **Evidence to prove personal knowledge** may be given by the witness's own testimony.

Mr. Bailey immediately shared this with both APD Jennifer M. Marshall & Dr. Gretchen Moy. On the police report I **did,** "**NOT** "see it showing that he is an authorized **member of Christ Fellowship Church,** Royal Palm Beach, Florida campus, who **serves for the church.** Creating an arrest by opinion of **Christ Fellowship staff.** Lacking both knowledge & position Mr. Bailey holds within the church. When he wrote this information, he had now been incarcerated for **95 days,** held in two different detention centers in Palm Beach County & this was the first time Mr. Bailey had a chance to see the police report. To his dissatisfaction the report was incorrect after review.

It also, doesn't show that Mr. Bailey was self-employed as a business owner with the **State of Florida.** Holding a business license through Department of State, known as **SUNBIZ.** Still an administrator, while being injured & awaiting surgery, during a financial loss. While being able to provide proof, showing the business taxes form 1099, in 2019.

Brian Bailey

Police Report
(Information)

8/5/2019

Case # 50-2019-MM-005685-AXXX-MB

On the morning of 8/8/2019, during a meeting with Assistant Public Defender: Ms. Jennifer Marshall, Doctor Gretchen Moy and myself. I was given the opportunity to read, recite and review, the police report taken on 5/12/2019. After doing so, I noticed the report was incorrect with improper information, violating statue # 90.604 Lack of knowledge. I immediately shared this with both (APD) Ms. Marshall and Dr. Moy. On the police report I did not see it showing that I'm a member of Christ Fellowship Church, Royal Palm Beach Campus, who serves for the church.

Creating an arrest by opinion of Christ Fellowship staff, Lacking both knowledge and position I hold within the church. When I wrote this information, I had now been incarcerated for 95 days, held in two different detention centers in Palm Beach County and this was the first time I had a chance to see the police reports. To my dissatisfaction the report was incorrect after review.

Statue Violation:

333

Google
PO Box 1870
Ashland VA 23005-4870

6742

BRIAN BAILEY
3200 SUMMIT BLVD UNIT 15532
WEST PALM BEACH FL 33416-4021

1410300.2020011103501.06742

PAYER'S name, street address, city, state, and ZIP code	1 Rents	OMB No. 1545-0115	
XXVI HOLDINGS INC. 1600 AMPHITHEATRE PARKWAY MOUNTAIN VIEW, CA 94043 650-253-0000	2 Royalties $ 0.00	**2019** 1099-MISC	**Miscellaneous Income**
	3 Other Income	4 Fed income tax withheld $ 0.00	**Copy B For Recipient**
PAYER'S Federal Tax ID RECIPIENT'S identification No. 82-2182297 XXXXX4912	5 Fishing boat proceeds	6 Med & health care pmts	This is important tax information and is being furnished to the Internal Revenue Service. If you are required to file a return, a negligence penalty or other sanction may be imposed on you if this income is taxable and the IRS determines that it has not been reported.
RECIPIENT'S Name and Address	7 Nonemployee Compensation $ 919.68	8 Pmts in lieu of Div or Int	
	9 Payer made direct sales of $5000 or more of consumer products ☐	10 Crop insurance proceeds	
BRIAN BAILEY 3200 SUMMIT BLVD. SUITE 15532 WEST PALM BEACH, FL 33416	11	12	
	13 Excess Golden Par Pmts	14 Gross paid to an attorney	
Account Number 15a Sec 409A deferrals 15b Sec 409A Income 488988246132	16 State tax withheld	17 State/Payer's state no.	18 State income
Form **1099-MISC**	(Keep for your records.)	Department of the Treasury - Internal Revenue Service	

*Leading up to the arrest that took place at **Christ Fellowship Church**, while being an enrolled student at **Palm Beach State College**, holding a high GPA. Looking to make honor role, including a career change. Below is the documentation providing proof of business taxes being settled for 2018, during the year of 2019. While still working the administration & closing lose ends as the President Owner of, "**Blackwater Dive Experts.**" And being self-employed through Google AdSense, a video production company. Also, reaching out to the **Social Security Administration** just months before & having an open case, while being disabled & explaining to the government, that he was seriously injured & needs help or assistance.*

334

Mary Ann Phillips CPA PA
1931 Commerce Lane Ste 6
Jupiter FL 33458
561-747-5431

Taxpayer Information

Credit Card Holder Information
Brian Bailey

Card Info Visa 6320

Amount: $500.00

Date/Time: 03-04-2019 / 10:17:14
Transaction ID: 61594737030
Transaction Type: Manual

X_____
I confirm the use of the card and agree to be bound by all agreements governing the issuance and use of
the card. I agree to pay the amount above in accordance with such agreements.

Customer Copy

SOCIAL SECURITY ADMINISTRATION

Supplemental Security Income
Notice of Disapproved Claim   **3/5/2019**

DATE: March 5, 2019
Claim Number:

BRIAN DALE BAILEY
SUITE 15532
3200 SUMMIT BLVD
WEST PALM BEACH FL 33416-4021

We are writing about your claim for Supplemental Security Income (SSI) payments.
Based on a review of your health problems you do not qualify for payments on this
claim. This is because you are not disabled or blind under our rules.

We have enclosed information about the disability and blindness rules and more
details about the decision on your claim.

ABOUT THE DECISION
Trained staff looked at your case and made this decision. They work for your State
but used our rules.

Please remember that there are many types of disability programs, both government
and private, which use different rules. A person may be receiving benefits under
another program and still not be entitled under our rules. This may be true in
this case.

INFORMATION ABOUT MEDICAID
Although you are not eligible for SSI payments, you may be eligible for medical
assistance (Medicaid). If you have any questions about your eligibility for
Medicaid or you need medical assistance you should get in touch with the
Department of Children and Families.

IF YOU DISAGREE WITH THE DECISION
If you disagree with this decision, you have the right to appeal. We will review
your case and consider any new facts you have. A person who did not make the first
decision will decide your case.

- o   You have 60 days to ask for an appeal.

- o   The 60 days start the day after you get this letter. We assume you got this
      letter 5 days after the date on it unless you show us that you did not get
      it within the 5-day period.

- o   You must have a good reason for waiting more than 60 days to ask for an
      appeal.

- o   You have to ask for an appeal in writing. We will ask you to complete a form
      SSA-561-U2, called "Request for Reconsideration". You may contact one of our
      offices or call 1-800-772-1213 to request this form. Or you may complete
      this form online at http://www.socialsecurity.gov/disability/appeal. Contact
      one of our offices if you want help.

BAILEY, BRIAN DALE

o   In addition, you should complete a "Disability Report - Appeal" to tell us
     about your medical condition since you filed your claim. You may contact
     one of our offices or call 1-800-772-1213 to request this form. Or, you may
     complete this report online after you complete the online Request for
     Reconsideration.

HOW THE APPEAL WORKS
You have the right to review the facts in your case. You can give us more facts to
add to your file. Then we will decide your case again. You will not meet the
person who will decide your case.

NEW APPLICATION
You have the right to file a new application at any time, but filing a new
application is not the same as appealing this decision. If you disagree with this
decision and you file a new application instead of appealing, you might lose some
benefits, or not qualify for any benefits. So, if you disagree with this decision,
you should ask for an appeal within 60 days.

IF YOU WANT HELP WITH YOUR APPEAL
You can have a friend, lawyer, or someone else help you. There are groups that can
help you find a lawyer or give you free legal services if you qualify. There are
also lawyers who do not charge unless you win your appeal. Your local Social
Security office has a list of groups that can help you with your appeal.

If you get someone to help you, you should let us know. If you hire someone, we
must approve the fee before he or she can collect it.

SOCIAL SECURITY BENEFITS
The application you filed for SSI was also a claim for Social Security benefits.
We looked into this, and decided you can't get any Social Security benefits
besides those you may already be getting. If you disagree with this decision, you
have the right to appeal. The appeal was described earlier in this letter.

IF YOU HAVE ANY QUESTIONS
If you have any questions, you may call us toll-free at 1-800-772-1213, or call
your local Social Security office at (866) 783-7339. We can answer most questions
over the phone. You can also write or visit any Social Security office. The office
that serves your area is located at:

                    801 CLEMATIS STREET STE 2
                    WEST PALM BEACH, FL 33401

If you do call or visit an office, please have this letter with you. It will help
us answer your questions. Also, if you plan to visit an office, you may call ahead
to make an appointment. This will help us serve you more quickly.

SUSPECT SOCIAL SECURITY FRAUD?
If you suspect Social Security fraud, please visit http://oig.ssa.gov/r or call
the Inspector General's Fraud Hotline at 1-800-269-0271 (TTY 1-866-501-2101).

                    Social Security Administration

Enclosures: Explanation of Decision   SSA-L444 (09/15)
             SSI Disability Rules Factsheet
                                                  661

8223

BAILEY, BRIAN DALE

RULES FOR SSI DISABILITY AND BLINDNESS

You must meet certain rules to qualify for SSI payments based on disability:

For Payments as a Disabled Adult:

If you are age 18 or older your health problems must:

o Keep you from doing any kind of substantial work (described below), and

o Last, or be expected to last, for at least 12 months in a row, or be expected to result in death.

For Payments as a Disabled Child:

If you are under age 18 your health problems must:

o Be as severe as those that would keep an adult from doing any kind of substantial work. This means that your health problems must limit you from doing things that other children the same age normally can do, to the extent required by our rules, and

o Last, or be expected to last, for at least 12 months in a row, or be expected to result in death.

You must meet certain rules to qualify for SSI payments based on blindness:

o Your eyesight must be no better than 20/200 in the better eye with the use of a corrective lens, OR

o Your visual fields must be restricted to 20 degrees or less.

You can qualify for SSI benefits due to blindness even if you can do substantial work.

Information About Substantial Work

Generally, substantial work is physical or mental work you are paid to do. Work can be substantial even if it is part-time. To decide if your work is substantial, we consider the nature of the job duties, the skills and experience you need to do the job, and how much you actually earn.

Usually, we find that your work is substantial if your gross earnings average over $1180 per month after we deduct allowable amounts. Your work may be different than before your health problems began. It may not be as hard to do and your pay may be less. However, we may still find that your work is substantial under our rules.

If you are self-employed, we consider the kind and value of your work, including your part in the management of the business, as well as your income, to decide if your work is substantial.

SSA-L444 Title XVI Factsheet (1/19)

BAILEY, BRIAN DALE

SOCIAL SECURITY ADMINISTRATION

          E X P L A N A T I O N   O F   D E T E R M I N A T I O N

Name: NH's Name [CDB/DWB]:   SSN: Claim Type:
BRIAN BAILEY   DI

The following evidence was used to decide your claim:

JFK MEDICAL CENTER report received 01/19/2019
ST MARYS MEDICAL CENTER report received 01/21/2019
MOREHEAD MEMORIAL HOSPITAL report received 01/15/2019
C L BRUMBACK PRIMARY CARE CLINICS report received 02/11/2019
DERMATOLOGY ASSOCIATES OF PALM BEACH report received 02/06/2019
ER DOCTORS URGENT CARE report received 02/04/2019
FYZICAL THERAPY AND BALANCE CENTERS report received 02/14/2019-02/21/2019
CITY DENTAL OF WELLINGTON report received 02/08/2019
MIDTOWN IMAGING report received 02/10/2019

We have determined that your condition is not severe enough to keep you from
working. We considered the medical record and other information, your age,
education, training, and work experience in determining how your condition affects
your ability to work.

You state that you are disabled and unable to work because of problems with the
left shoulder and arm, right knee problems, hip issues, sleep apnea, wrist
problems, and a limited learning capacity. We realize you are concerned about your
condition and how it affects your ability to complete tasks. However, based on our
review of the information in your case file, we have determined that you are
capable of understanding and carrying out instructions, meeting general production
and quality standards, and reporting to work on a regular and continuing basis.
Although you may need treatment for your condition, and it may limit your ability
to perform your past work, disability cannot be established because you are still
capable of performing work that requires less physical effort, and only a very
short, on-the-job training period.

If your condition gets worse and keeps you from working, call or visit any Social
Security Office about filing another application.

8223

BAILEY, BRIAN DALE

339

April 11, 2019

Blackwater Dive Experts Inc
c/o Brian Bailey
3200 Summit Blvd STE 15532
West Palm Beach, FL 33416

Brian:

Enclosed is the 2018 Form 1120S, U.S. Income Tax Return for an S Corporation, prepared for Blackwater Dive Experts Inc from the information provided. **This return will be e-filed with the IRS once we receive a signed Form 8879-S, IRS e-file Signature Authorization for Form 1120S.** {ENCLOSED -- URGENT]

The corporation's federal **return reflects neither a refund nor a balance due**.

Also enclosed are letters to the shareholders and their copies of the Schedule K-1, to be distributed to the shareholders.

Thank you for the opportunity to be of service. For further assistance with your tax needs, please contact this office at (561)747-5431.

Sincerely,

Alycia Phillips
Mary Ann Phillips CPA PA

340

On the date of 5/8/2019, a letter of documentation was created by the IRS, stating that Brian Dale Bailey only had 20 days to reply with proper forms & documentation. This takes place just days before the arrest at a religious location, known as

Christ Fellowship Church.

IRS Department of the Treasury
Internal Revenue Service
OSC
OGDEN UT 84201-0034

5/8/2019

027460.148035.476463.2214 2 AB 0.412 1180

BRIAN BAILEY
3200 SUMMIT BLVD STE 15532
WEST PALM BEACH FL 33416

027460

CUT OUT AND RETURN THE VOUCHER BELOW IF YOU HAVE AN INQUIRY OR A RESPONSE.
DO NOT USE IF YOU ARE MAKING A PAYMENT.

The IRS address must appear in the window.
32221-502-78461-9   0425809591
BODCD-SB

Use for inquiries only
Letter Number: LTR0012C
Letter Date : 2019-05-08
Tax Period   : 201712

INTERNAL REVENUE SERVICE
OSC
OGDEN UT 84201-0034

BRIAN BAILEY
3200 SUMMIT BLVD STE 15532
WEST PALM BEACH FL 33416

592644912 JS BAIL 30 0 201712 670 00000000000

341

 **IRS** Department of the Treasury
Internal Revenue Service

5/8/2019   OMB Clearance No.:   1545-0074

OSC
OGDEN   UT   84201-0034

In reply refer to: 0425809591
May 08, 2019   LTR 12C   0 R
                 201712 30
Input Op: 0425809591 00004631
                              BODC: SB

BRIAN BAILEY
3200 SUMMIT BLVD STE 15532
WEST PALM BEACH FL 33416

027460

Social Security number:

32221-502-78461-9

Dear Taxpayer:

We received your Dec. 31, 2017, Form 1040 federal individual
income tax return, but we need more information to process the return
accurately. Unless required otherwise, send us your reply within 20
days from the date of this letter.

Enclose only the information requested and any forms, schedules or
other information required to support your entries and a copy of this
letter. Don't send a copy of your return unless we ask you to do so.
Don't respond with a Form 1040X, Amended U.S. Individual Income Tax
Return. We'll issue any refund due to you in about 6 to 8 weeks from
the time we receive your response. If we don't receive a response from
you, we may have to increase the tax you owe or reduce your refund.

To obtain the forms, schedules, or publications to respond to this
letter, visit www.irs.gov or call 800-TAX-FORM (800-829-3676).

According to our records, advance payments of the premium tax credit
were made for health care coverage from the Health Insurance
Marketplace for you or someone listed on your return. If advanced
payments of the premium tax credit were made for you or someone else
listed on your return, you must use Form 8962, Premium Tax Credit, to
reconcile the advance credit payments with the amount of the premium
tax credit you are allowed for the year.

You should have received a Form 1095-A, Health Insurance Marketplace
Statement, from the Health Insurance Marketplace. Refer to the Form
1095-A and Form 8962 instructions to help you complete Form 8962. If
you didn't receive a Form 1095-A, visit www.healthcare.gov or your
state Marketplace website.

Send us the following documents:

- a completed Form 8962
- a copy of your Form 1095-A

If you don't reconcile, you won't be eligible for advance payments of
the premium tax credit or cost-sharing reductions to help pay for your
Marketplace health insurance coverage and other medical expenses in

BRIAN BAILEY
3200 SUMMIT BLVD STE 15532
WEST PALM BEACH FL   33416

future years. You may also be required to pay back all or part of the
advance payments, which could result in an additional tax due or a
reduction of your refund.

If you have questions, you can visit www.irs.gov/ltr0012C or call us
at 866-682-7451, extension 568.

If you have questions about this letter, call the appropriate
telephone number listed below:

   - 800-829-0922 (Individual-Wage Earners)
   - 800-829-8374 (Individual-Self Employed/Business Owners)
   - 800-829-4059 (Telecommunication Device for the Deaf, TDD)
   - +1-267-941-1000 (Outside of the United States), not toll-free

If you prefer, you can write to us at the address shown at the
beginning of this letter.

If you want to send the information by fax, our fax number is
855-309-9361. Due to the high volume, we can't acknowledge receipt of
your fax. Your faxed signatures will become a permanent part of your
filing. Don't send another copy by mail. Doing so could delay the
processing of your return. Be sure to put your taxpayer identification
number on each page faxed. Include a cover sheet with the following
information:

Date: _____
Attention: ICO Rejects Team OSPC
BATCH: .
Control number: 32221-502-78461-9
Your name: _____
Your taxpayer ID: _____
(Social Security or individual taxpayer identification number)
Tax period: _____
Number of pages faxed: _____

If you didn't file your tax return electronically and your filing
requirements allow you this option, please consider this in the
future. The e-file program will guide you through the steps of
completing your tax return, so that you can help to avoid
correspondence delays. For more information about electronic filing,
ask your tax preparer or visit www.irs.gov.

When you write, include a copy of this letter, and provide your
telephone number and the hours we can reach you in the spaces below.

343

0425809591
May 08, 2019   LTR 12C   0 R
201712 30
Input Op: 0425809591 00004633

BRIAN BAILEY
3200 SUMMIT BLVD STE 15532
WEST PALM BEACH FL 33416

027460

Telephone number ( )_____ Hours _____

Keep a copy of this letter for your records.

Thank you for your cooperation.

Sincerely yours,

Karen E. Peat

Karen E. Peat
Department Manager, ICO ERS/Rejects

BATCH .
32221-502-78461-9

Enclosures:
Copy of this letter
Envelope

5/12/2019

Sheriff's Department "Lack of Knowledge"

Case# 50-2019-MM-005685-AXXX-MB

On the date of **5/12/2019**, Sheriff's Department unaware of the facts, before this became a case. Needing to be advised by an employee of Christ Fellowship Church, Royal Palm Beach campus, before carrying out this arrest. Mr. Bailey had never received any documentation or paperwork with a (No Trespass Warning) or case number. Therefore, still being an authorized member of Christ Fellowship Church. On the day of **5/12/2019**, only doing what the Sheriff's Department ask of me. Which was to put my hands behind my back & sit down in the back of a Sheriff's Department automobile. **Violating statutes 90.604 & 90.702**

Statute violation:

1) *Statute* **90.604 – Lack of Personal Knowledge**
   *Except as otherwise provided in s. 90.702,
   a witness may not testify to a matter
   unless evidence is introduced which is
   sufficient to support a finding that the
   witness has personal knowledge of the
   matter. Evidence to prove personal
   knowledge may be given by the witness's
   own testimony.*

2) *Statute* **90.702 – Testimony by experts**
   *If scientific, technical, or other specialized
   knowledge will assist the trier of fact in
   understanding the evidence or in
   determining a fact in issue, a witness
   qualified as an expert by knowledge, skill,
   experience, training or education may
   testify about it in the form of an opinion
   or otherwise, if;*
   *(1) The testimony is based upon sufficient facts
   or data.*

Brian Bailey

History Report MDC   8/19/2019

Date	Exercise	Reading (writing)	Holy Bible	Law	Misc.
8/19/2019	squats ✓	writing		Inmates (Smoking Drugs)	Working on case defense writing (Vegen Diet Plan)
8/19/2019	"Denied" to the Program for chaplan				Due to (No Wristband)
8/20/2019	Legal Request forms for Definition				Statue for evidence cpd. 27.405
8/20/2019	squats ABS ✓	Obdained Indigent Package	Samuel (2) Kings (1) ✓ reading		Called father 3:15 Writing recipes for (Phone Use)
8/21/2019	squats ✓		✓	Requesting legal Definition	Statue for (False Imprisonment) 960.COVE speedy trail
8/22/2019	Legal request form			Requesting Definitions	90.601 Lack of personal know 393.17 Behavioral programs
8/21/2019	Returned legal request form			Definitions Arrived	27.50 / 490.05 27.51
8/21/2019	Returned legal request forms			No Definitions attained	393.17 393.18
8/22/2019	squats ✓	writing letter to Capel fellowship Church	2 Kings ✓		Did not recieve Indigent Package/Due to No I.D. wristb

Released from incarceration 8/23/2019

Case# 50-2019-MM-005685-AXXX-MB

CHARGE DROPPED

Unable to provide prima facie evidencie

On the morning of 8/23/2019, C.E.R.T. team was in the process of searching the East 4A dorm. When Mr. Bailey was called outside the vest by C.E.R.T. Team. Where one of the C.E.R.T. Team members handed him a yellow sheet of paper, then saying your being released. Guiding him in the direction of a woman holding a clipboard, requesting his signature for an S.O.R. After Mr. Bailey signed this yellow form, he was giving a copy & asked by the C.E.R.T. Team to return back into East 4A dorm. Mr. Bailey wasn't released right away, so he continued working on a project, back in the cell.

This went on for several hours, until it was around 5:00pm & dinner was being served. When he finished his tray, it wasn't long after that his name was called over the intercom system for released. Then Mr. Bailey packed any personal property, making his way out of the dorm. He was met by a woman officer on the outside of the bars, who escorted him downstairs to the lobby. Where he retrieved the rest of his personal property.
The officers were polite enough to allow him to go through the belongs verifying everything, that wasn't considered **contraband**.

The items considered to be contraband, were things like his wallet, bank cards, cell phones, recorder, etc. While going through these items, he found his shoes in an airtight bag sealed. When he opened the bag, a foul odor hit his sense of smell, when touching the inside of the shoe it was damp. When he turned in this personal property over to the Sheriff's Department, on **5/12/2019**, the day of the arrest. The shoes were dry & in a like new condition, not damp or wet at all. Mr. Bailey went ahead & put on the damp shoes, with extreme odor. Putting on the clothes he was holding before being arrested back on.

Mr. Bailey was instructed not to open the contraband items till he left the building. Once he finished signing all the paperwork & packing his bags, he made his way to the exit doors. The first place he headed was to the United States Post Office, once making it inside the building, he set his backpack on the table & decided to go ahead an open the bag with his wallet in it. When doing so, he put everything back in its place organizing his bank cards, & medical information. But, to his dissatisfaction he realized that there was one thing missing, **93 cents** from the zipper pouch of the wallet. **Petty theft** was committed while the personal property was in the position of **Palm Beach County Sheriff's Office.** While saving to pay back the Government for college financial loans.

Statute violation: **Committed by Palm Beach County Sheriff's Office**

1) **812.014 Theft**

   3 (A) *Theft of any property not specified in subsection (2) is petit theft of the second degree & a misdemeanor of the second degree, punishable as provided in s. 775.082 or s. 775.083, and as provided in subsection (5), as applicable.*

The officer made a report of what was in the wallet, totaling **93 cents** *on his report, which never turned up in the rest of the personal property. Now, he made his way over to the mailbox & to his surprise, it was full of mail. Mr. Bailey emptied the box, then going through each piece seeing what had been delivered. Once he was done, he made his way to the teller, returning mail that didn't have his name on it & paying for a year of service, covering 2020. When he left the post office, he made his way west on Summit Blvd. Coming to a Publix grocery store, thinking of sweet carrot cake.*

After 3 months of incarceration, eating a lean diet. He put few items in the basket, & because he was eating vegan he forgot to check the ingredients for milk or soy until he was outside. He then realized that what he had starting eating had milk products in it. This was a big no no for him, Mr. Bailey had made a vow of dedication to God & himself, since State cam is watching all of us. Taking things very seriously, knowing the superior power those satellites had on me, with tight cables.

Here he was starting at square one all over again. As he was walking south on Military trail, towards Forest Hill Blvd. He felt his feet starting to blister & felt pain, with the shoes being damp, blisters started growing, & he had a long walk ahead, with a destination of over several miles.

Ephesians 6:12

For our struggle is not against flesh & blood, but against the rulers, against the authorities, against the power of this dark world & against the spiritual forces of evil in the heavenly realms.

8/23/2019

Publix.

Polo Grounds
926 South Military Trail
West Palm Beach, FL 33415
Store Manager: Bob Miller
561-616-2563

BAR CAKE CARROT	4.99	F
You Saved	1.50	
NV PROTEIN COC ALM	3.99	F
NV GRAN BAR ALMOND	3.59	F
Promotion	-3.59	F
CELERY HEARTS	2.49	F
PEANUT BUTTER DELI	3.35	F
SMARTWATER 1 LTR	1.99	F
CARROTS BABY CUT	1.29	F
You Saved	0.70	
BANANAS		
2.00 lb @ 0.68/ lb	1.36	F

Order Total	19.46
Sales Tax	0.00
Grand Total	19.46
EBT Food Payment	19.46
Change	0.00
F/S Total	19.46

Savings Summary
    Special Price Savings   5.79
****
*   Your Savings at Publix   *
*   5.79   *
****

PRESTO!
Trace #: 058331
Reference #: 1635017898
Acct #: XXXXXXXXXXXXXXXX1992
EBT Food Purchase
Amount: $19.46
Auth #: 352960

AVAIL.BALANCE(FOOD): $372.99

Your cashier was Christian

08/23/2019 20:38 S1104 R105 0255 C0239

Explore the many ways to save at Publix.
View bargains at publix.com/savingstyle

Publix Super Markets, Inc.

Statute Violations

Fifteenth Judicial Circuit of Florida

Case# 50-2019-MM-005685-AXXX-MB

During this case, there were a number of **Statute violations** that were violated & dismissed when brought to the attention of Officials. This has created a distrust between **civilians** & **Law Enforcement**. Not relieving **the truth of the courts** & their hidden secrets behind the walls of authority. This story is true & only comes from one set of eyes, while during his lifetime being moved around by the government, only to have his artistic abilities & tools removed from his position. Leading the surrounding personal to see an individual with very little personal property & to become **indigent** & **considered** a **migrant**.

Raised in **Palm Beach County** & seeing what is offered to our youth as they grow in a town with slim **natural environment**. Without a higher income, this town has little to offer to those with free spirits or explorers of this planet. The system has been designed to seek out those individuals who know how to create new sources of income. Then having those with **power** & **money**, tiering over these talented individuals who aren't financially stable, but yet extremely skilled.

Challenging them both mentally & physically, with their authority figures. Pushing around paperwork, dragging out the lives of the human race. The Department showing signs of dishonesty by theft, loss of data, not hearing the voice of the honest. This world of success revolves around science & technology, being able to analyze & predict. This is all ran by our government, which is designed so that no one individual can create a source of income without sharing with others or providing for the community. While we have so many opportunities leading to believe that there is opportunity for an individual. After experience of being able to create new sources of income, Mr. Bailey has been drawn back & had to use all funds necessary into the **Judicial System**.

Paying the Sheriff's Department after having all charges dropped & after spending his last few years rebuilding with injuries. Having the unknown on the backside of his computer screen that is a building platform, while working to create stability. Living with limited shelter & food, watching the system degenerate the human body, this is a form of **manslaughter**, that has a slow process & is difficult to prove in the eyes of Law. Showing proof of accomplishments & having dedication to a goal, with the government blocking these artists & creating new challenging, for the Laws they also break on the daily bases. While in uniform & presiding to show leadership throughout the community.

There is no reason that Mr. Bailey should be paying to wear handcuffs after the charges have been dismissed! Only creating, time loss only while he now has recently received a Government Loan for college & the Government is the one holding him hostage. Mr. Bailey now a project of his environment being removed of any financial status. At the same time, proving that he's injured & still unable to receive the medical attention needed to complete a successful surgery. The United States of America is using him for advertisement worldwide on the internet, after having thousands of hours with no logged time. That same body that is making other companies' monetary income, is now being destroyed through the system by our Government. This goes with the phrase, "Used & Abused" be careful who your trusting, no matter what uniform is being presented.

Statute violations:

Christ Fellowship Church, Palm Beach County Sheriff's Office, Public Defender & Assistants to Carey Haughwout of Palm Beach County, Department of Corrections, Fifteenth Judicial Circuit of Florida.

1) 27.0065 - Witness Coordination
2) 27.151 (1)(2)(3) Confidentially of Specified executive orders; criteria
3) 27.16 - Appointment of Acting State Attorney
4) 27.18 - Assistance to State Attorney
5) 27.40 (1)(B,1)(9) - Court-appointed counsel; circuit registries; minimum requirements; appointment by court.
6) 27.401 (2)(A) - Cross-circuit conflict representation pilot program
7) 27.405 (1) - Court-appointed counsel; Justice Administrative commission tracking and reporting
8) 27.50 - Public defender; qualifications; election
9) 27.51 (1)(B) 1. - Duties of public defenders
10) 90.105 - Preliminary question
11) 90.202 (1)(2)(12) - Matters which may be Judicially noticed
12) 90.302 - Classification of rebuttable presumptions
13) 90.401 - Definition of Relevant Evidence
14) 90.604 - Lack of Personal Knowledge
15) 90.612 - Mode and order of interrogation and presentation
16) 90.702 - Testimony by Expert
17) 92.525 (1)(A)(4)(A)(B)(C) - Verification of documents; perjury by false written declaration, penalty
18) 393.17 (1) - Behavioral program; certification of behavior analysts
19) 393.18 - Comprehensive transitional education
20) 458.311 - Licensure by Examination; requirements; fees
21) 458.313 - licensure by Endorsement; requirement; fees
22) 458.3165 - Public Psychiatry Certificate
23) 458.3175 - Expert Witness Certificate
24) 460.0015 (B) - Victim's right to a speedy trial
25) 490.005 - Licensure by examiner
26) 490.009 - Discipline
27) 627.732 (16) Emergency Medical Condition
28) 800.03 - Exposer of Sexual Organs
29) 812.014 (3)(A) - Theft
30) 836.05 - Threats; extortion
31) 944.012 - Legislative Intent
32) 950.04 - **Penalty for Neglect** of duty in keeping prisoners of the **United States**

Officials & Agents involved

Case# 50-2019-MM-005685-AXXX-MB

1) Christ Fellowship Church - Pastor **Oscar Soto**
2) Christ Fellowship Church - Security **Don Edward Helvey**
3) Christ Fellowship Church - Security **Gerald Charles**
4) Christ Fellowship Church - Youth Minster **Gregory Reade**
5) Christ Fellowship Church - Member **Gary Borge**
6) Palm Beach Sheriff Office - **Joshua Carmenate**
7) Palm Beach Sheriff Office - **Robert Peitz**
8) Fifteenth Judicial Circuit of Florida - Judge **Leonard Hanser**
9) Fifteenth Judicial Circuit of Florida - **Paulina Pasuarelli**
     (Court Administrator)
10) State Attorney - **David Andrew Aronberg**
11) Assistant State Attorney - **Ryan Glenn Myers**
12) Assistant State Attorney - **Carson Kinnear Kern**
13) Assistant State Attorney - **Robert Seebold Jaegers**
     (Government Attorney)
14) Public Defender - **Carey Haughtwout**
15) Assistant Public Defender - **Jonell Anthony Shih**
16) Assistant Public Defender - **Raymon A. Burns**
17) Assistant Public Defender - **Ilana Felice Marcus**
18) Assistant Public Defender -**John Rivera**
19) Assistant Public Defender - **Jennifer Marie Marshall**
20) Assistant Public Defender - **Lesli Karen Shalloway Fagon**
21) Lifespan Health Services - **Dr. Lisa A. Faraldo**
22) West Detention Center - **Mary Foss**
     (Mental Illness)
23) Augustine Recovery - **Dr. Gretchen Michelle Moy**
     (Psychologist)
24) Internal Revenue Service (Manager) - **Karen E. Peat**
25) Business Owner - **Daniel L. Coston**
26) Inmate - (Houseman) **Patrick**
27) Inmate - **James Lynch**
28) Inmate - **Dunn. C Quinn**

Palm Beach County Sheriff's Officers

Case# 50-2019-MM-005685-AXXX-MB

(Arresting Officers)
1) Palm Beach Sheriff Office - **Joshua Carmenate**
2) Palm Beach Sheriff Office - **Robert Peitz**

(Correction Officers)
3) Palm Beach Sheriff's Office - **Sergeant Bryant**
4) Palm Beach Sheriff's Office - **Deputy Taylor**
5) Palm Beach Sheriff's Office - **Officer Ferguson**
6) Palm Beach Sheriff's Office - **Officer Smith**
7) Palm Beach Sheriff's Office - **Officer Harris**
8) Palm Beach Sheriff's Office - **Officer Cooper**
9) Palm Beach Sheriff's Office - **Officer McWilliams**
10) Palm Beach Sheriff's Office - **Officer Sneed**
11) Palm Beach Sheriff's Office - **Officer Lopez**
12) Palm Beach Sheriff's Office - **Officer Mondragon**
13) Palm Beach Sheriff's Office - **Officer Chiquito**

Doctors & Medical Staff

Case# 50-2019-MM-005685-AXXX-MB

(Correction Medical Staff)

1) Armor Correctional Health - **Dr. Louidor Alliance**
2) Armor Correctional Health - **Dr. Chadia Wilson Morcos**
3) Armor Correctional Health - **Dr. Burgess**
4) Armor Correctional Health - **ARNP Lillian Dent**
5) Armor Correctional Health - **RN Ruth Ihinger**
6) Armor Correctional Health - **RN Marcia Phillips**
7) Armor Correctional Health - **RN Melvia Guillame**
8) Armor Correctional Health - **RN Mioche Remy**
9) Armor Correctional Health - **LPN Elizabeth Lisanti**
10) Armor Correctional Health - **LPN Janet Gomez**

During Mr. Bailey's incarceration at both detention centers, he took the time to write. Below you will find a link to **The Book of Poems, Way of Life**, through **Amazon Publishing** at **Kindle Direct Publishing**. Mr. Bailey shares this with you to help others understand, what some go through while facing the challenges in life. Being seen by the eyes of others at a time when dealing with hardship. If you have the opportunity, please take a moment & view the book through the **Amazon link**. Thank you for taking the time to read this story Mr. Brian Dale Bailey just shared with you.

Have a great day & God Bless!

Amazon Publishing: Way of Life

https://www.amazon.com/Way-Life-Book-Poems-Ultimate-ebook/dp/B089Q8YHJX/ref=sr_1_1?dchild=1&keywords=the+book+of+poems+brian+bailey&qid=1592076175&sr=8-1

YouTube
BB's Life
https://www.youtube.com/c/BBsLIFE/playlists

Blackwater Dive Experts
https://www.youtube.com/watch?v=HzKnD-sFsIw&list=PLN9owjatRoeqBo1GFVmCmDnlvWtdZoBeM

Respectfully,
Brian Dale Bailey

IN THE COUNTY COURT OF THE FIFTEENTH
JUDICIAL CIRCUIT, CRIMINAL DIVISION
IN AND FOR PALM BEACH COUNTY, FLORIDA

TO: GERALD CHARLES C\
C/O CHRIST FELLOWSHIP CHURCH SECURITY
9905 SOUTHER BLVD
ROYAL PALM BEACH, FL 33411
PALM BEACH

CASE NO. 2019MM005685AMB
DIVISION: "B"
Police Case No 06-19-070132
ME. No.

STATE OF FLORIDA
vs.
BRIAN DALE BAILEY

CALENDAR CALL
2 WEEK DOCKET - REMAIN ON CALL
COUNTY COURT - DIVISION B

You are commanded to appear at the Palm Beach County Courthouse, 205 North Dixie
Highway, West Palm Beach, FL 33401, COURTROOM 2E, beginning at 8:30 AM, on
08/27/2019. **PLEASE DO NOT APPEAR BEFORE CALLING: (561) 355-7413 (or 1-(800)
353-3859 7413 if out of the area) to verify if you will be needed for the trial.**

Failure to appear will subject you to contempt of Court. This subpoena is binding day to
day and week to week until the case is closed.

Victoria Suarez

VICTORIA SUAREZ
Assistant State Attorney
Fla Bar No.1010141

August 13, 2019

I received this subpoena on the _15_ day of _Aug_, 2019, and executed the same on the _22_ day
of _Aug_, 2019, in Palm Beach County, Florida.

13762 Aldsworth CT
Wellington 33414

SHERIFF, PALM BEACH COUNTY

By: _____ 7835
Deputy Sheriff

8/19 12:11
8/20 7:05
8/22 5:20 Post

If you are a person with a disability who needs any accommodation in order to participate
in this proceeding, you are entitled, at no cost to you, to the provision of certain assistance.
Please contact the ADA Coordinator in the Administrative Office of the Court, Palm
Beach County Courthouse, 205 North Dixie Highway, Room 5.2500, West Palm Beach,
Florida, 33401; telephone number (561) 355-4380 at least 7 days before your scheduled
court appearance, or immediately upon receiving this notification if the time before the
scheduled appearance is less than 7 days; if you are hearing or voice impaired, call 1-800-
955-8771.

SCANNED
AUG 2 6 2019
DT

8/26/2019

REPORTING CONDITIONS OF SUPERVISION

PALM BEACH COUNTY PRETRIAL SERVICES
Supervised O.R. Program
205 North Dixie Highway, Room 2.2400
West Palm Beach, FL 33401

259394

CASE # 2019mm005685Axx   BOOKING # 2019015844   CHARGE(S): MF Trespass Aft. Warning

A. You have been released on Level: IV   Supervised O.R. by Judge: Collins

B. You MUST do the following until further order of the Court: 8, 26, 2019 at 11:00 a.m. to:

1. You MUST report for an orientation interview on _____ at _____ m. to:
   - ☑ Palm Beach County Courthouse, 205 North Dixie Highway, Room 2.2400, West Palm Beach, FL 33401 (561) 355-6308
   - ☐ South County Courthouse, 200 West Atlantic Avenue, Room 1E-201, Delray Beach, FL 33444 (561) 274-1412
   - ☐ West County Courthouse, 2950 State Road 15, Room #5101, Belle Glade, FL 33430 (561) 992-1120

2. You MUST appear at all future hearings of any kind or nature at the specific time scheduled.

3. You MUST immediately report S.O.R. in person after each court appearance.

4. You MUST NOT VIOLATE ANY City, County, State or Federal LAW.

5. You MUST notify Pretrial Services, in person, if you plan to leave the Palm Beach, Broward, or Martin county area.
   - a. If you plan to travel outside of the Palm Beach, Broward or Martin county area for more than 24 hours, you MUST obtain a travel permit from the S.O.R. office prior to travel.

6. You MUST complete the "CLIENT ASSOCIATIONS AND PLACES FREQUENTED" form prior to release.

7. You MUST follow the following standard program conditions:
   - a. You MUST PAY $10.00 (NO personal checks) each week for the cost of supervision unless otherwise ordered by the Court. This payment starts with your orientation interview.
   - b. You must report in person at a frequency based on your level of supervision.

8. You MUST notify the Clerk of Court and Supervised O.R. of any change of address. (Supervised O.R. will also notify the clerk, as the mailing of any notice of the last address furnished by you to the Court shall constitute service of notice).

C. The following checked conditions of pretrial release are Court imposed and MAY BE MODIFIED ONLY BY THE COURT:

SCANNED AUG 28 2019

- ☐ You shall not possess or carry any type of weapons or firearms.
- ☐ You shall not possess or consume alcoholic beverages and/or chemical substances in the absence of a doctor's prescription.
- ☐ You shall not visit any bars or liquor lounges. ☐ You shall submit to random drug/alcohol testing at your own expense.
- ☐ You shall ☐ complete a mental health evaluation ☐ complete a mental health assessment within _____ of release.
- ☐ You shall promptly engage in any recommended treatment.
- ☐ You shall, within _____ hours of the date of this order or within the same period of time from your release from custody, whichever occurs first, enroll, register, and attend ☐ inpatient ☐ outpatient treatment at _____ and shall maintain such treatment until further order of the Court.
- ☐ You shall maintain a curfew and be in your residence (the address given to the Clerk of Court) by _____ ☐ a.m./☐ p.m. until _____ ☐ a.m./☐ p.m
- ☑ You shall have ☑ no contact ☐ no violent contact with the alleged victim in this case.
- ☐ Other: _____

D. I hereby agree to abide by the above conditions which were thoroughly explained to me. I also understand that my failure to follow the above conditions could result in a warrant being issued and the revocation of my Supervised O.R. bond. I also understand that my willful failure to appear at any future court hearing will result in the revocation of my Supervised O.R. bond.

X _____ (Defendant Signature)   _____ (Pretrial Services Counselor/Interviewer)

Brian Bailey (Defendant Name)   8/23/2019 (Date)

E. Next Scheduled Court Information (to be completed at Orientation Interview)

1. YOUR NEXT SCHEDULED COURT DATE IS ON: _____ per Clerks AT (561) 355-2994

2. THE LOCATION OF YOUR NEXT COURT APPEARANCE IS CHECKED BELOW:
   - ☐ Criminal Justice Complex Courtroom, 3228 Gun Club Road, West Palm Beach, Florida
   - ☐ Central Courthouse, Room/Division _____, 205 North Dixie Highway, West Palm Beach, Florida
   - ☐ South County Courthouse, 200 West Atlantic Avenue, Delray Beach, Florida
   - ☐ North County Courthouse, 3188 PGA Boulevard, Palm Beach Gardens, Florida
   - ☐ West County Courthouse, 2950 State Road 15, Belle Glade, Florida

X _____ (Defendant Signature)   8/26/2019 (Date)   _____ (Pretrial Services Counselor)

"If you are a person with a disability who needs any accommodation in order to participate in this proceeding, you are entitled, at no cost to you, to the provision of certain assistance. Please contact the ADA Coordinator in the Administrative Office of the Court, Palm Beach County Courthouse, 205 North Dixie Highway, West Palm Beach, Florida 33401; telephone number (561) 355-4380 within seven (7) working days of your receipt of this form. If you are hearing or voice impaired, call 711."

PTS Form: SORCOND-2018

FILED: PALM BEACH COUNTY, FL, SHARON R. BOCK, CLERK. 8/27/2019 3:31:00 PM

363

8/27/2019

IN THE COUNTY COURT OF THE FIFTEENTH JUDICIAL CIRCUIT
IN AND FOR PALM BEACH COUNTY, FLORIDA - CRIMINAL DIVISION
CIRCUIT/COUNTY COURT
Court Event Form

DEFENDANT: BRIAN DALE BAILEY
CASE NO: 50-2019-MM-005685-AXXX-MB

STATE OF FLORIDA   DATE: 8/27/2019
vs.
DEFENDANT: BRIAN DALE BAILEY   JACKET #: 0403731
CASE NO: 50-2019-MM-005685-AXXX-MB   BOOKING #: 2019015844
DIVISION: B: Cnty Crim - B (County)

PRESIDING JUDGE: HANSER, JUDGELEONARD   START TIME: 9:21 AM
ASA: MYERS, RYAN   END TIME: 9:23 AM
ATTORNEY:
PUBLIC DEFENDER: BURNS, RAYMON
CO-COUNSEL: COURT REPORTER
DEPUTY CLERK: CB   COURT TYPE: CC
                                                              CALENDAR
                                                              CALL

COURT ROOM: 2E (Main Branch)

Speedy Trial Waived
Reset For
Court Date Scheduled - STCK - STATUS CHECK - 11/25/2019 8:30 AM - 2E (Main Branch) MB, 205 N. Dixie
Highway West Palm Beach FL 33401 - DPA

Other: DEFENDANT PRESENT
Other: STAND IN ATTORNEY ASA SUARZ PRESENT
Total Criminal Court Costs and Fines: $150.00 - Due Date: 11/25/2019
Other Fees: $150.00
PD App Fee: $50.00
Cost of Prosecution: $100.00

Count 1 - MF TRESPASS AFTER WARNING 810.09(2A)
Court Action: PRE-TRIAL DIVERSION

Tuesday, August 27, 2019   Page 1 of 1

364

IN THE CIRCUIT/COUNTY COURT OF THE FIFTEENTH JUDICIAL CIRCUIT
IN AND FOR PALM BEACH COUNTY, FLORIDA

STATE OF FLORIDA

-Vs-

Date: 08/27/2019

Case No: 50-2019-MM-005685-AXXX-MB

Division: B: Cnty Crim - B (County)

BRIAN DALE BAILEY
GENERAL DELIVERY
WEST PALM BEACH, FL 32200

NOTICE OF HEARING
THE DEFENDANT MUST BE PRESENT AT THIS HEARING

For Criminal Charges: Failure to Appear will result in a Bond Forfeiture or
revocation of own recognizance (O.R.) and a Capias/Warrant being issued for your arrest.
For Civil Traffic Charges: Failure to appear may result in the suspension of your driver's license.
IF YOUR CASE IS ON-CALL, CONTACT YOUR ATTORNEY FOR THE TIME TO APPEAR
YOU ARE HEREBY NOTIFIED that this case is scheduled

DATE:	TIME:	HEARING TYPE:	LOCATION:
11/25/2019	8:30 AM	STCK - STATUS CHECK	2E (Main Branch) MB, 205 N. Dixie Highway West Palm Beach FL 33401

BE PREPARED TO PAY COURT COSTS AND FINES ASSESSED BY THE COURT AT THIS HEARING
"IF YOU INTEND TO REQUEST THE SERVICES OF THE PUBLIC DEFENDER, YOU MUST FILE AN APPLICATION AT THE CLERK &
COMPTROLLER'S OFFICE AND BE APPOINTED THE PUBLIC DEFENDER BEFORE YOUR COURT DATE. THE APPLICATION FEE IS $50.00."
Civil Traffic Charges are not eligible for a Public Defender.

SHARON R. BOCK,
CLERK & COMPTROLLER
BY: CB

Deputy Clerk

Deft/Atty:

cc: RYAN MYERS
        BURNS, RAYMON A

FILED: PALM BEACH COUNTY, FL SHARON R BOCK, CLERK 08/27/2019 09:23:07 AM

IN THE CIRCUIT/COUNTY COURT OF THE FIFTEENTH JUDICIAL CIRCUIT
IN AND FOR PALM BEACH COUNTY, FLORIDA

"If you are a person with a disability who needs any accommodation in order to participate in this proceeding, you are entitled, at no cost to you, to the provision of certain assistance. Please contact Tammy Anton, Americans with Disabilities Act Coordinator, Palm Beach County Courthouse, 205 North Dixie Hwy, West Palm Beach, FL 33401; telephone number (561) 355-4380 at least 7 days before your scheduled court appearance, or immediately upon receiving this notification if the time before the scheduled appearance is less than 7 days; if you are hearing or voice impaired, call 711."

"Si usted es una persona minusválida que necesita algún acomodamiento para poder participar en este procedimiento, usted tiene derecho, sin tener gastos propios, a que se le provea cierta ayuda. Tenga la amabilidad de ponerse en contacto con Tammy Anton, 205 N. Dixie Highway, West Palm Beach, Florida 33401; teléfono número (561) 355-4380, por lo menos 7 días antes de la cita fijada para su comparecencia en los tribunales, o inmediatamente después de recibir esta notificación si el tiempo antes de la comparecencia que se ha programado es menos de 7 días; si usted tiene discapacitación del oído o de la voz, llame al 711."

"Si ou se yon moun ki enfim ki bezwen akomodasyon pou w ka patisipe nan pwosedi sa, ou kalifye san ou pa gen okenn lajan pou w peye, gen pwovizyon pou jwen kèk èd. Tanpri kontakte Tammy Anton, kòòdonatè pwogram Lwa pou amerìken ki Enfim yo nan Tribinal Konte Palm Beach la ki nan 205 North Dixie Highway, West Palm Beach, Florida 33401; telefòn li se (561) 355-4380 nan 7 jou anvan dat ou gen randevou pou parèt nan tribinal la, oubyen imedyatman apre ou fin resevwa konvokasyon an si lè ou gen pou w parèt nan tribinal la mwens ke 7 jou; si ou gen pwoblèm pou w tande oubyen pale, rele 711."

366

8/27/2019

SHARON R. BOCK

CLERK & COMPTROLLER
PALM BEACH COUNTY, FLORIDA

RECEIPT
3306658

Printed On:
08/27/2019 09:11
Page 1 of 1

Receipt Number: 3306658 - Date 08/27/2019 Time 9:11AM	
Received of:	BRIAN DALE BAILEY
	GENERAL DELIVERY
	WEST PALM BEACH, FL 32200

Cashier Name:	RAHayes	**Balance Owed:**	150.00
Cashier Location:	County Criminal - Front Counter	**Total Amount Paid:**	100.00
Receipt ID:	9594205	**Remaining Balance:**	50.00
Division:	B: Cnty Crim - B(County)		

Case# 50-2019-MM-005685-AXXX-MB -- DEFENDANT: BAILEY, BRIAN DALE			
Item	Balance	Paid	Bal Remaining
Fees	150.00	100.00	50.00
Case Total	150.00	100.00	50.00

Payments		
Type	Ref#	Amount
CREDIT	2559	100.00
Total Received		100.00
Total Paid		100.00

How was your service today? Please visit www.mypalmbeachclerk.com/survey or send your
feedback to clerkweb@mypalmbeachclerk.com.
For office locations and information about Clerk & Comptroller services:
Visit www.mypalmbeachclerk.com or call (561) 355-2996.

367

IN THE COUNTY COURT – 15th JUDICIAL CIRCUIT
PALM BEACH COUNTY, FLORIDA
DIVISION "B"

STATE OF FLORIDA

CASE NO: 19MM005685

vs

CHARGES: 1) Trespass
2)
3)
4)

BRIAN Bailey
Defendant

PRE-TRIAL AGREEMENT / STIPULATION FOR DEFERRED PROSECUTION RE: NOTICE TO APPEAR / UNIFORM TRAFFIC CITATION / INFORMATION

This matter comes before the Court upon stipulation between the State of Florida and the defendant to redirect this case into an alternative resolution/diversion program.

By entering into this agreement, the defendant agrees to waive his/her right to a speedy trial as provided for by F.R.C.P. 3.191. Further, by entering this agreement, the parties stipulate as follows:

1. It is agreed that this case shall be continued for the purpose of successfully completing all terms of this agreement by your next court date which is now scheduled for _____ / _____ / 20_____ at _____ : _____ AM / PM in Courtroom 2E.
2. It is agreed that if all conditions are successfully completed in a timely manner and the defendant has not been arrested for new charges, has not received any additional Notices to Appear or Uniform Traffic Citations, has not been convicted of any new crimes, and does not fail to appear, the State will abandon prosecution of this case.
3. Extensions of this agreement may be granted upon the discretion of the prosecutor.
4. Defendant shall provide or show proof of completion of the items checked below:

☐ Community Service _____ Hours ☒ Cost of Prosecution ($100 to Clerk)
☐ Anger Management Course _____ Hours ☐ Valid Driver's License
☐ Defensive Driving Course _____ Hours ☐ Valid Vehicle Registration
☐ DEP Course _____ Hours ☐ Valid Vehicle Insurance
☐ Theft Abatement Course _____ Hours ☐ Successful P&P Agreement
☒ No Contact with CHRist Fellowship
☐ Letter of Apology to _____
☐ Restitution: $ _____ to _____
☐ No new arrests or criminal law violations since _____ / _____ / 20_____.
☐ OTHER: _____

ASSISTANT STATE ATTORNEY

DEFENDANT

8/27/19
DATE

ATTORNEY FOR DEFENDANT

UPDATED: 08/01/18

368

8/30/2021

Notice of Case Action
State of Florida Department
of Children and Families

ACCESS CENTRAL MAIL CENTER
P.O. BOX 1770
OCALA FL 34478

August 30, 2019   9/13/2019   Case: 1540732843   Phone: (954) 626-5927

3644 - (Olavo)   couldn't - (LM)
        Customer Service   9/13/2019 - 9:04 A.M.

BRIAN D BAILEY
3200 SUMMIT BL 15532
WEST PALM BEACH FL 33416

Dear Brian D Bailey

The following is information about your eligibility.

Food Assistance

Your application for Food Assistance dated August 28, 2019 is **approved**. You are eligible for the months listed below:

Name	Aug, 2019	Sep, 2019	Oct, 2019 Thru January 31, 2020
Brian Bailey	Eligible	Eligible	Eligible
Benefit Amount	$19.00	$192.00	$194.00

Certain food assistance recipients, known as Able-Bodied Adults Without Dependents (ABAWDs) will have to meet work requirements to be eligible to receive food assistance benefits. An ABAWD is an able-bodied adult without a dependent who is age 18 through 49; physically and mentally able to work; not living and eating with a child under age 18; not pregnant; and not exempt from food assistance general employment program work requirements. **If you are identified as an ABAWD, you will be referred to participate in the SNAP Employment and Training program, operated by local workforce development areas (LWDA) also known as CareerSource. To find your local LWDA or to learn more about services offered, please visit:** http://www.floridajobs.org/onestop/onestopdir/.

If you are identified as an ABAWD and fail to comply with work requirements, or do not have good reason not to participate, a sanction will be imposed that stops or reduces food assistance benefits. If your case is closed, you can reapply if you are exempt from work requirements, have good reason to not participate, or are working or volunteering 20 hours per week, averaged 80 hours per month.

More information about food assistance work activities, including exemptions and reasons for good cause, can be found at http://www.myflfamilies.com/service-programs/access-florida/abawdfaq.

Before your eligibility ends, we will send you a letter telling you what to do to keep getting Food Assistance. To keep your Food Assistance from ending, you will need to complete a review by January 31, 2020. You can use the web site at www.myflorida.com/accessflorida to do this on My ACCESS Account.

AE01   FORM : CF-ES 103 03 2009

For Food Assistance benefits, the only change you must report during your certification period is when your household's monthly gross income is more than your income limit of $1,354.00. You must report this change within 10 days following the end of the month the change happens. If your household income was higher than this amount at the time of your last application or review, you should report changes at the next review. If you fail to report changes as required, or if the information you provide is not correct, you may have to repay any benefits you receive for which you were not eligible and you may be prosecuted for fraud. You must report other changes and your household's situation at the time of the next recertification. If you have access to a computer, you may report your changes online at the ACCESS Florida website www.myflorida.com/accessflorida. You may also report changes by calling the ACCESS Florida Customer Call Center toll free at 1-866-762-2237, or by mail to the return address at the top of this notice.

If this is the first time you have been approved for food or cash benefits, your EBT Card will be mailed to you. If you received benefits before and had a card but have lost or misplaced it, please call EBT Customer Service at 888-356-3281 to ask for a replacement card.

Go to www.myflorida.com/accessflorida and update your MyACCESS account. You will need your case number, 1540732843, to validate your account. Once you have validated your account you will be able to see the status of your benefits, view notices, renew benefits, request additional benefits, report changes, and upload documents.

Once being approved & receiving **SNAP Food Assistance** through an **EBT Card**. Mr. Bailey was required to volunteer or prove employment for at least 20 hours a week, while being **disabled** under section 1614(a)(3)(A) with a left shoulder needing a total reconstruction & right fractured wrist that wasn't healing. Causing him extreme amounts of pain to move either arm. Unable to seek medical attention or prove to the **Department of Children & Families** that he is indeed injured.

ACCESS Central Mail Center
P.O. BOX 1770
Ocala, FL 34478-1770

Notice of Case Action
State of Florida Department
of Children and Families

_91_

September 03, 2019

Medicaid Denied

BRIAN D BAILEY
3200 SUMMIT BL 15532
WEST PALM BEACH FL 33416

Dear Brian D Bailey,

The following is information about your eligibility.

Information About Medicaid

Name: Brian D Bailey
SSI Application Date: January 03, 2019
PIN: 8678838736

SSN: XXX-XX- 4912
SSI Denial Date: March 05, 2019
Birth Date: February 24, 1979

The application you filed for Supplemental Security Income (SSI) is also an application for Medicaid. Medicaid is a joint federal and state medical assistance program. Although you were denied SSI payments, you may still be eligible for Medicaid.

Call the ACCESS Florida Customer Call Center toll free at 1-866-762-2237 within 30 days if you would like us to determine your eligibility for Medicaid. If you already receive Medicaid, you do not need to call us unless you have unpaid medical bills.

If the Social Security Administration (SSA) decided you are not disabled, we may not be able to provide you with Medicaid based on disability, but there are exceptions. If you have questions, call one of our Customer Call Center agents.

Enfòmasyon sou Medicaid

Non: Brian D Bailey
Dat aplikasyon pou SSI: January 03, 2019
PIN: 8678838736

SSN: XXX-XX-4912
Dat Refi pou SSI: March 05, 2019
Dat li fèt: February 24, 1979

Aplikasyon ou te ranpli pou Revni Sekirite Siplemantè (SSI) reprezante yon aplikasyon tou pou Medicaid. Medicaid se yon pwogram asistans medikal komen federal ak leta. Menmsi ou te jwenn refi pou resevwa peman SSI, ou kapab toujou kalifye pou Medicaid.

Rele Sant Apèl Kliyan ACCESS Florida gratis nan nimewo 1-866-762-2237 nan 30 jou si ou ta renmen pou nou detèmine kalifikasyon ou pou Medicaid. Si ou deja ap resevwa Medicaid, ou pa bezwen rele nou sof si ou genyen bòdwo medikal ou poko peye.

Si Administrasyon Sekirite Sosyal (SSA) te deside ou pa yon moun ki andikape, nou pa kapab anmezi pou ofri ou Medicaid dapre andikap ou, men genyen eksepsyon. Si ou genyen kesyon, rele youn nan ajan Sant Apèl Kliyan nou.

*Mr. Brian Dale Bailey the claimant has been **disabled under Section 1614(a)(3)(A)** of the Social Security Act since January 3, 2019 & was "**unable to receive a surgery**" with government assistance through **Department of Children & Families**. While being Self - Employed with multiple companies & holding a valid **State of Florida** license for corporation.*

Información sobre Medicaid

Nombre: Brian D Bailey
Fecha de solicitud de SSI: January 03, 2019
PIN: 8678838736

Número de Seguro Social (SSN): XXX-XX-4912
Fecha de negativa de SSI: March 05, 2019
Fecha de nacimiento: February 24, 1979

La solicitud de Ingresos por Seguro Suplementario (SSI) es también una solicitud de Medicaid. Medicaid es un programa de asistencia médica conjunta federal y estatal. Si bien se le denegó el pago de SSI, aún puede resultar apto para recibir el beneficio de Medicaid.

Llame al número gratuito 1-866-762-2237 del Centro de Atención al Cliente de ACCESS Florida dentro de los 30 días si desea que determinemos si cumple los requisitos para recibir Medicaid. Si ya recibe Medicaid, no es necesario que nos llame a menos que tenga facturas médicas impagas.

Si la Administración del Seguro Social (SSA) decidió que usted no tiene discapacidad alguna, es posible que no podamos darle Medicaid por discapacidad, pero hay excepciones. Si desea hacer alguna consulta, comuníquese con alguno de nuestros agentes del Centro de Atención al Cliente.

Health Care District of Palm Beach County
1150 45th Street
West Palm Beach, FL 33407
(561) 804-4117

09/19/2019

BRIAN BAILEY
3200 SUMMIT BLVD STE 15532
WEST PALM BEACH, FL 33416

MEMBER NO.: 1000315673 - 01
SUBJECT: NEED ADDITIONAL INFORMATION TO PROCESS APPLICATION

Dear BRIAN BAILEY

We need more information before we can complete your application. You
must send the information listed below:
IDENTIFICATION [] -- [] Wage form
RESIDENCY [] -- [] Homeless form
INCOME [] -- [] Living arrangement
OTHER [SEE BELOW]
Note: We need a copy of...

  1. Please provide a support letter by the person you are living with
     and helping you with your monthly expenses.

When you have all of the requested information, please mail, fax or
bring the information to the address listed at the top of this letter.
The fax number is (561) 804-5639.
All offices are open Monday through Friday, 8:00 am - 5:00 pm.except
holidays.

While we are reviewing your application, If you need to see a doctor,
call (561) 642-1000. The doctors at C.L. Brumback Primary Care
Clinics are available regardless of your ability to pay.

Sincerely,
West Palm Beach Eligibility Office
GD/MS

Si-w bezwen moun ede-w an kreyol, tanpri rele 1-866-930-0035.
Si necesita asistencia en espanol, favor de llamar al 1-866-930-0035.
Letter2W   Enclosure

The *Palm Beach County Health Care District*
*continually having Mr. Bailey send documentation
& letters explaining his living situation. Requesting
the owners or lease holders of each location he stayed
sign letters that were being provided as proof. In some
cases, he stay was no longer than 30 days. In order to
keep a valid Florida driver license.*

373

Filing # 96187460 E-Filed 09/24/2019 11:22:24 AM

IN THE CIRCUIT COURT OF THE FIFTEENTH JUDICIAL CIRCUIT
IN AND FOR PALM BEACH COUNTY, FLORIDA
CRIMINAL DIVISION "B"

CASE NO. 2019MM005685AMB

STATE OF FLORIDA,

vs.

BRIAN DALE BAILEY.

_____/

ORDER DIRECTING PAYMENT OF EXPERT.

THIS MATTER, having come before the Court, *sua sponte,* and the Court being otherwise fully advised in the premises, it is hereby

ORDERED AND ADJUDGED that Court Administration is to pay $250.00 to Dr. Lisa Faraldo, the expert appointed to evaluate Defendant's Competency to Proceed, in accordance with this Court's order of July 8, 2019. This amount is in accordance with Administrative Order 2.601 and covers payment for the attempted evaluation and travel fee to Belle Glade, FL.

DONE AND ORDERED in Chambers, West Palm Beach, Palm Beach County, Florida this 24 day of September, 2019.

LEONARD HANSER
County Court Judge

Copies furnished to:
Dr. Lisa Faraldo, lwretzel@gmail.com
Ryan Myers, Assistant State Attorney
Raymon Burns, Assistant Public Defender
Court Administration- Court Finance
Paulina Pasquarelli, Mental Health Case Manager

374

ACCESS Central Mail Center
P.O. BOX 1770
Ocala, FL 34478-1770

Notice of Case Action
State of Florida Department
of Children and Families

September 30, 2019

BRIAN D BAILEY
3200 SUMMIT BLVD
SUITE 15532
WEST PALM BEACH FL 33416

Dear Brian D Bailey,

The following is information about your eligibility.

Information About Medicaid

Name: Brian D Bailey
SSI Application Date: January 03, 2019
PIN: 8678838736

SSN: XXX-XX- 4912
SSI Denial Date: March 05, 2019
Birth Date: February 24, 1979

The application you filed for Supplemental Security Income (SSI) is also an application for Medicaid. Medicaid is a joint federal and state medical assistance program. Although you were denied SSI payments, you may still be eligible for Medicaid.

Call the ACCESS Florida Customer Call Center toll free at 1-866-762-2237 within 30 days if you would like us to determine your eligibility for Medicaid. If you already receive Medicaid, you do not need to call us unless you have unpaid medical bills.

If the Social Security Administration (SSA) decided you are not disabled, we may not be able to provide you with Medicaid based on disability, but there are exceptions. If you have questions, call one of our Customer Call Center agents.

Enfòmasyon sou Medicaid

Non: Brian D Bailey
Dat aplikasyon pou SSI: January 03, 2019
PIN: 8678838736

SSN: XXX-XX-4912
Dat Refi pou SSI: March 05, 2019
Dat li fèt: February 24, 1979

Aplikasyon ou te ranpli pou Revni Sekirite Siplemantè (SSI) reprezante yon aplikasyon tou pou Medicaid. Medicaid se yon pwogram asistans medikal komen federal ak leta. Menmsi ou te jwenn refi pou resevwa peman SSI, ou kapab toujou kalifye pou Medicaid.

Rele Sant Apèl Kliyan ACCESS Florida gratis nan nimewo 1-866-762-2237 nan 30 jou si ou ta renmen pou nou detèmine kalifikasyon ou pou Medicaid. Si ou deja ap resevwa Medicaid, ou pa bezwen rele nou sof si ou genyen bòdwo medikal ou poko peye.

Si Administrasyon Sekirite Sosyal (SSA) te deside ou pa yon moun ki andikape, nou pa kapab anmezi pou ofri ou Medicaid dapre andikap ou, men genyen eksepsyon. Si ou genyen kesyon, rele youn nan ajan Sant Apèl Kliyan nou.

Información sobre Medicaid

Nombre: Brian D Bailey
Fecha de solicitud de SSI: January 03, 2019
PIN: 8678838736

Número de Seguro Social (SSN): XXX-XX-4912
Fecha de negativa de SSI: March 05, 2019
Fecha de nacimiento: February 24, 1979

La solicitud de Ingresos por Seguro Suplementario (SSI) es también una solicitud de Medicaid. Medicaid es un programa de asistencia médica conjunta federal y estatal. Si bien se le denegó el pago de SSI, aún puede resultar apto para recibir el beneficio de Medicaid.

Llame al número gratuito 1-866-762-2237 del Centro de Atención al Cliente de ACCESS Florida dentro de los 30 días si desea que determinemos si cumple los requisitos para recibir Medicaid. Si ya recibe Medicaid, no es necesario que nos llame a menos que tenga facturas médicas impagas.

Si la Administración del Seguro Social (SSA) decidió que usted no tiene discapacidad alguna, es posible que no podamos darle Medicaid por discapacidad, pero hay excepciones. Si desea hacer alguna consulta, comuníquese con alguno de nuestros agentes del Centro de Atención al Cliente.

10/19/2019
Brian Bailey
3200 Summit Blvd., Suite 15532
West Palm Beach, FL 33416

Health Care District of Palm Beach County

Dear Ms. Marley,

The reason for this letter is to provide you with as much information in detail. First, I would like to explain the current living arrangements. I live at Brenda Taft's home – address 6110 Silver Oaks Dr. Lake Worth, FL 33467. I've lived here since the date of 8/24/2019, I'm on a day to day terms with no written agreement. I'm currently looking for residence while staying with Ms.Taft. She has **not** requested any money from me, but I have offered her an amount of 500.00 a month and will continue to due so until I able to find new residence. Attached is a number of different items ranging from bank statements to state license from sunbiz and the latest tax information for myself.

I'm currently a full-time student enrolled in Palm Beach State College, taking 12 credits online. At this time, I'm in the process of an appeal for disability, this case started 1/1/2019. Now continues through the court system till the hearing. At this time, I'm currently injured in multiple places on my body having serious injury. One is my left shoulder having (L) shoulder syndrome and could possible need a complete rebuild. The second is my (R) wrist is fractured due to an auto accident. It hasn't had surgery or been casted and has not healed correctly. My (aunt) Brenda Taft and myself do not share accounts, nor does she give me any cash. I am in need of health care and would like any help possible being a part of C. L. Brumback Primary Care Clinics, known as District Cares.

I am working towards being able to afford paid health care through the marketplace. I will be enrolling when open enrollment opens up 11/1/2019. If there is a number you can provide for low-income due to my current situation, could you please provide.

If you have any questions, please feel free to contact me in regard to District Cares coverage. My contact information is: hawaiianchristian@hotmail.com, (561) 720-0787
Thank you for your time and review of this information, have a great day and God Bless!

Respectfully,
Brian Bailey

10/19/2019

10/19/2019
Brian Bailey
3200 Summit Blvd., Suite 15532
West Palm Beach, FL 33416

Health Care District of Palm Beach County

Dear Ms. Monica,

The reason for this letter is to provide you with as much information in detail. First, I would like to explain the current living arrangements. I live at Brenda Taft's home – address 6110 Silver Oaks Dr. Lake Worth, FL 33467. I've lived here since the date of 8/24/2019, I'm on a day to day terms with no written agreement. I'm currently looking for residence while staying with Ms.Taft. She has **not** requested any money from me, but I have offered her an amount of 500.00 a month and will continue to due so until I able to find new residence. Attached is a number of different items ranging from bank statements to state license from sunbiz and the latest tax information for myself.

I'm currently a full-time student enrolled in Palm Beach State College, taking 12 credits online. At this time, I'm in the process of an appeal for disability, this case started 1/1/2019. Now continues through the court system till the hearing. At this time, I'm currently injured in multiple places on my body having serious injury. One is my left shoulder having (L) shoulder syndrome and could possible need a complete rebuild. The second is my (R) wrist is fractured due to an auto accident. It hasn't had surgery or been casted and has not healed correctly. My (aunt) Brenda Taft and myself do not share accounts, nor does she give me any cash. I am in need of health care and would like any help possible being a part of C. L. Brumback Primary Care Clinics, known as District Cares.

I am working towards being able to afford paid health care through the marketplace. I will be enrolling when open enrollment opens up 11/1/2019. If there is a number you can provide for low-income due to my current situation, could you please provide.

If you have any questions, please feel free to contact me in regard to District Cares coverage. My contact information is: hawaiianchristian@hotmail.com, (561) 720-0787
Thank you for your time and review of this information, have a great day and God Bless!

Respectfully,
Brian Bailey

11/7/2019

*After being released on the date of 8/23/2019 & spending the next few weeks. Reenrolling in Palm Beach State College &, then reapplying for health care with our county, through, "District Cares" after being denied surgery. As well as **Department of Children & Families**, in hope of receiving EBT SNAP food assistance. While using public transportation & minimal funds available. Starting the college semester later than other students & then drowned in government, state & county paperwork.*

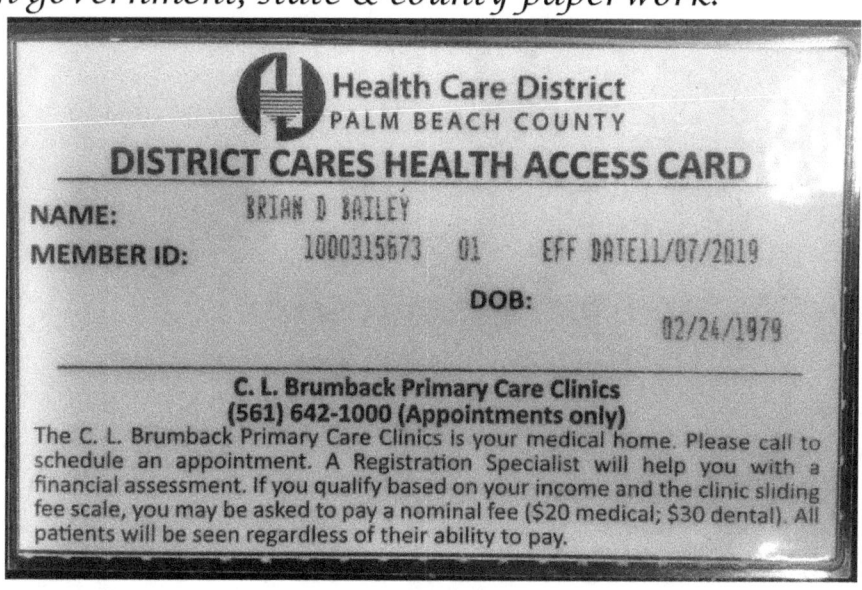

*Without the college financial assistance, Mr. Bailey wouldn't have had the opportunity to seek medical attention, while sustaining bodily injury. **The Palm Beach County Health Care District's** policy is that in order to receive health care. The individual must have proof of employment.*

11/25/2019

IN THE COUNTY COURT OF THE FIFTEENTH JUDICIAL CIRCUIT
IN AND FOR PALM BEACH COUNTY, FLORIDA - CRIMINAL DIVISION
CIRCUIT/COUNTY COURT
Court Event Form

DEFENDANT: BRIAN DALE BAILEY
CASE NO: 50-2019-MM-005685-AXXX-MB

STATE OF FLORIDA
vs.
DEFENDANT: BRIAN DALE BAILEY
CASE NO: 50-2019-MM-005685-AXXX-MB
DIVISION: B: Cnty Crim - B (County)

DATE: 11/25/2019

JACKET #: 0403731
BOOKING #: 2019015844

PRESIDING JUDGE: HANSER, JUDGELEONARD
ASA: MYERS, RYAN
ATTORNEY:
PUBLIC DEFENDER: BURNS, RAYMON
CO-COUNSEL:
DEPUTY CLERK: MED

START TIME: 8:56 AM
END TIME: 8:56 AM

COURT REPORTER
COURT TYPE: STCK - STATUS
CHECK

COURT ROOM: 2E (Main Branch)

Other: NOLLE PROSSE FILED
Other: DEFENDANT NOT PRESENT
Other: STAND IN ATTORNEY KERN PRESENT

Monday, November 25, 2019

Page 1 of 1

380

11/25/2019

CASE NUMBER: 19MM005685

_____ RECALL CAPIAS _____ RECALL D-6's

STATE OF FLORIDA

vs

Defendant **BRIAN Bailey**

Notice to Appear/Uniform Traffic Citation FOR:

___ DWLS/C/R   RESIST W/O VIOLENCE
___ VIO. OF D/L REST.   ☒ TRESPASS
___ NO VALID OR EXP. REG.   ___ RETAIL THEFT
___ ATT. TAG NOT ASSIGNED   ___ OPEN CONTAINER
___ IMP. OR EXP. TAG   ___ POSS. OF MARIJ
___ NO VALID D/L   ___ POSS. OF PARA.
___ EXPIRED D/L   ___ PROSTITUTION
___ NO INSURANCE   ___ SOLIC. PROSTITUTION
___ _____   ___ BATTERY
    ___ PETIT THEFT
___ PAY FOR INFRACTION(S)

Nolle Prosequi for Deferred Prosecution/PTI/Diversion

THIS CASE IS NOLLE PROSSED DUE TO THE FOLLOWING REASON(S):

☒ SUCCESSFUL COMPLETION OF DIVERSION PROGRAM IN LIEU OF JUDICIAL DISPOSITION
___ SUCCESSFUL COMPLETION OF DIVERSION SPECIFIED CLASSES
☒ COST OF PROSECUTION PAID
___ RESTITUTION PAID
___ SUCCESSFUL COMPLETION OF COMMUNITY SERVICE HOURS
___ SUCCESSFUL COMPLETION OF DEFENSIVE DRIVING SCHOOL

FILED
NOV 2 5 2019
SHARON R. BOCK, CLERK
PALM BEACH COUNTY, FL
COUNTY CRIMINAL

___ LICENSE OR PRIVILEGE TO DRIVE REINSTATED   ___ VALID REGISTRATION SHOWN
___ VALID LICENSE SHOWN   ___ PROOF OF INSURANCE SHOWN
☒ OTHER No Contact with Christ Fellowship

DATE: 11/25/19

DAVID ARONBERG
State Attorney

Victoria J Mc

ASSISTANT STATE ATTORNEY

SCANNED
NOV 2 6 2019

381

⭘   ⭘

IN THE CIRCUIT COURT IN AND FOR
PALM BEACH COUNTY, FLORIDA

BOOKING NO.: _____

CASE NO.: 19MM005685AMB

DIVISION: B

STATE OF FLORIDA

v. Bailey, Brian
_____
(last name)   (first name)
DEFENDANT

ORDER RESCINDING NO CONTACT ORDER

This matter having come before the Court, the Court finds that:

[X] the State Attorney has entered a nolle prosse as to the charges
[ ] the State Attorney has entered a "No File" as to the charges
[ ] the case has been concluded by plea
[ ] the Defendant has been found not guilty at trial
[ ] a motion to rescind the No Contact Order has been granted
[ ] probation has been revoked or terminated

Wherefore, it is hereby **ORDERED** and **ADJUDGED** that the No Contact Order previously entered in this case is hereby rescinded.

DONE and **ORDERED** in ~~Chambers~~ Open Court in Palm Beach County, Florida this 25 day of Nov. , 20 19 .

_____
JUDGE

BLUE - Palm Beach Sheriff's Office Communication
GREEN - Complainant
CANARY - Public Defender/Defense Attorney
PINK - State Attorney
GOLD - Defendant

April 2017

EMAILED
PBSO ✗
OTHER _____
DATE 11/25/19
INITIALS MD

FILED
NOV 25 2019
SHARON R. BOCK, CLERK
PALM BEACH COUNTY, FL
COUNTY CRIMINAL

SCANNED
NOV 25 2019

Form 38

382

While creating the content for "**Indigent Truth of the Court**" by Brian Dale Bailey the files on Mr. Bailey's Seagate external hard drive were being removed, disassembled or deleted.

As he was gathering the evidence, just after enrolling **Palm Beach State College,** he had multiple laptops stop working correctly & required the manufactures attention. Blocking him from studies & being able to work on the project consistently.

While Mr. Bailey was a member of **Christ Fellowship Church** & serving on traffic outside the building. Another individual went through his backpack & disassembled a new **Dell** personal computer. Paid for with a **Government** loan by **Palm Beach State College.**

After being released from incarceration Mr. Bailey had an external **4TB Seagte Hard Drive** go down. Making it unusable even after being sent back to the manufacture **Seagate Technology.** This hard drive was holding multiple Legal cases with providing evidence, with the capabilities Of proving the difficulty of using the system in place. While coming from a **low - income** family & using the government assistance that's in place.

Below is the list of debts for **Brian Dale Bailey**, in order by date, showing that after the first auto accident, taking place on the Florida Turnpike, during the year 2013. On the same day as his mother's funeral, the medical debt began to build & with injuries leading to inconsistent employment. Followed by financial debts left outstanding in a variety of places.

The total amount showing $36,146.38

On 5/12/2019, this was the indebted amount owed before accepting college loans & receiving surgery.

Mr. Bailey also shared his indebted amount with **Members of Christ Fellowship Church,** who were grouped to enhance financial income. But, in order to participate Mr. Bailey was required to purchase a costly book for the class & already ready had a backpack filled with higher education books.

These are the tales from **Palm Beach County**, Florida & shares a small-scale version of how the system. Has the capability of shutting out individuals through the power of business & financial need. Leaving people pushed off the grid & left to be saved by our community & used as labors. Creating a force to be reconned with, when unable to afford fighting the system with the Judicial Courts. While the same system drains us of funds, when working for hourly wages, labor or piece work.

Defeat evil with the "**Power of Love**."

www.ingramcontent.com/pod-product-compliance
Lightning Source LLC
Chambersburg PA
CBHW072144230526
45467CB00040B/12